ACLS History E-Book Project

Reprint Series

The ACLS History E-Book Project (www.historyebook.org) collaborates with constituent societies of the American Council of Learned Societies, publishers, librarians and historians to create an electronic collection of works of high quality in the field of history. This volume is produced from digital images created for the Project by the Scholarly Publishing Office and the Digital Library Production Service at the University of Michigan, Ann Arbor. The digital reformatting process results in an electronic version of the text that can be both accessed online and used to create new print copies. This book and hundreds of others are available online in the History E-Book Project through subscription.

Many of the works in the History E-Book Project are available in print and can be ordered either directly from their publishers or as part of this series. For information refer to the online Title Record page for each book. Inquiries regarding this series can be directed to info@hebook.org.

ACLS
HISTORY E-BOOK

I0833760

http://www.historyebook.org

Denne afhandling er af det filosofiske fakultet ved Københavns universitet antaget til offentligt at forsvares for den filosofiske doktorgrad.

København, den 17. februar 1964

C. J. Becker
h.a.dec.

Translated by
P. LAMPE CHRISTENSEN

PRINTED IN DENMARK BY
AARHUUS STIFTSBOGTRYKKERIE A·S 448.64

ʿALĪ AND MUʿĀWIYA
IN EARLY ARABIC TRADITION

Studies on the Genesis and Growth of

ISLAMIC HISTORICAL WRITING

until the End af the Ninth Century

By

ERLING LADEWIG PETERSEN

MUNKSGAARD

COPENHAGEN 1964

have made it possible for me to undertake supplementary studies of literature. In conclusion I wish to extend my warm thanks to *Statens almindelige Videnskabsfond* and the *British Council* for economic support towards the research indispensable to the book. The English translation has been undertaken by Mr. P. Lampe Christensen, whom I wish to thank heartily for his careful and patient work.

Lyngby, May 1964

E. Ladewig Petersen

Preface

The first civil war 656–61 and the party antagonisms emerging from it have proved to be of crucial importance to the development of Islam. No wonder, then, that subsequent interpretations of the ʿAlī-Muʿāwiya conflict provoked serious misrepresentations of the actual course of events. In a previous study I have tried to reconstruct some trends and problems of this conflict on the basis of the primary sources. This book presents an attempt to trace the formation of the historical tradition associated with the first civil war by applying modern standards of historical method. I have finally tried to establish an outline of the genesis of "profane" historical writing in Islam, in so far as the ʿAlī-Mu'āwiya conflict can be considered paradigmatic. The book thus aims at combining a "historiographical" and methodical study of the early conflicts in Islam.

My manuscript was finished in the summer of 1962, and I have therefore been unable to utilize more recent publications. I especially regret not having had access to "*Historians of the Middle East*" (ed. by B. Lewis and P. M. Holt, London 1962). However, by courtesy of Professor Lewis I have had the opportunity to consult two of the essays from this work in a duplicate of the manuscript.—Except for the most common names and terms Oriental words are here presented in the transliteration used by *The Encyclopaedia of Islam, New edition.*

It remains for me to thank all my teachers in the *University of Copenhagen*, the Professors Astrid Friis, Aksel E. Christensen, Povl Bagge, Sven Henningsen, Kristof Glamann, and the late lecturer Erik Bach. I feel particularly indebted to Professor Christensen and Professor Frede Løkkegaard for inspiration and constant encouragement. I am anxious, also, to thank my parents, chief engineer and Mrs. S. W. Petersen, cordially for their efforts in my behalf. *The Royal Library* of Copenhagen has greatly eased my work by procuring books not available here. I likewise wish to thank Professor Bernard Lewis and the staff of *The School of Oriental and African Studies*, London, who

Contents

Introduction

1.

The murder of ʿUthmān in Medina in June 656 proved to be of epoch-making significance in the history of Islam, an event which in the words of Arab historians formed the threshold of that religio-political schism *(fitna)* which gave rise not only to a series of bitter conflicts in the following years, but also to a lasting division of the Moslem community into irreconcilable factions[1]. At the same time, the murder itself was prokoved by latent elements of tension already in existence within the Arab community: dissensions among the newly created Islamic theocracy, Muhammad's Meccan and Medinese associates, the old patriciate in Mecca under Umayyad leadership, and the Arabian Bedouin communities. At a somewhat later stage, this state of tension seems to have been aggravated by a new group, the exponents of the incipient principle of legitimacy, with ʿAlī b. Abī Ṭālib, the Prophet's cousin and son-in-law, as the central figure. Abū Bakr and ʿUmar had so far succeeded in upholding a *modus vivendi* by identifying Islam's religious programme with the warlike instincts of the Arab tribes, a policy the direct result of which was the first great wave of expansion in the 630's. The first five caliphs at the same time had to pay regard to the Umayyads whose commercial interests in Syria naturally placed the leadership and organization of the conquest of this province in their hands.

Still, already during ʿUmar's (634–44) and especially during his successor ʿUthmān's reign do we find evidence of a budding disaffection among those Arab tribes that had participated in the expansion, both because of the severe military regimentation and the economic advantages which the new Islamic aristocracy in the Ḥijāz and, in the reign of ʿUthmān, the Umayyads, too, reaped from the conquests. These circumstances appear to have provided material for the revolution against ʿUthmān. In this situation ʿAlī's election

1 The actual meaning of *fitna* is "scruple", in casu: defining one's attitude to the religious problems arising from the murder; cf. Wellhausen: Kingdom, 50 *sqq*; Wensinck, 78 *sq*. As to the following, cf. Gibb, 5 *sqq*.

to Caliph could hardly be due so much to any wish of acknowledging the legitimacy principle as to the bedouin's—particularly the Iraqi tribes'—and the Medinese Helpers' *(Anṣār's)* endeavour to utilize the possibilities of the immediate circumstances and to carry the development back to older and more pietistic channels[2]. In any case, ʿAlī's authority as Caliph could only be maintained in close collaboration with the circles behind the slaying of ʿUthmān, and so he encountered resistance among the Meccan companions *(Muhājirūn)* who had benefited from the expansion, and he also had to face a rebellion on the part of Ṭalḥa and az-Zubayr in the autumn of 656. Their somewhat vague demands for reforms *(iṣlāḥ)* are presumably expressive of their reluctance to reconcile themselves to the programme implied by ʿAlī's election. However, in the given circumstances they would hardly be able to carry through their demands, and their rebellion was suppressed already in December at the battle of the Camel (near Basra)[3].

More natural and far more important was the strong Umayyad reaction headed by the leading personality of the dynasty, the Syrian governor Muʿāwiya b. Abī Sufyān. As the murdered Caliph's kinsman *(walī)*, and pursuant to the Quran, Muʿāwiya, presumably in Januar 657, raised the claim for blood vengeance on the Caliph's murderers as he did not recognize any religious justification of their act. By all accounts he regarded ʿAlī as an accomplice in the murder inasmuch as the latter did indeed lean on the murderers' circle and must, therefore, be religiously compromised[4]. On the other hand, ʿAlī and his adherents denied that the Quran's *lex talionis* could in fact be applied to this case seeing that ʿUthmān's own arbitrariness *(iḥdāth)* had given occasion for the murder, and so Muʿāwiya might be looked upon as a rebel against the lawful religious authority, the fight against whom was sanctioned by the Quran "until he reverts to obedience to God"[5].

There is hardly any doubt that this *fitna* had shaken the very foundation of the Islamic community, and these scruples re-emerged spontaneously in both Muʿāwiya's and ʿAlī's camp when the two parties met at Ṣiffīn on the Euphrates in the summer of 657. ʿAlī was forced to agree to having the justification of the Caliph murder and his own attitude to it referred to arbitration *(ḥukūma)* on the basis of the Quran[6]. Either party appointed its own umpire

2 As to the flwg.; see Vaglieri I, *passim*; same in *E. I.*[2] I, 381 *sqq*; Veselý, 36 *sqq*; *AO* XXIII, 157–96.

3 cf. Caetani IX, 3 *sqq*., 72 *sqq*., 216 *sqq*.

4 Ṣāliḥ b. Kaysān in Bal. 504 v; cf. Muh. b. Isḥāq *ibid*. 502 r (Caetani IX, 289, 284 *sq*.); *Waq. Siff*., 36 *sq*. As warrant for his demand for blood vengeance Muʿāwiya cited the Quran's sure 17:32–35, which permits blood vengeance to the murdered man's *walī*, provided that the murder is unjust *(maẓlūm[an])*.

5 *Waq. Siff*., 33 *sq*., 212, 570, 590 *sqq*.; cf. the Quran, *sure* 49:8–9.

6 Vaglieri I, 26 *sqq*.; *AO* XXIII, 182 *sqq*.

(ḥakam), the Syrians 'Amr b. al-'Āṣ, and 'Alī's army Abū Mūsā al-Ash'arī, who had been among those Companions that for religious reasons wanted to stand aloof from the *fitna*. 'Alī's camp was, however, no longer in unison concerning this decision; one group—first and foremost among the Bedouin—later to be known as the Khārijites seceded because they considered the agreement incompatible with the Caliph's religious office; they had made sacrifices in the fight against Mu'āwiya's unlawful rebellion and would recognize only a military decision, God's judgement in the conflict[7]. There is, again, hardly any doubt that the Khārijites' simultaneous insistence on a far-reaching democratization of Islam represented one side of the opposition against 'Uthmān and the ideas that stood behind 'Alī's Caliphate.

Khārijite opposition seems to have caused postponement of the arbitration until January 659 when 'Amr and Abū Mūsā met at Adhruḥ (an oasis between Ma'ān and Petra). The award appears to have been to the effect that the caliph murder was unlawful and that 'Alī had compromised himself religiously by his collaboration with the murderers[8]. By his—even if somewhat vacillating—observance of the agreement of Ṣiffīn 'Alī had already incurred Khārijite denunciation for infidelity *(kufr)*. This altercation issued in the battle of an-Nahrawān (near Kufa) in July 658, where the Khārijites were routed. The subsequent arbitration apparently caused a heavy defection from 'Alī, and the remaining two years of his caliphate took the shape of a progressive disintegration until he fell a victim to a Khārijite assassination in January 661. In the preceding summer, however, Mu'āwiya had already received the oath of allegiance at Jerusalem[9].

In this civil war the basic elements of Islam had collided into an irreconcilable conflict. We should bear in mind that Ali's defensive war aimed at "maintenance of the faith and (his obligation to) carry the right guidance to victory"[10]. This obligation rested upon him automatically because he was in possession of *dīn*, the religious burden which God enjoined upon him in his capacity of *Imām*[11]. It is, on the other hand, manifest that his attitude to the *fitna* influenced contemporaneous judgment of his religious prestige to a marked degree. The mere doubt as to his possible complicity in the caliph murder—if this was *maẓlūm*[an]—seems to have induced a number of prominent Companions of the Prophet (Sa'd b. Abī Waqqāṣ, 'Abdallāh b. 'Umar among

7 Gabrieli: *Origini*, 110 *sqq.*; Vaglieri I, 31 *sqq.*

8 *Ibid.* I, 85 *sqq.*; *AO* XXIII, 192 *sqq.* – L. Veccia Vaglieri's chronology is hardly tenable, *inter alia* because it is based on secondary sources.—On the site of Adhruḥ, which is unprecisely given by Arab geographers, see Vaglieri in *E. I.*[2] I, 194.

9 *AO* XXIII, 196.

10 Bal. 441 v (Caetani X, 418).

11 For this concept, see L. Gardet s. v. *dīn* in *E. I.*[2] II, 293 *sq.*; cf. Buhl: 'Alī, 41, 55, 57.

others) to withhold their recognition of him and to prefer to remain neutral[12]; similarly, his part in the shedding of his fellow believers' blood in the battles of the Camel, Ṣiffīn and an-Nahrawān evoked a progressive scepticism regarding his *dīn*. Concerning the Khārijites, he forfeited his *dīn* by accepting arbitration, and the two umpires likewise considered his attitude to the *fitna* so religiously compromising as to disqualify him for the caliphate.

The crumbling of ʿAlī's *dīn* is, however, only one aspect in the accounting for the Umayyad victory. The other is to be found in Muʿāwiya's personal qualities. In his case, too, we find no reason to doubt the sincerity of his motives, nor any basis for the idea that he openly aspired to the Caliphate until much later—probably not until the award had called ʿAlī's *dīn* in question. The successful outcome of Muʿāwiya's fight must indeed be ascribed to his political shrewdness, calm deliberation, and tolerance, all manifestations of qualities epitomized by the Arab concept of *ḥilm*[13]. Muʿāwiya's opportunism made him wait until ʿAlī compromised himself by his conduct before intervening in the course of events.

It was, then, the old Meccan aristocracy headed by Muʿāwiya which in 660–61 attained to the Caliphate. It is, however, a moot question to what extent the civil war and the Umayyad assumption of power altered Islam's political and social structure. Muʿāwiya and his immediate successors obviously endeavoured to pursue the line of the first caliphs, i.e. to co-ordinate Islam's and the Bedouin's interests in the expansion that was gathering new momentum. At the same time, Muʿāwiya's personal calibre enabled him to maintain the balance in the traditional tribal institutions and to organize the aristocratic Arab community in the new environments. Nevertheless, the pro-ʿAlī (Shīʿi) and Khārijite revolts that very soon sprang up in Iraq go to show that this balance was unstable, especially when assimilation of the Arabs into the eastern provinces and the gradual conversion of the indigenous population deepened the religious antagonisms and added social difficulties to the political ones. The discontent among Arabs and *mawālī* (sing. *mawlā*, client) rallied round the Shīʿi opposition, so the state of conflict from ʿAlī's caliphate had not ebbed away with his murder; it retained its formal actuality, even if the antagonisms had assumed a somewhat different character. The *fitna* provoked by ʿUthmān's murder was, by virtue of the Islamic society's peculiar structure and its concatenation of religion and politics, of such fundamental significance that it continued not only to call for interpretation *a posteriori*, but also ruled out loyalty to the past. The history and historiography civil-war of the are thus two widely different things, either of which is entitled to discussion.

---

12 Nawbakhtī, 5 (*RHR* 153, 179 *sq.*); Tab. I. 3072 (Caetani VIII, 327); cf. Buhl: *ʿAlī*, 37, 46 *sq.*

13 For this concept, see Lammens: *Moʿāwia*, 66 *sqq.*

2.

Every historical account can be classified and analysed from two chief points of view, depending on whether it is regarded as a source of knowledge of the subject described, or as a historiographic monument. Obviously, these two classification principles are not mutually irrelevant and sliding transitions do occur, but the distinction is nevertheless of fundamental interest. Historiographically the dependence of the exposition on its sources and the author's physiognomy will invariably play a decisive role in placing the work, whereas the exposition's value as a source to modern research has no relevance to the historiographic inquiry. Where the exposition is considered as a historiographic monument our attention will be focused on its placement by virtue of its evidence of the standard of the contemporaneous historians—their methods, their ideology. No inquiry of this nature can be accomplished by bibliographical compilation or a review of the historian's data only; an appraisal must assume that the historical recordings are dealt with as a product of the society from which they emanate and in which they had their functions[14].

The social and didactic function of historical writing is a well-known phenomenon in mediaeval Europe where its characteristic presentation is primarily a product of Christianity's victory in the 4th century, and where the theologically couloured aspects still stand out significantly[15]. The philosophy underlying the mediaeval historians' work derives from St. Augustine's dualistic system, which was first applied to a profane-historical material and for polemic purposes by his disciple Paulus Orosius while their chronology—also employed by Orosius—is based on Eusebios' synchronization of the classical and the biblical tradition. The synthesis of these elements was accomplished definitely in the early 7th century by Isidore of Seville. The teleological demarcation, however, did in no case preclude a certain margin for the historian's personal contribution. Mediaeval accounts do indeed leave the impression that by means of combinations and harmonization or by constructions on the source material at his disposal the historian devised that particular interpretation of the past which served his purpose and his political points of view.

This intimate concatenation of actual political views and the writing of history within the frames of terminology and religion is, however, no specially European phenomenon. Features entirely parallel occur in classical Islamic historiography, even though the demarcations are cast in a somewhat different

14 cf. Herbert Butterfield's theoretical reflections in "The History of the Writing of History" (*XIe Congr. int. des Sciences hist., Rapp.* I (1960)), 25 *sqq.*—Incidentally, the term historiography, as used now-a-days, is highly ambivalent; it is used both of the history of historical writing and of the research or exposition dealing with the latter. The second and derivative meaning is as far as possible avoided in this work.

15 For the following, cf. e.g. E. Bernheim, *passim; HT* 11:V, 455 *sq.*

mould in the Orient, where the religious incentive in every political consideration or action—at any theoretically—is bound up with Islam's concatenation of state and religion, in the tradition characteristically described as twins *(dawla wa dīn)*. The analogy can hardly be ascribed to any immediate classical or Christian influence[16]; it is due, primarily, to the facts that Muhammad's preaching originated in a milieu religiously akin to the Christian and that his views framed the religious foundations of the Arabic conception of history. The conception of history with which the Arab historian of the Middle Ages operates is thus of a specifically Islamic mould, just as the European conception is fundamentally Christian, and both have their place in the teleological systems of the Middle Ages.

The pre-Islamic north Arabian communities did indeed possess a not inconsiderable historical tradition which dealt chiefly with tribal genealogy or the tribes' warlike deeds (the *ayyām al-ʿarab* tradition)[17]. This tradition no doubt served the tribes as far as practical matters or prestige were concerned; but it never developed any concepts expressive of firmly framed ideas of the past, and for that reason alone limited the scope of such impulses as the later Islamic historians may have found here. True, the Umayyad court maintained the interest in the pre-Islamic past *(jāhiliyya)*, and the preoccupation with the Prophet's military actions (the *maghāzī* literature), the Islamic expansion, and the early conflicts must likewise presuppose influence from the technique of the *ayyām al-ʿarab* tradition[18]. But the Bedouin's interest in tribal prosperity is entirely devoid of the unifying religious incitement inherent in Muhammad's teachings and in the first organization of the Arab Empire under Islamic auspices. It was not until the advent of Muhammad that historical concepts crystallized and were incorporated in the practical norms governing the new society in a way that was to exert a decisive influence on posterity. Theoretically the objective ascertainment of facts was of no importance to him, but they enter—despite modifications in his argumentation where influenced by external circumstances—as an organic element in his preaching.

It is of paramount importance that Muhammad himself expresses the idea of the historical continuity very cogently; it was a leading principle in his doctrine of revelation that the revelation which he experienced did not in its essence differ from the ones that other peoples had received, but that he him-

16 It is probable—at any rate at a later date—that Islamic historians knew elements of classical historical writing through Byzantine or Syrian-Christian intermediaries (cf. Spuler, 125 *sqq.*).—Of Christian sources only Orosius seems to have been translated; cf. *HT* 11:VI, 153 with note 3.

17 cf. Caskel, *passim*; M. Plessner s.v. *taʾrīkh* in *E.I.(S)*, 230 *sqq.*; Obermann, 239–64.

18 For the following, see Rosenthal: *Historiography*, 22–28; Obermann, 264–80; *HT* 11:V, 456 *sq.*

self consummated the prophetical tradition which the Old-Testament prophets and Christ had initiated[19]. This very insistence on the identity of all revelations explains how the accumulated historical experience—the predecessors' warnings, history's lessons *('ibra)*—comes to carry such distinctive weight in his own preaching[20]. His knowledge of the past and its purport is an organic element of the revelation on a parity with any other part of the divinely revealed law[21], and it can be taken for granted that this strict historical continuity and its accentuation of the *'ibra* of the past must likewise have influenced the ideology within the new social structure.

From the outset Muhammad's preaching had been individualistic, a line which if carried to its logical conclusion would demolish the existing collectivistic tribal structure. Even before his *hijra* the conflicts and the breach with the Meccans were engendering an Islamic founding of institutions, which was given full scope in the theocratic social order of Medina. In consequence hereof his teachings gradually took on unmistakable elements of collectivism; they were subjected to a kind of arabizing process, which, again, brought Muhammad nearer to the tribal institutions. His prophetical universalism was maintained, though in the nature of things the Arab roots and the accumulation of history's *'ibra* stood out more clearly than before. In his Medina period, however, he had to formulate a more clear-cut distinction between heathenism and Islam, between barbarity *(jāhiliyya)* and clemency *(ḥilm)* as reflected in the manifestation of two contradictory attitudes to life as separated by his own advent.

The conception of history that forms part of Muhammad's teachings maintains, as does the Augustinian doctrine, that the historical process is a realization of eternal or universal norms, the embodiment of God's will—"this is the path of God; to you it is already so, and God's path never changes", as a Quran passage has it. The Islamic community is *ummat Allāh*, God's followers, and his creative power does not cease manifesting itself in all their activities. Interest in their thriving and in the interpretation of God's will as revealed in the course of events is therefore not merely a matter of piety but simply a necessity for those that will submit themselves to God. In this way the Muhammadan social order's concatenation of state and religion gives the historical tradition an important function from the very beginning, a tendency naturally favoured by the religious *fitna* and political schism that set in at 'Uthmān's death. Though ideally incompatible with Islam's fundamental principles, *fitna* does nevertheless exist, a fact which at a very early stage

19 Thus e.g. the Quran, *sure* 42:11.

20 e.g. *ibid*, *sure* 12:111.—For the meaning and development of the *'ibra* concept, see Mahdi, 63 *sqq.*; Abbott, 6 with note 12, and 7 with note 1.

21 Cf. e.g. the Quran, *sure* 11:51.

claimed all believers' attention and conscience and called for their personal engagements. Any political and physical conflict must in the nature of things assume a fundamentally religious aspect; any opinion is a legal constituent of Islamic society and is by its very essence entitled to that religious legitimacy which is obtainable only by invocation of the prophet tradition or the views of the very early generations. The latter's political distinctions are brought into the argumentation on topical controversial issues, and the conflicts are generally so alternative that their very nature prevents loyalty to the past.

This particular position of Arabic historical writing within the Islamic society also serves to explain its external features. The Arab's disclination to deviate from the traditionally established authority by his own initiative (*ra'y*, personal opinion, *opinio*) or by any innovation (*bid'a*) is very closely bound up with his basic view of the concept of "knowledge". By knowledge, *'ilm*, especially in relation to religious matters, the Arab does not generally mean the result of independent reasoning but merely the ability to cite some competent authority – the Quran's commandment or the transmission (*ḥadīth*) of the Prophet or his Companions' practice (*sunna*) – for his assertion under all due formality, i. e. with a trustworthy chain of transmitters (*isnād*) enumerating the intermediate links which the tradition has passed before reaching the informant. "No people (except the Arab) since the creation of Adam possessed trustworthy men that could guard the Prophet's words", writes the bibliographical author Muhammad b. 'Abd ar-Raḥmān as-Sakhāwī, "were it not for the *isnād*, then everybody would say what suited him. A man who studies the facts of his religion without (applying) *isnād* is like the one who climbs a roof without a ladder"[22].

What in this and similar contexts applies to exegesis and jurisprudence does also in principle apply to the historical transmission; the course of history is indeed the manifestation of God's will and thus subsists objectively, independent of the observer. The narrator, in keeping with the classical connotation of scholarly tradition, merely hands down the *'ilm* that he is in possession of. As in the other *ḥadīth* disciplines, these basic concepts are phenomena gradually taking root in that tradition-technique which the historical recorders, too, work out – at any rate from the end of the 8th century. Correspondingly, *'ilm al-akhbār*[23], knowledge of noteworthy occurrences or events, will not generally indicate results of study of the sources or of empirical research but merely a capability to cite authoritative informants – recognized historians or, a little later, eywitnesses – referring to an *isnād* satisfying such formal demands as might be made.

22 D. S. Margoliouth in *The Moslem World* II (1912), 120; cf. also Goldziher: *Islam*, 38 *sqq*.
23 For this concept, see Rosenthal: *Historiography*, 10 *sq*., 59 *sqq*.

It is, then, innate in Arabic recording of history that its relation to the source is not that of the researcher. Neither documents nor monuments are on principle looked for by the early Arabic historians[24]). Material of this kind is given no methodical preference, a fact hardly ascribable to lack of dramatizing qualities, but rather to its failure in immediately satisfying such function or such essence as the historian would require from his subject-matter. Such letters or speeches as he quotes will no doubt in most cases depend upon a fiction that is adopted because it is expressive of the historian's own conception of characters of the past[25]. No more was it possible for the Arab historian to distinguish critically concerning age and nature of the tradition. Although tradition, like jurisprudence, in the earliest Abbasid period tends to prefer evidence – which is here taken to be narrations the *isnād* of which could be traced back to a contemporary or an eye witness – this process remains secondary and fictitious[26]; it may be assumed to reflect the religious nature of the concept of cognition, the need of procuring such *'ilm* as the observer might yield. Formal demands were, admittedly, made on the outward appearance of historical transmission, but this material was not subjected to such rigorous criticism of tradition as was in principle applied to jurisprudence and dogmatics in the 9th century. Even such scrupulous authorities as Sufyān ath-Thawrī (d. 777/78) and Aḥmad b. Ḥanbal (d. 855) considered absolute accuracy obligatory only where the case relates to a right or a wrong whereas other matters, including the recording of history, did not call for the same care[27]. Although scepticism and formal criticism are not infrequently met with, and respect for the transmission is theoretically established, the Arab historian tends to take a somewhat freer stand in relation to his source material than do the authors on jurisprudence and exegesis. The traditionist never relinquishes his right to personal political or religious commitment to the subject he deals with.

From a very early time—the transition from the seventh to the eight century—we know of *ruwāt* (sing. *rāwī*), persons who orally carry or transmit individual reports (genealogy, *akhbār* or *ayyām* narrations), and, not much later, records, *kutub* (sing. *kitāb*), which deal monographically with *akhbār,* make their appearance[28]. The title indexes in the bibliographical literature—*akhbār Ṣiffīn, kitāb an-Nahrawān, kitāb al-Karbalā',* etc.—afford circumstantial evidence that the written monograph or pamphlet was the normal mode of expression

24 Margoliouth: *Lectures*, 50; Rosenthal: *Historiography*, 105 *sqq*. Purely antiquarian studies may occasionally embrace monuments and inscriptions; cf. *HT* 11:V, 458 *cum* note 2.

25 A case in point is Mas. IV, 393 *sqq*., which unlike all earlier traditions has the umpires in Adruḥ take down a record of the negotiations.

26 cf. *infra* p. 63.

27 Sprenger: *Trad.wes*., 16 *sq*.; cf. Rosenthal: *Historiography*, 56 *sq*.; *Scholarship*, 41 *sqq*.

28 cf. Duri: *The Iraq School.*

from the middle of the 8th century, even if the transmissal is still effected by dictation, and subject to the teacher's authorization or licence to his disciple to pass on his tradition material *(ijāza)*[29]. The earliest preserved manuscripts or fragments of a historical nature do indeed belong to the early Abbasid period[30], which is borne out by the fact that such works of the ninth-century historians as are known to us frequently invoke the eighth-century traditionists in a form—without any connecting *isnād*—which proves that they must have known and made use of these written works. The Arab transmission retains its monographical form for a very long time to come, and even when the 9th and 10th centuries saw it replaced by chronologically systematizing presentations*(ta'rīkh)* it does not renounce its character of *ḥadīth* learning. This development appears to be due to a progressive compilatory process in the 9th century, no doubt favoured by the growth of the paper industry, which provided cheaper writing materials and facilitated manifolding. However, these physical processes did not alter the pecular character of the tradition, nor, again, did they at any stage preclude adaptations *ad hoc* of the tradition.

3.

The status of historical recording in the Islamic society as well as its potentialities left a wide margin for tendentious presentation. In this respect ʿAlī's fateful Caliphate and the outbreak of the *fitna* mark the momentous cross-roads in the historical writing, also irrespective of the evident fact that actual knowledge of the conflicts soon faded. Most of the important parties in Islam stem in some way or other from the events of those years, which despite all varying extraneous situations are taken to be their theoretical point of departure. The real elements in the conflicts issuing from the murder of ʿUthmān were clearly incident to the immediate situation and hardly able to arouse any historiographical interest, especially not after the fall of the Umayyad Caliphate. It is nevertheless possible to continue following the historiographical debate on ʿAlī's Caliphate through the Abbasid period in its undiminished vehemence; there exists, as we know, an obvious disparity between our knowledge of these years and the interest that the Islamic historical recorders bestowed upon them[31].

---

29 Rosenthal: *Historiography*, 61 *sqq.*; *Scholarship*, 7 *sqq.*; Abbott, 22 *sqq*; cf. Johs. Pedersen, 17–30 *cum* notes pp. 143 *sqq*.

30 Abbott, *passim.*—The earliest known monographs of this type are Naṣr b. Muzāḥim's (d. 828), *Waqʿat Ṣiffīn*, and Muhammad b. ʿUthmān al Kalbī's as yet unpublished *Akhbār Ṣiffīn* (cf. *GAL(S)*, 212) from the early 9th century.

31 Even in quite modern times these lines of distinction divide Arab historical research; cf. N. A. Faris: *Development in Arab Historiography as reflected in the struggle between ʿAlī and Muʿāwiyah.*

It is, however, long since established that the legendary ʿAlī figure, which the Arab—and particularly the Shīʿi—tradition operated with, has nothing in common with the ʿAlī of real life. Neither he nor his descendants were distinguished by such political sagacity as would qualify them to occupy that headship in Islam to which the Shīʿa considered them entitled[32]. All the research available is, directly or indirectly, the fruit of the critical work of unravelment pioneered in the first decades of this century by the publication of Ṭabarī's (d. 923) Annals during the years 1879–1901. By his detailed investigations Wellhausen broke new ground in the study of the earliest Caliphate and the Umayyad period[33]. At about the same time (1898) Th. Noeldeke formulated an outline of the conflicting politico-religious Shīʿi and pro-Abbasid interests represented in the building up of a tradition around ʿAlī[34]. Scholars soon became aware that the Abbasid period's political situations might have influenced the historical recorders' changing attitudes to the earliest history of Islam[35]. The same cognition underlies the temperamental Belgian orientalist Henri Lammens' extensive critical studies on the traditions and his in many ways meritorious rehabilitation of the Umayyads. His work was accomplished with a fascinating intuition, an often unerring sensibility to the tradition's party-political function, and with particular accentuation of the religious and personal aspects of the events—though, also, without systematical methods in his handling of his subject-matter[36]. All the immensely comprehensive material for Islam's earliest history—printed and unprinted—was finally collocated and systematized by Leone Caetani, who furnished it with numerous critical comments and often perspicacious analyses of the political tendencies of the sources[37].

So the publication of Ṭabarī's work enabled scholars not only to rid the Iraqi tradition—on which he relied—of many of its later and secondary adaptions, but also obtain an insight into the historical recorder's workshop in the reign of the Abbasids and a provisional impression of the unreliability of this late tradition. However, even the possibility of reconstructing the earliest

32 cf. especially Buhl: *Aliderne*, 355 *sqq*.

33 Wellhausen: *Prolegomena* (1899); *Opp. parteien* (1901); *Das arabische Reich und sein Sturz* (1902; English edition 1927).

34 Noeldeke: *Zur tendentiösen Gestaltung der Urgeschịchte Islams* (1898).

35 Thus W. Sarasin: *Das Bild Alis* (1907), which likewise emphasizes that the mythogenesis is a secondary feature, whereas his late dating of its formation is less convincing. Cf. also I. Friedlaender: *Muhammedanische Geschichtskonstruktionen* (1911, orig. a lecture delivered in 1902), which like his later works (*Heterodoxies, b. Saba*' 1909–11) deals with the ʿAlī myths.

36 Cf. C. H. Becker, 263–69.—The most important of Lammens' works in this connection are: *Moʿāwia* (1908), *Yazīd* (1921), and *Omayyades* (1930).

37 Caetani: *Annali dell'Islām*, I–X (1905–1926).

Iraqi tradition—as done by Wellhausen—failed to dispose of all the problems relating to the sources, for this transmission is no less one-sided than the secondary one[38]. Not until the publication of Balādhurī's *kitāb Ansāb al-Asrāf,* which like Ṭabarī's work stems from the late 9th century, were we given the necessary correctives to the Iraqi transmission insofar as it contains copious fragments of the early pro-Umayyad version of the same events[39]. Knowledge of this material provides not only better means of determining the reliability of the earliest tradition, but also of following and explaining the genesis of the historical tradition fairly adequately. Knowledge of both versions of 'Alī's Caliphate and of their subsequent fate in the Abbasid period enables us to establish the circumstances under which the Arab historical writing was shaped and to what extent it was influenced by Islam's political and religious evolution, until it was brought into full play at the end of the 9th century. It must be stressed, however, that this study is not a matter of more or less radical scepticism concerning the Arab tradition, but fundamentally of application of this material to modern historical and critical methods.

The tradition on 'Alī's Caliphate, particularly on his relations with Mu'āwiya, gives ample scope and justification for studies on the main features of the genesis and growth of Arabic historical recording. The subject is primarily of vital interest concerning Islam's internal political and religious development for the very reason that it coincides with the opening stages of the *fitna*, and because it might occasion theoretical discussions on which dynasty—the Umayyads, the Abbasids, or the Alids—was entitled to the Caliphate. Unlike, for instance, the description of 'Umar's share in the political organization of the Empire in the years of conquest, it is influenced neither by discussions on the origin of the administrative and fiscal machinery, nor on the rights of subjugated peoples and non-Arab converts, nor by any aspects whatsoever of foreign policy. On the whole, then, all circumstances point to the conclusion that the 'Alī-tradition's evolution may offer an adequate and representative elucidation of an important aspect of the growth of Arab historical writing.

---

38 cf. *AO* XXIII, 163 *sq.*

39 The publication of Balādhurī's work was introduced by W. Ahlwardt's edition of the section on 'Abd al-Malik's Caliphate (*Anonyme arabische Chronik* (Lpz. 1883)) and of deGoeje's brief survey on its contents (*ZDMG* 38 (1884)). Later a number of sections have been produced in translation (by Caetani, della Vida, and O. Pinto), but the complete edition undertaken by Hebrew University under the leadership of S. D. Goitein is still unfinished.

PART I

GENESIS OF THE TRADITION

1. General Background

Regrets are sometimes voiced by late traditionists that not until very late, and, as it seems, reluctantly, was the transmission—and particularly that of the Prophet—comitted to writing[1]. Seen in the light of the insecurity or doubt that must arise from the contradictions of *ḥadīths* this reaction is but natural. However, such credence as might in the Abbasid period be placed in the idea that an authentic and first-hand Prophet *sunna* did exist is untenable. The various forms of tradition do not appear to have crystallized until a practical need for an authoritative transmission arose. As regards the Quran tradition this happened, as could be expected, very early; as regards the Prophet tradition (insofar as it did exist) at a considerably later stage and, as it seems, occasioned by collocation of juristic and dogmatic *ḥadīths* with such biographical elements as may have existed, especially in the shape of accounts of the Prophet's military expeditions (*maghāzī*). Finally, the historical tradition did no doubt crystallize at a late stage[2].

The dating of the tradition's commitment to writing, again, affords no reliable quidance as to its age. Concerning the early tradition, its written form did not ensure the transimission's authencity, but rather helped to substantiate its oral narrative, which continued to be the normal procedure[3]. The first record of the historical tradition belongs, as mentioned above, to the transition period between the Umayyad and the Abbasid Caliphate; the earliest and more consistent presentation of the prose tradition and those intimations which we know in poetical form can be definitely traced to the preceding generation. Among the earliest traditionists is the Kufic *muḥaddith* ash-Sha'bī (d. ca. 104 A.H./725), whereas az-Zuhrī (d. 124/742), for instance, a Medinese scholar, to all appearances represents a transitional stage[4]. Irrespective of their outward

1 e.g. Sprenger: *Trad. wes.*, 4 *sq.*; Rosenthal: *Scholarship*, 42; cf. adh-Dhahabī cited by as-Sakhāwī: *I'lān*, 160 (Rosenthal: *Historiography*, 433).

2 cf. Becker, 263 *sq.*; Margoliouth: *Mohammedanism*, 18 *sqq.*, 63 *sqq.*

3 Johs. Pedersen: *Den arabiske Bog*, 26 *sqq.*

4 Sprenger: *Origins*, 303 *sqq.*, 375 *sqq.*; Abbott, 17 *sqq.*—It seems beyond doubt that al-Balādhurī (d. 892) utilized the written tradition from the eighth century; cf. *infra*, p. 138.

framing, none of the sources with which we are dealing can be less than one or two generations removed from the events described; although primary to us, they are in no way first-hand accounts. This being so, the questions arise whether it will be possible to form any idea of the basis underlying this transmission and under what circumstances the tradition took the shape in which it exists in the first half of the 8th century. Then again, any conceivable knowledge that may be obtained concerning this genesis will depend on what can be gleaned form the earliest known narratives, by inference from the known to the unknown.

For a fact-finding study it will often—as asserted by Wellhausen—suffice to excerpt and treat the earliest known coherent tradition as definitive sources. It, too, was admittedly built on the spoken or writen words of former or contemporaneous narrators, but it was also the first to compile the individual accounts with variants into a comprehensive picture, which the earliest informants, *ruwāt* or *akhbāriyyūn*, were unable to grasp or not interested in[5]. We must, however, recognize the obvious fact that our difficulties with regard to the sources cannot be surmounted by a reconstruction of the earliest collected tradition seeing that it, too, bears the stamp of individual points of view that have to be determined by confrontation with other sources or a probing of their inherent probability[6]. Moreover, the new material now made available in Balādhurī and in the Iraqi historian Naṣr b. Muzāḥim's (d. 828) *Waq'at Ṣiffīn* has revealed a close inner relationship between the earliest *muḥaddithūn*'s narratives. This relationship, in evidence in both the Iraqi and the pro-Syrian transmission, would suggest that the tradition must have been established in its main features at a very early stage—presumably in the late Umayyad period. We are thus most likely confronted with the traditions of certain schools which—with all due reservations—might be described as a kind of historiographical *sunna*, a generally recognized reading within a certain circle of events of the past.

It seems now fully established that the earliest generations did not attach to the *sunna* conception that same narrow meaning of "the Prophet's normative practice in authentically transmitted form" as did the classical jurisprudence of the 9th century. The *sunna* has been regarded as the rules in force in Islam. There cannot have been question of any universal *sunna*, only of a living tradition or a tradition of regional character ascribed *per fas et nefas* to local authorities, and still without the later tradition's rigidity[7]. This definition of

5 Wellhausen: *Prolegomena*, 4; *Kingdom*, introduction, viii *sqq*.

6 Wellhausen, too, was obliged to do so insofar as he was able to compare az-Zuhrī's pro-Syrian version (in Ṭabarī's quotations) with the Iraqian version in Abū Mikhnaf and others.

7 Margoliouth: *Mohammedanism*, 69 *sq*., 75; Schacht: *Origins*, 58 *sqq*.

the *sunna*, concept applies, strictly speaking, only to the *fiqh* doctrine, the normative ethics and jurisprudence, because only it served the social adjustment. In this shape the concept of *sunna* has also exercised an undoubted influence on the historical or pseudohistorical Prophet transmission as presented in the *sīra* (the Prophet biography), in which locally or politico-religiously accentuated impulses and differences can be observed. Also as regards the "profane" recording of history would there be every reason to apply this fundamental concept to the transmission of Islam's earliest history inasmuch as it, too, gradually assumed the character of *ḥadīth* discipline.

It will probably not be possible to trace the application of *isnād* to jurisprudence farther back than to the beginning of the 2nd century after the *hijra*[8], and the same, more or less, is true of the historical writing. The Medinese traditionist Ṣāliḥ b. Kaysān (d. 758) still considered *isnād* unnecessary in the Prophet tradition, whereas posterity (wrongly, we think) credited az-Zuhrī, his contemporary, with having taken the opposite view[9]. The early Abbasid period's historians do indeed very frequently quote traditionists from the late Umayyad period as definitive authorities. This applies, for instance, to the above-mentioned Ṣāliḥ b. Kaysān and az-Zuhrī, both of the Medinese school; and to ash-Sha'bī, 'Awāna b. 'Abd al-Ḥakam al-Kalbī (d. 751), Muhammed b. as-Sā'ib al-Kalbī (d. 763), and to some extent Abū Mikhnaf (d. 774) from the Iraqi circle. Naṣr b. Muzāḥim and, later, aṭ-Ṭabarī and al-Balādhurī normally quote these traditionists without tracing the *isnād* back further, to eyewitnesses or contemporaries. The chain of transmitters which those compilers make use of will in most cases be acceptable; very often the material of both schools follows homogenous courses and invariably with the same traditionists as intermediaries. In ash-Sha'bī the two Kufic traditionists al-Mujālid b. Sa'īd (d. 751/52) and Numayr b. Wā'ila (no date) appear most frequently as intermediaries from whom his material is taken over by compilers of the 9th century. In exactly the same way the Medinese tradition is quoted in the names of Ṣāliḥ b. Kaysān and az-Zuhrī by a purely Basrian school with great regularity and invariably as definitive authorities[10]. The conclusion must be that the 8th and, partly, even the 9th century considered an individual—the recognized local traditionist's authority—as an adequate and valid warrant for information concerning the past[11]. The normal practice in the earliest historical tradition thus appears to have been the same as that applied to jurisprudence: to quote an individual, a recognized scholar, as proof of the genuineness of a

8 Schacht: *Origins*, 36 *sq.*

9 Sprenger: *Origins*, 211; cf. also Caetani's comments in *Annali dell' Islām* I, introduzione, § 11.

10 cf. *infra* p. 109 *sqq.*

11 Even as-Sakhāwī can at the end of the 15th century draw up a list of the authors who quote tradition on one man's authority (*I'lān*, 118; Rosenthal: *Historiography*, 375).

narration or opinion, quite irrespective of the fact that he is no eyewitness or not even contemporaneous with the events that he describes. It is with these reservations that one is tempted to characterize the earliest *muḥaddithūn*'s transmission as a type of historical convention, a general historical idea bearing a regional or partisan stamp.

A qualitative reservation is, however, called for. As mentioned above, this definition of the earliest tradition's character is only partly true in the case of Abū Mikhnaf, for in numerous instances Ṭabarī quotes him as merely the unifying intermediary to earlier narratives that are traced back to eyewitnesses and contemporaries. In the authentic transmission such practice is of rare occurrence in those sections which deal with the political aspects of ʿAlī's Caliphate, the Caliph's administrative measures, his negotiations with his adversaries, and internal conditions—it is normally met with only in reports on military events[12]. It applies to the frequently circumstantial accounts of the combats of ʿAlī's troops at Basra, at Ṣiffīn, and at an-Nahrawān, and likewise to other military events in the first century of Islam. These same features can be observed in Naṣr b. Muzāḥim, whose account of the political development follows ash-Shaʿbī and a few other contemporary Kufic authorities, whereas the treatment of the clash at Ṣiffīn rests on different and earlier informants. It is thus natural to assume the existence of a difference as regards the handing down or quality between descriptions of the two themes of tradition as far back as the earliest narrations.

These battlefield reports bear all the factual and stylistic marks that distinguish the *ayyām al-ʿarab* presentation of the classical type: the Arab warrior's exploits, his courtesy, his observance of the formal rules pertaining to combat, and the frequent use of rhetoric and verse[13]. The chief deviation from the common *ayyām* account is that in Abū Mikhnaf and Naṣr b. Muzāḥim these tales sometimes touch on the *jihād* idea, the notion that the fight against the Caliph's antagonists is righteous, but, again, without their ever formulating precisely the standpoints of the two parties. To all appearances we are thus confronted with an element of very ancient origin, *ayyām* presentations based on the Iraqi *ruwāt*'s narratives, which are committed to paper in Abū Mikhnaf and Naṣr b. Muzāḥim. Our supposition is borne out by analysis—in such measure as is possible—of the *isnāds* used by these two traditionists, for they, too, show a certain uniform quality, the many varying names notwithstanding. The informants are often, like Abū Mikhnaf himself, persons belonging to the same tribe (Azd) or group of tribes in Iraq and distinguished by their anti-Umayyad

12 In Balādhurī, who, incidentally, is briefer than Ṭabarī on the military clashes, he is, on the other hand, invariably quoted as the definitive source.

13 cf. Caskel, 9 *sqq.*, 43 *sqq.*

feelings[14]. On comparing Abū Mikhnaf's presentation of the skirmishes and the combats at Ṣiffīn with Naṣr b. Muzāḥim's we find long passages to be in obvious agreement[15]. Naṣr very rarely quotes Abū Mikhnaf, and even though we cannot rule out the possibility of his having known the latter's presentation, we are taken back to informants who according to the context must be Iraqi *ruwāt* of the traditional type, carriers of the viva voce *ayyām* tradition.

All the known battle reports of this pattern are of Iraqi provenance whereas the corresponding Syrian transmission is now missing although we know for certain that this genre was cultivated for choice at the Caliph's Court in Damascus. It is, moreover, a striking fact that the handing down of the earliest *ayyām* tradition appears not to have followed the same channels as the pre-Islamic *ayyām* transmission, but to be due to Iraqi tribal traditions. Not until the advent of the controversial Kufic traditionists and genealogists Muhammed b. as-Sā'ib al-Kalbī and, especially, his son Abū Mundhir Hishām b. Muhammed (d. 819 or 821) do the two streams converge in the Kufic tradition. These two traditionists serve in large measure as links in the pre-Islamic *ayyām* tradition and—through Abū Mikhnaf—in the historical transmission of Islam's earliest years[16].

As regards the historical tradition, two different currents are thus unified in the first half of the 8th century in the nascent historical writing: an *ayyām* tradition of the well-known type and a presentation of politico-historical information[17]. In contrast to the first element, which represents nothing really new, the second element has been related to—or, if you like: one aspect of—the juristic and dogmatic traditional substance, carried by *muḥaddithūn* of local importance. To these must be added yet an element, namely the fragments of poetical transmission by a number of poets from the decades round the year 700. Their relations to the *ayyām* tradition are hardly of any decisive significance in this connexion, but it is, on the other hand, of great interest that in these poets we meet with opinions or points of view akin to those found in the strictly historical tradition both in Iraq and in Syria.

---

14 On banū Azd in the Umayyad period, see G. Strenziok in *E.I.*[2], 812 *sq.*

15 Brockelmann, 9 *sqq.*, 19 *sqq.*, and *infra* pp. 105 *sq.*

16 Caskel, 85 *sqq.*

17 cf. also Duri: *The Iraq School.*

2. Genesis of the Tradition

Even the earliest elements of the Kufic tradition, to which we shall for the present isolate the investigation, are available in various and somewhat divergent versions. The records that will come into consideration originate in ash-Sha'bī, al-Jurjānī (data unknown)[1], 'Awāna b. 'Abd al-Ḥakam al-Kalbī[2], an anonymous version from al-Balādhurī[3], and in 'Īsā b. Yazīd b. Da'b al-Kinānī (ca. 750)[4]. Common features are very much in evidence—concrete details as well as motivations—and even though the individual adaptations vary constantly, there must somehow exist a connexion. We cannot, of course, leave off here on the plea that these *muḥaddithūn* express a comprehensive idea of Kufic observance. It is, on the other hand, clear that the earliest Arab tradition's character of regional or partisan *opinio* will somewhat impede a mechanical isolation of one particular tradition as the primary one, a procedure that in practice will often be hampered in consequence of the tradition's immense scattering, its migrations along unverifiable channels, its cross-currents or interpolations. A comparison of accounts that have relevance in this connexion must above all aim at discovering their primary elements or motives. We shall then find that ash-Sha'bī's account on the whole represents the primary stage, those of the other authors the secondary stages.

As our point of departure for the comparison it may be expedient to isolate ash-Sha'bī's version. A continuous reconstruction of it may admittedly be out of reach for the following reasons: the transmission is fragmentary; ash-Sha'bī's chronologic disposition of the subject-matter has been lost in his successors' episodic quotations; and, finally, the veneration of ash-Sha'bī because of his legendary piety has resulted in his name being frequently lent to late and false traditions[5]. As regards the main features it will, nevertheless,

1 *Waq. Siff.*, 18–21, 37–42, 50 *sqq.* 58 *sqq.*

2 Tab. I. 3255–56 (Caetani IX, 234).

3 Bal. 494 r–v; b. al-Athīr III, 229 *sq.* (Caetani IX, 253, 238 *sq.*).

4 Bal. 498r–99v; cf. Ya'q. II, 214–17 (Caetani IX, 239 *sqq.* and § 329, note 1).

5 On ash-Sha'bī, see b. Khall, no. 316 (de Slane II, 4 *sqq*); F. Krenkow in *E.I*[1]. IV, 260 *sq.*— On the false ash-Sha'bī traditions, cf. Friedlaender: *Heterodoxies* II, 19, 77, 86, 95, 135,

be possible to eliminate the falsifications and to form a fairly reliable idea of his estimation of the events of these years. As was to be expected, ash-Sha'bī emphasizes the Kufians' share in the rebellion against 'Uthmān, the Kufic Quran readers' irritation at the Quraysh' alleged exploitation of as-Sawād without, however, mentioning the Kufians as directly implicated in the caliph murder[6]. In an exactly corresponding way he stresses the Kufic leader al-Ashtar's decisive effort in favour of 'Alī's election to Caliph, although the latter for fear of the Qurayshites' and, especially banū Umayya's reaction had desired a *shūrā*, an election conclave of competent men[7].

We have no knowledge of ash-Sha'bī's position on Ṭalḥa's and az-Zubayr's rebellion[8]. It appears, however, consistently from his material that Mu'āwiya's motivation of his hostile attitude to 'Alī was the demand for vengeance for the wrongfully murdered caliph's blood. A detached tradition according to which 'Uthmān's widow, Nā'ila, forwards to Mu'āwiya the victim's blood-stained shirt *(qamīṣ)* accompanied by a circumstantial account of his innocence and an intimation of 'Alī's indirect complicity cannot be placed chronologically, but it is instrumental to ash-Sha'bī's subsequent presentation, into which these elements keep entering[9]. After the battle of the Camel when 'Alī sent an envoy, Jarīr b. 'Abdallāh al-Bajalī, to Syria in order to request homage *(bay'a)* from Mu'āwiya, the latter in his capacity of 'Uthmān's *walī* raised the demand for vengeance, launched on his own initiative the agitation in Syria, accepted homage from the Syrians—though intrinsic details of this action are lacking—and, finally, entered into an alliance with 'Amr b. al-'Āṣ, who was promised Egypt. Already in his message to Mu'āwiya did 'Alī repudiate the accusations of complicity in the caliph murder as false. He vigorously asserted his legitimate right to the Caliphate seeing that *Muhājirūn* and *Anṣār* —who alone were entitled to vote—stood behind his election, whereas Mu'āwiya belonged to the freedmen *(ṭulaqā'; sing. ṭalīq)*, to whom the Caliphate is inadmissible. He who turns away from the *Imām* acceptable to God shall be brought back by force[10]. ash-Sha'bī's rendering of the Syrian governor's connection and agreement with 'Amr b. al-'Āṣ is not known; the only fact established is that Mu'āwiya's agitation in Syria catches Jarīr unawares, and he has to return without having accomplished his object. He was subsequently

142, 144; Schacht: *Origins*, 230 *sq.*; *AO* XXVII, 111.—In Bal: *Mu'āw.*, the two traditions on Mu'āwiya (nos. 132 and 143) are most likely false; the first anecdote is found also in *'Iqd* II, 299 referring to 'Amr b. al-'Āṣ.

6 *Agh.* XI, 30; Tab. I. 2915–21 (Caetani VIII, 86 *sq.*, 38 *sqq.*)

7 Bal. 465r–v; cf. Tab. I. 3074–75 (Caetani VIII, 328 *sq.*, 333).

8 A few details of minor importance are found in Tab. I. 3140, 3173–74 (factitious?) and 3189–90 (Caetani IX, 120 *sq.*, 127, 139 *sq.*).

9 *Agh.* XV, 71 *sq.* (Caetani VIII, 305 *sq.*); cf. *AO* XXIII, 166 *cum* note 5.

10 *Waq. Siff.*, 32 *sqq.*

taken to task by 'Alī and al-Ashtar, who accused him of being in league with Mu'āwiya[11].

Apart from one or two insignifant details the next we know of ash-Sha'bī's rendering is the arbitration agreement (the *ṣulḥ* letter) at Ṣiffīn[12]. According to this version the meeting is appointed for the next Ramaḍān (i.e. 37 A.H. = 12. Jan.–9. Febr., 658) at Dūmat al-Jandal. The two parties will submit to the Quran's judgment. They both undertake to resign themselves to the award pronounced by the two arbitrators, 'Amr b. al-'Āṣ and Abū Mūsā al-Ash'arī, and to refrain from any resumption of war. In ash-Sha'bī the climax is reached in his account of the proceedings before the arbitrators, which take place at Adhruḥ where either party sends a delegation of 400 men headed by respectively 'Abdallāh b. 'Abbās and 'Amr b. al-'Āṣ[13]. A great number of prominent Arabs attended the meeting, but Sa'd b. Abī Waqqāṣ deliberately stayed away in order to avoid contact with the *fitna*. During the hearing 'Amr b. al-'Āṣ again raised the question of 'Uthmān's innocence and Mu'āwiya's claim to vengeance. Abū Mūsā admitted both points, but refused to entrust the power to Mu'āwiya and instead put forward 'Abdallāh b. 'Umar as a candidate. At this point ash-Sha'bī's rendering is broken off so that we cannot be sure whether he has given any information on the two arbitrators' decision to set up a *shūrā* for a new caliph election, or on the famous report of 'Amr's deception in handing over the power to Mu'āwiya after his opponent had declared both 'Alī and Mu'āwiya deposed[14]. Subsequent allusions in ash-Sha'bī's account to 'Alī's relations to the Khārijites indicate that at any rate he knew the latter of these reports[15]. Chronologically ash-Sha'bī places 'Alī's clash with the Khārijites after the arbitration meeting, which in consonance with the *ṣulḥ* letter is fixed for Ramaḍān, 37 A.H.; the Khārijites' definitive break with 'Alī and their choice of 'Abdallāh b. Wahb al-Rāsibī for *Imām* is

11 *Waq. Siff.*, 66 *sqq.*

12 Ibid. 584–86; cf. Abū Mikhnaf's analogous version in Tab. I. 3336–38 (Caetani IX, 478 *sq.*). —The subject of the dispute is not mentioned in ash-Sha'bī's rendering, but it appears from his account of 'Alī's showdown with the Khārijites that it is still the question of the justification of 'Uthmān's murder.

13 Tab. I. 3354–56; cf. b. Sa'd IV.2.4. (Caetani X, 18 *sqq.*, corr. e agg., xxv). Whereas Ṭabarī states the meeting place to be "Dūmat al-Jandal, in Adhruh", b. Sa'd has only Adhruḥ. Ṭabarī's statement is due more likely to his own attempt to harmonize conflicting information; cf. *AO* XXIII, 186.

14 Cf. 'Awāna and Abū Janāb al-Kalbī in Tab. I. 3358–60 (Caetani X, 22 *sqq.*).

15 Cf. Bal. 532r (Caetani X, 103), where 'Alī informs the Khārijites that the two umpires have parted without agreeing, so he can now resume the war against Syria. Cf. also Bal. 534r–v (Caetani X, 83 *cum* note to § 96), where 'Alī in his *khuṭba* before an-Nahrawān reproaches the two umpires with having given their award in defiance of the Quran and the tradition; later they disagreed about the award. This source thus shows the well-known duplicity: award–violation; see also *AO* XXIII, 189 *sq.*

set down as the 10. Shawwāl, 37 A.H. (21. March, 658) and the battle at an-Nahrawān as the 9. Safar, 38 A.H. (17. July, 658)[16].

Despite occasional inconsistencies and uncertainties, ash-Sha'bī's basic view is clearly discernible. The conflict concerned the justification of 'Uthmān's murder, Mu'āwiya's claim to revenge and right to oppose 'Alī. ash-Sha'bī had hardly much liking for Mu'āwiya, let alone for 'Amr b. al-'Āṣ, whose worldliness and dishonesty he distinctly emphasizes, but the religious motives surrounding 'Uthmān's guilt or innocence remain the central factor. There is every probability that ash-Sha'bī dated the breach between the two parties to the time after the battle of the Camel; only then does Mu'āwiya launch his agitation for vengeance in Syria, and receive homage. It is noteworthy, however, that 'Amr b. al-'Āṣ plays no prominent part by Mu'āwiya's side except, inevitably, at the arbitration meeting. Characteristic of ash-Sha'bī's judgment of their mutual relations is an anecdote from the battle at Ṣiffīn where Mu'āwiya, as previously done by 'Alī, sets the Iraqi prisoners free in defiance of 'Amr's brutal advice to have them killed. The Syrian governor still observes the rules of combat. He is, moreover, sufficiently independent of 'Amr to be able to point to the predicament with which he might find himself confronted by following that advice[17]. On the other hand, ash-Sha'bī has no doubt whatever about 'Alī's legitimate title to the power and the unlawfulness of Mu'āwiya's rebellion. He does indeed stress the acceptableness to God of 'Alī's Imāmate, and that God will punish 'him that turns away from 'Alī's cause', Mu'āwiya as well as Ṭalḥa and az-Zubayr. On the whole, then, this rendering reflects an ideological cohesion of Kufic observance, even if it is not carried to extremes[18].

On confronting this presentation in ash-Sha'bī with such other versions as can come into consideration we find that three of them in their special framing, namely al-Jurjānī's, Balādhurī's, and 'Awāna's differ from ash-Sha'bī's in that they eliminate Mu'āwiya's initiative in the vengeance agitation in Syria and transfer it to 'Amr b. al-'Āṣ. He advises Mu'āwiya to initiate the action by influencing Shurāḥbīl b. as-Simṭ al-Kindī, "the leader of the Syrians", in favour of the vengeance claim[19]. On the other hand, they all give prominence to the fact that *Muhājirūn* and *Anṣār* had sworn allegiance to 'Alī, though, unlike ash-Sha'bī, without drawing the conclusions of their argumentation: That by

16 Bal. 530r–31r; 531r–32r (Caetani X, 101 *sqq.*). On the chronological modifications in this schedule cf. below pp. 38 *sq.*, 54 *sqq.*

17 Tab. I.3339–40 (Caetani IX, 480).

18 b. Ḥajār's information (*Tadhib* I, no 77, cf. Vaglieri II, 67, note 3) that ash-Sha'bī said himself that "he hates him who hates 'Alī and 'Uthmān" can hardly find direct substantiation in the material at hand.

19 In 'Awāna, however, merely: "the coryphæi among the Syrian chiefs".

its authoritative character the election is binding also on Muʿāwiya. Balādhurī's and ʿAwāna's renderings coincide with ash-Shaʿbī's in that they place these arguments on the occasion of ʿAlī's instructions to Jarīr b. ʿAbdallāh. al-Jurjānī, however, uses them on a few occasions, in one instance already after the battle of the Camel when ʿAlī appeals to Jarīr, who as governor in Hamadhān applies them to win his own people over for ʿAlī; and in another when he—somewhat illogically—makes a Syrian, ʿAbd ar-Raḥmān b. Ghann al-Azdī, impress on Shurāḥbīl b. as-Simṭ that *Muhājirūn* and *Anṣār* had elected ʿAlī despite the accusations of complicity in the caliph murder, accusations which if untenable would be one more reason for not trusting Muʿāwiya. Even this spreading of particular data, which varies from historian to historian, would indicate arbitrary shifts. This is especially true of the argumentation for the legitimacy of ʿAlī's election to Caliph, where the moral cogency of the Meccans' and Medinians' choice evanesces because of the alterations.

Muʿāwiya's motivation for his opposition to the caliph is still dealt with in these three versions, but it, too, gradually fades away. Outside this group is ʿĪsā b. Yazīd's version, even though still in many ways in close contact with al-Jurjānī's. Like the latter he makes ʿAmr b. al-ʿĀṣ responsible for the agitation against ʿAlī, and follows al-Jurjānī's account according to which ʿAmr consults with his sons about the opportuneness of ranging himself behind Muʿāwiya. He, also like al-Jurjānī, makes ʿAmr maintain that from the religious point of view the Syrian governor is not ʿAlī's equal. Moreover, ʿĪsā b. Yazīd makes use of the same—qualitatively rather insignificant—poetical sprinklings, which, incidentally, are not found in either Balādhurī's or ʿAwāna's version. Then again, the story about Shuraḥbīl b. as-Simṭ does not appear in ʿĪsā b. Yazīd. He, on the other hand, brings on a report that Muʿāwiya's half-brother Marwān b. al-Ḥakam, who had fled from Basra, felt slighted in favour of ʿAmr[20]. Of great significance, however, is the fact that ʿĪsā breaks the hitherto accepted view of the Syrian governor's stand by making ʿAmr render homage to him as Caliph—the former traditionists only discussed Muʿāwiya's right to act as ʿUthmān's *walī*. This dissociation from the Umayyads thus represents a far more extremist, or entirely Shīʿi point of view, remote from ash-Shaʿbī's appreciation[21].

20 This report probably reflects the division between the earlier and the later branch of the Umayyad dynasty, the Sufyānids and the Marwānids—Marwān b. al-Ḥakam was the founder of the latter—and their divergent interests; cf. Lammens: *Omayyades*, 391 *sqq.*; *AO* XXVII, 110.

21 Some of the features found in ʿĪsā b. Yazīd are met with again in a tradition in b. ʿAbd Rabbihi under al-Ḥasan al-Baṣrī's name (*ʿIqd* II, 290; Caetani IX, 252). It has no value as an independent source, and is most likely a fake (akin to b. Yazīd's version) to which the pious al-Ḥasan has had to lend his name.

To sum up the main features of the study of sources as rendered above: It is clear that ash-Sha'bī represents a less complicated, though more homogeneous—even if hardly chronologically older—stage than other historians in the Iraqian tradition. On certain points we have been able to demonstrate that, by comparison with his, any other tradition betrays a spreading of particular data and of motives, a fact that seems to indicate that ash-Sha'bī is expressive of a primary stage. However, the main factor is undoubtedly that the motive power and consequently also in some degree the responsibility for the Syrian rebellion is attributed variously in the five versions here discussed. In ash-Sha'bī we still find a full account of Mu'āwiya's motives and see how his actions are independent of his entourage, even though we may already observe attempts at an unfavourable depiction of 'Amr b. al-'Āṣ. In 'Awāna, Jurjānī, Balādhurī, and 'Īsā b. Yazīd, on the contrary, it is no longer Mu'āwiya, but 'Amr who makes the final decisions or adopts measures for the combats against 'Alī. It is 'Amr who gradually takes the initiative in the agreement with Mu'āwiya, and it is he who initiates and organizes the agitation in Syria. There is hardly any reason to think that the discrepance in question may be accidental; once more the circumstances indicate that ash-Sha'bī's description represents the primary version, an assumption confirmed by the fact that a few points lend themselves to a demonstration of the mechanism of this process of misrepresentation.

An approach to the legendary 'Amr figure is found in the otherwise comparatively sober-minded ash-Sha'bī's narrative of his consultation with his sons on the opportuneness of ranging himself behind Mu'āwiya and his agreement with the latter on Egypt. There is hardly reason to assume that these tales have any value as a source, but already in ash-Sha'bī the point of the anecdote is to establish that Mu'āwiya, unlike 'Alī, is religiously unworthy; that in this religious dilemma 'Amr "sells his religion for paltry worldly gains" held out by the Syrian governor; and that because of his patent worldliness he is destined to become the conflict's evil genius. In ash-Sha'bī this episode is not yet merged organically into the body of his rendering, the initiative in the agitation emanates from Mu'āwiya himself, and his motive is invariably the demand for blood vengeance. Proceeding to 'Īsā b. Yazīd we find the initiative in the agreement on Egypt transferred to 'Amr, and Mu'āwiya's motive is now his desire to attain the caliphate. What has happened, then, is an aggravation of the conflict's religious character, it is now a question of the struggle between the Prophet family's legitimate claim to sovereignty and the Umayyads' usurpation.

An Iraqi poet, an-Najāshī, intimates somewhere that Shuraḥbīl b. as-Simṭ has sided with Mu'āwiya, not because he felt convinced of 'Uhtmān's innocence, but on account of his personal hatred of Jarīr b. 'Abdallāh and al-

Ash'ath b. Qays, one of 'Alī's Iraqi followers[22]. The story of Shuraḥbīl is, as mentioned above, found again in Balādhurī; but neither of these authors gives the slightest hint on 'Amr's initiative in summoning him[23]. The first intimation of the hostility between Shuraḥbīl and Jarīr is found in al-Jurjānī, and not until then do we meet with also 'Amr's initiative and 'Amr's endeavour to utilize this antagonism in favour of Mu'āwiya[24]. In all probability, then, al-Jurjānī and an-Najāshī draw on the common tradition, which does not necessarily mean that they are dependent on each other. There is at any rate very little doubt that in this case the architects of the tradition operate with entirely arbitrary constructions over the available elements. an-Najāshī merely avails himself of the widely known antagonisms to make Shuraḥbīl's partisanship suspect, and Balādhurī merely has a report that Shuraḥbīl's attitude to the conflict makes Jarīr realize that he can achieve nothing; but al-Jurjānī combines these details with the tale of 'Amr's initiative in winning Shuraḥbil over to the demand for blood vengeance, and that, of course, presupposes 'Amr's acquaintance with his ill-will towards Jarīr.

On a preliminary recapitulation of the shift that has thus taken place in the earliest Kufic tradition we find the decisive factor to be the very mythogenesis surrounding 'Amr b. al-'Āṣ. There is no denying that he took an active part in the combat on Mu'āwiya's side, but the unreliable and wordly figure gradually emerging in the tradition is entirely due to Iraqi constructions in the transmission and to the attempts to motivate a contrast between 'Alī's rightful struggle and 'freedmen's rebellion'. A similar development—to which we shall revert below[25]—is observable on a few other points. We see it primarily in the famous report on 'Amr's exploitation of the Quran for his stratagem at Ṣiffīn: Advising Mu'āwiya to have the Syrian troops fasten Qurans to their lances in order to break off the fighting and cause dissension in 'Alī's camp. We likewise see it in the report on 'Amr's deception in respect of the arbitration award at Adhruḥ. On the whole, then, ash-Sha'bī's version and, especially, his attitude no doubt represent the primary stage in the Iraqi tradition, even though we can already here observe attempts at adaptation of the tradition.

In addition to this Iraqi tradition we are able to draw on another fairly contemporaneous material, the pro-Umayyad transmission, preserved chiefly

22 b. al-Athīr III, 230 (Schultess, 463; Caetani IX, 239); cf. below, p. 45.

23 Bal 494r–v and presumably from this b. al-Athīr, *loc. cit.* (Caetani IX, 253, 238 *sq.*).

24 *Wab. Siff.*, 54 *sqq.*—This element disappears again in Din., 169 *sq.* (Caetani IX, 246). The account of Shuraḥbīl's hatred of al-Ash'ath b. Qays is, on the other hand, found only in b. al-Athīr, where it may have arisen by learned combinations of other traditional material in order to explain an-Najāshī's hints; cf. Caetani IX, 239, 230 note 1.

25 cf. below, pp. 40 *sqq.*, 48 *sqq.*

through Balādhurī's quotations in his *kitāb ansāb al-ashrāf*, and also, occasionally, in Ṭabarī. This tradition, too, exists in two somewhat divergent versions, both formulated by prominent Medinese traditionists, viz. Ṣāliḥ b. Kaysān and b. Shihāb az-Zuhrī[26].

Concerning the Caliph election after 'Uthmān's murder Ṣāliḥ b. Kaysān states that 'Alī himself took the initiative[27], and that immediately after the election he offered the Syrian governor his friendship if the latter would only swear *bay'a* to him in the normal way, which Mu'āwiya indirectly refused in that he omitted 'Alī's Caliph title in his letter of reply. On 'Alī's receipt of this reply, the bearer exclaimed: "Oh, Quraysh's tribe. The horsemen, the horsemen. By God, there they shall be upon you with 40,000 horsemen!"[28]. It was not, however, until information on the battle of the Camel arrived that Mu'āwiya summoned the Syrians to battle for vengeance on 'Uthmān's blood, and for the demand that a *shūrā*, an election conclave, should be set up for the purpose of nominating an untarnished caliph. In support of his claims M'āwiya received oath of allegiance as *Amīr*, though not as Caliph; "so passed six months or more after 'Uthmān's murder", whereupon 'Alī started moving, and the two parties met at Ṣiffīn[29]. Ṣāliḥ b. Kaysān's report on the battle is unknown. In Balādhurī it is already replaced by another Syrian version from 'Iyāḍ b. Khalīfa (data unknown), who states that the battle did not get under way until the armies had faced each other for some time. After two days' fighting the Syrians began to give ground. Then a Syrian, b. Lahīya by name, rode forward with a copy of the Quran fastened to the ears of his horse. Others followed his example, and a cleavage arose in 'Alī's camp. So the Caliph had to agree to "having the Quran decide the dispute between the two parties". The Syrians rejected a proposal to choose two *Anṣār* for arbitrators because their objectiveness was considered questionable. Instead, 'Amr b. al-'Āṣ and Abū Mūsā were appointed. An arbitration document specifying the conditions

26 On him, see b. Khall. no. 574 (de Slane II, 581 *sqq.*); Horowitz: *Biographies*, 33 *sqq.*; same in *E.I.*[1] IV, 1342 *sq.*; Duri: *al-Zuhrī*, 1–12. az-Zuhrī's traditional material has like ash-Sha'bī's been subject to later adaptations; cf. Schacht: *Origins*, 175, 246 sq.; Mūsā b. 'Uqba, 291 *sq.*; *AO* XXVII, 99 *sqq.*

27 Bal. 464v–65r (Caetani VIII, 328). For the following cf. *AO* XXIII, 164 *sq.*, 187 *sq.*

28 Bal. 457v–68v (Caetani IX, 18–20). The bearer's outcry refers no doubt to the Umayyad massacre at al-Ḥarra in 683; cf. *AO* XXIII, 164, 170 *sq.*, and below p. 57.—Ṣāliḥ b. Kaysān's version of Ṭalḥa's and az-Zubayr's rebellion is known interpolated only in Abū Mikhnaf's version in Balādhurī (472r–75r; Caetani IX, 63 *sq.*) in such a manner that the two constituents cannot be distinguished with certainty.

29 Bal. 504r; cf. az-Zuhrī *ibid* 498r, 516v–17r (Caetani IX, 289, 488 sq.; della Vida, 453); cf. also Abu-l-Faraj Bar Hebræus: *Historia compendiosa Dynastarum*, ed. E. Pocock, 188 *sq.* (*versio*, 119 *sq.*), where this tradition is interpolated in other versions, probably al-Mas'ūdī's.

was drawn up. The contents of this arbitration agreement, however, are not stated[30].

Ṣāliḥ b. Kaysān says that the two arbitrators met at Tadmur in Ramaḍān, 37 A.H., but negotiations were postponed to the next year, when they met, first, at Dūmat al-Jandal and, finally, at Adhruḥ in Shaʿbān, 38 A.H., i.e. January 659. He thus seems to place the Khārijite rebellion and the battle at an-Nahrawān antecedent to the definitive meeting. Muʿāwiya arrives accompanied by a number of prominent Qurayshites, whereas ʿAlī fails to appear. Saʿd b. Abī Waqqāṣ claims to be entitled to the Caliphate because of his dissociation from the *fitna*. During the deliberations Abū Mūsā puts ʿAbd ar-Raḥmān b. al-Aswad az-Zuhrī, a prominent Qurayshite, forward as a candidate for the Caliphate, but this is turned down by ʿAmr, who enjoins upon his opponent the duty to re-establish the unity of Islam. ʿAmr then moves that one of them nominate the person that he considers the best qualified candidate. On Abū Mūsā's refusal ʿAmr takes the task upon himself so that his opponent should hereupon bind himself to accept ʿAmr's proposal. Then Abū Mūsā realizes his mistake, and the meeting breaks up in a quarrel during which the two umpires exchange insulting Quran verses. Ṣāliḥ b. Kaysān, nevertheless, concludes his rendering by having ʿAmr inform ʿAbdallāh b. ʿUmar that he is the nearest to the Caliphate, an idea that ʿAbdallāh b. ʿUmar indignantly rejects[31].

Broadly speaking, az-Zuhrī's rendering and reasoning follow Ṣāliḥ b. Kaysān's fairly closely despite discrepancies on certain points. In az-Zuhrī's version az-Zubayr and Ṭalḥa very soon broke their oath to ʿAlī, but did not leave Medina until four months after the caliph election[32]. Of greater significance, however, is the fact that his rendering differs from Ṣāliḥ b. Kaysān's in respect of the events at Ṣiffīn and in Adhruḥ. As regards the former case, az-Zuhrī says that when the Syrians feared being overwhelmed by their opponents, ʿAmr b. al-ʿĀṣ advised Muʿāwiya to have his men carry the Quran into the battlefield in order to appeal to its decision; he anticipates a consequent "cleavage among them (ʿAlī's troops), whereas Syrian unity and obedience would be strenghtened". On this point, then, az-Zuhrī comes near to the Iraqi version. In his report on the arbitration he says that "the two umpires were to judge according to God's Book and the common sunna *(al-jāmiʿa)*, not according to the particular (*al-mufarriqa:* the not generally adopted) *sunna*"[33]. az-Zuhrī's version of the arbitration meeting in Adhruḥ is a much

30 Bal. 515v–16r (Caetani IX, 489 *sq.*).

31 Bal. 521v–23r (Caetani X, 28 sqq.); cf. az-Zuhrī in Tab. I. 3341–43 (Caetani X, 26 *sqq.*).

32 Tab. I.3102–03; Bal. 481v–82r (Caetani IX, 53). We shall (below p. 58) revert to this point. In Balādhurī's contamination of Ṣāliḥ b. Kaysān and Abū Mikhnaf this feature is not found.

33 Bal. 514v–15r and in abbreviated form in Tab. I.3341–42 (Caetani IX, 488 *sq.*; X, 25 *sq.*); in an adapted form the same tradition is found also in b. Saʿd IV.2.3 (Caetani IX, 531).

abridged rendering of Ṣāliḥ b. Kaysān's[34]. The latter's circumstantial account of the outer framework of the meeting is almost entirely passed over; but he ascribes to al-Mughīra b. Shuʿba[35] the initiative in persuading the two arbitrators to invite ʿAbdallāh b. ʿUmar and ʿAbdallāh b. az-Zubayr[36] "accompanied by many", and makes him, in consequence of questions put to members of the meeting, a priori ascertain the impossibility of reaching a positive result from the negotiations. Finally, az-Zuhrī—in correspondence with the Kufic tradition—introduces ʿAbdallāh b. ʿUmar's candidature, while, on the other hand, leaving out ʿAbd ar-Raḥmān b. al-Aswad's. Such discrepances as are here ascertainable between the two pro-Umayyad accounts can hardly be explained otherwise than by adaption of traditions in the same way as in the Iraqi transmission. az-Zuhrī is apparently not uninfluenced by particular instances in the Kufic version. The point of the story comes out far more cogently here, and Ṣāliḥ b. Kaysān, thus, represents the primary version.

An exhaustive analysis of the primary Syrian-Medinese and Iraqi versions is made difficult by the fact that the former uses a very succinct and lapidary style, in contrast to ash-Shaʿbī's broad descriptions with numerous, often anecdotal, details and careful motivations. A provisional confrontation of the concrete information in ash-Shaʿbī's with that in Ṣāliḥ b. Kaysān's version will immediately expose a number of parallel features and some discrepances. Both versions date the breach between ʿAlī and Muʿāwiya after the battle at Basra, in which respect they agree with all other sources included into this study. Intrinsic criteria and independent testimonies in the sources constitute a strong case for the historical correctness of this dating[37]. Both versions likewise agree that Muʿāwiya himself took the initiative in the rebellion against ʿAlī, and in support of his demands on the Caliph received homage in Syria. But while ash-Shaʿbī fails to specify its signification, Ṣāliḥ b. Kaysān states that the homage was given to Muawiya in his capacity of *Amīr*. In this instance, too, the Medinese—and to some extent the Kufic—renderings are supported by independent, even though not quite clear, evidences in Arabic and contemporaneous Syrian sources[38]. Finally, both versions are in agreement in stating that the arbitration meeting took place in Adhruḥ and that a number of Qurayshites—whose names are in most cases even given identically—attended the negotiations. Up to their recording of the external frame-

34 Tab. I.3341–43 (Caetani X, 26 *sq.*).

35 al-Mughīra b. Shuʿba is a Prophet Companion noted for his impudence (cf. H. Lammens in E.I.[1] III, 683). In the historical tradition he often appears as a kind of outside commentator on events; cf. e.g. *AO* XXVII, 88 *sqq.*

36 az-Zubayr's son, see H.A.R. Gibb in *E.I.*[2] I, 54 *sq.*

37 *AO* XXIII, 174 *sqq.*; cf. also the poet ash-Shannī in Din., 162 *sq.* (Caetani IX, 166).

38 *AO* XXIII, 176 *sq.*

work of the arbitration, the two versions thus follow the course of events in a fairly uniform manner.

Ṣāliḥ b. Kaysān, unlike ash-Sha'bī, presents a very succinct motivation of the object of the conflict and Mu'āwiya's incentives. Both versions agree that the latter's opposition to 'Alī was due to doubts about the justification of the caliph murder and 'Alī's possible share in it. The Syrian-Medinese version adds that Mu'āwiya desired a *shūrā* set up for the purpose of electing an untarnished Caliph and thus emphatically accentuates his doubt whether 'Alī's attitude to the murder would permit him to fill the Caliphate. The latter point is entirely passed over by ash-Sha'bī, even though he very carefully pleads for 'Alī's innocence. It is, however, conspicuous that in addition to the general reference to the assertion that none but "the men in these *amṣār* (verbally: cities, metropoles)" have so far failed to swear *bay'a* to 'Alī, ash-Sha'bī puts forward one further assertion: The letter which 'Alī instructs Jarīr b. 'Abdallāh to deliver to the Syrian governor said he was not allowed to refuse *bay'a* because *Muhājirūn* and *Anṣār*, who alone are entitled to elect the Caliph, are on an equal footing with a *shūrā*. Such argumentation cannot be *a priori* rejected as unhistorical, but on comparising this information with the fact that in his version of 'Alī's election ash-Sha'bī distinctly states that 'Alī would not be content with an election by those present and had desired a *shūrā* in order to prevent a *fitna*, the logical coherence fails. The contrast to Ṣāliḥ b. Kaysān, then, must be due rather to an indirect refutation of the latter.

Besides the factual discrepance here ascertained there are chronological inconsistencies concerning the placing and interpretation of the meeting of arbitration and the Khārijites' rebellion. Whereas Ṣāliḥ b. Kaysān has the final arbitration at Sha'bān 38 A.H., i.e. presumably after the massacre at an-Nahrawān in Ṣafar that same year[39], ash-Sha'bī dates the meeting as at Ramaḍān, 37 A.H., before the clash with the Khārijites[40]. This latter dating corresponds with the time prescribed by the *ṣulḥ* letter. Unlike the Syrian

39 Apart from a single fragment, the Medinese School's account of the Khārijite opposition and rebellion is unknown. Moreover, Ṣāliḥ b. Kaysān's brief comments (Bal. 521v; Caetani IX, 545 *sq.*) are rather obscure. He distinguishes between three oppositional groups: one that returns home in protest against the arbitration agreement, one that wants to await 'Alī's subsequent conduct, and, finally, those that declare 'Alī an infidel—and are defeated at an-Nahrawān.

40 According to ash-Sha'bī the oppositionists broke away when 'Alī sent Abū Mūsā to the arbitration meeting in Ramaḍān 37; they elected 'Abdallāh b. Wahb ar-Rāsibī their Imām on the 10. Shawwāl 37 A.H. (21. March 658), before the outcome of the arbitration was known. The battle at an-Nahrawān is dated at 9. Ṣafar 38 A.H. (17. July 658) (Bal. 531r–32r; Caetani X, 101 *sqq.*).—Cf. the discussion on the chronological shiftings in Wellhausen: *Kingdom*, 87 *sq.*; della Vida, 485 *sqq.*; Buhl: *'Alī*, 72 *sq.*; Caetani X, 73 *sqq.*, 139 *sqq.*; Vaglieri I, 4 *sqq.*, 78 *sqq.*

tradition, ash-Sha'bī fails to mention that a deferment had taken place, so he seems to have obtained his chronological schedule by strict adherence to the clauses of the agreement. There is, however, hardly any doubt that the modification already here observed in the Iraqi tradition cannot be ascribed to an opposite meaning in the Syrian-Medinese; it is above all expressive of deference to the Khārijites and their incipient historical tradition[41]. The earliest Khārijite transmission—in 'Abdallāh b. Yazīd al-Fazārī (d. ca. 700)—very strongly emphasizes their opposition to the arbitration for religious reasons, and their demand for a military decision to reflect God's judgment (*ḥukm Allāh*) on the Syrians[42]. The Kufic tradition, on the other hand, seeks rather to efface the religious incentive. ash-Sha'bī accentuates the Khārijite opposition to the idea of having man judge in God's cause *(ḥukm ar-rijāl)*; he has 'Alī assert that he had but unwillingly yielded to the majority's demand for arbitration, so that after the arbitration meeting had ended in shipwreck, he could declare that the two umpires had betrayed Islam. The Khārijites' qualms about following the Caliph into a new attack on Syria, and their demand to 'Alī that he apologize for his religious offence in accepting arbitration in preference to a military decision appear, therefore, quite absurd[43].

Whereas ash-Sha'bī's chronological placement of the arbitration primarily serves to justify 'Alī's attitude towards the Khārijites' argumentation, the case is different as regards the rendering of the arbitration meeting. Where ash -Sha'bī asserts that the old Sa'd b. Abī Waqqāṣ stayed away from the meeting in order to avoid any part in the *fitna*, Ṣāliḥ b. Kaysān declares explicitly that not only was he present, he also considered himself better qualified for the Caliphate than anybody else because he had kept away from the *fitna*. Where the Kufic version states that the two umpires had decided in favour of 'Abdallāh b. 'Umar, Ṣāliḥ b. Kaysān ends up by having 'Abdallāh b. 'Umar refuse the dignity of Caliph as an entirely absurd notion in the given situation. The chief difference between the two versions—we take it here that ash-Sha'bī follows Abū Janāb al-Kalbī's account—lies, however, in their divergent

41 I hope to be able to explain later how the Iraqian tradition on the Khārijites (in ash-Sha'bī, Abū Janāb al-Kalbī, and Abū Mikhnaf) seems to have originated in polemics against or as tendentious excerpts from the Khārijite (Ibāḍite) tradition. The Khārijite transmission exists only from the Ibāḍiyya sect, a moderate Khārijite group (cf. *E.I.*[1] III, 372 *sq.*); it is now only known interpolated in writings of a far later date, in al-Barrādī's *kitāb al-jawāhir* (ca. 1400), in ash-Shammākhī's *kitāb as-Siyar* (ca. 1500), and in theological adaptation in Abū Sa'īd al-Qalhātī (11th century) (Vaglieri I, 12 *sqq.*; Kafāfī's introduction to Qalhātī, 29 *sqq.*), which all seem to build on a certain 'Abdallāh b. Yazīd al-Fazārī, presumably identical with the Khārijite theologian 'Abdallāh b. Yazīd al-Ibāḍī who lived in Kufa about 700 (Mas. V, 442 sqq.; Vaglieri I, 14 *sqq.*).

42 Ibid. II, 23 *sqq.*, 81 *sqq.*; Qalhātī, 40 *sqq.*

43 Bal. 519v–20r, 530r–32r, 534r–v (Caetani IX, 545; X, 101 *sqq.*, 83).

reading of the course of the meeting. The Kufic tradition has it that the two umpires reached an agreement, which ʿAmr b. al-ʿĀṣ subsequently violated by swearing allegiance to Muʿāwiya as Caliph after Abū Mūsā's having published the result of the negotiations and deposed both ʿAlī and Muʿāwiya. Ṣāliḥ b. Kaysān, on his part, carries an anecdote to show that the outcome of the meeting was decided during the negotiations. He, as well as az-Zuhrī, has it that ʿAmr outmanoeuvered his opponent by sheer trickery.

The number of contradictions here established between the Syrian-Medinese and the Iraqi transmission in some way or other bears on the central points of the conflict between ʿAlī and Muʿāwiya and the question of ʿAlī's worthiness. If he himself—as Ṣāliḥ b. Kaysān has it—had taken the initiative in his election, he would from the very outset have found himself in a vulnerable position; this fact also accounts for ash-Shaʿbī's emphasizing that ʿAlī had, as it were, the dignity of the Caliphate thrust upon him despite his wish for a *shūrā*. As already mentioned, ash-Shaʿbī further emphasizes that not only did all Islam, apart from Syria, stand behind ʿAlī's caliphate but his election was as valid as if it had been undertaken by a *shūrā*, and had a *shūrā* been set up, the result would have been the same. It is, on the other hand, likewise natural for Ṣāliḥ b. Kaysān to call attention to Saʿd b. Abī b. Waqqāṣ as an obvious candidate for the Caliphate against ʿAlī. He was at that time the sole survivor of the *shūrā* that had elected ʿUthmān and had refused to commit himself to recognize ʿAlī[44]. Even these early discrepancies are thus most likely due to mutual contradictions of the two versions, which respectively attack and defend ʿAlī's position.

This also applies more or less to the presentation of the arbitration meeting. Neither of the versions found in the two earliest historians are of any historical verisimilitude[45]. Both narratives are apparently heterogeneous in themselves and composed of two or three elements: the account of the outer framework of the meeting, the report of the negotiations, and, in so far as the Kufic version is concerned, the famous scene on the publication. It is obvious that the Syrian-Medinese report, which contains but little concrete information on the negotiations, can serve no other purpose than to stultify Abū Mūsā and to demonstrate that the two umpires did not make any progress at all. It is, on the other hand, equally clear that the Kufic version's account of the negotiations and the publication is entirely inharmonious. Quite apart from ash-Shaʿbī's subsequent statement that ʿAlī's objections applied to either umpire's offence against the Quran and the tradition[46], ʿAmr's deceit, if histori-

---

44 A hardly much later pro-ʿAlī tradition accordingly makes Saʿd refuse participation in a *shūrā* (*Waq. Siff.*, 79 *sqq.*; Yaʿq. II, 217; Caetani IX, 263).

45 In contrast to Vaglieri I, 90 *sqq.*; *E.I.*² I, 384 *sq.*—On the flwg., see *AO* XXIII, 190 *sqq.*

46 Cf. Buhl: *ʿAlī*, 76 *sq.*

cally true, would by itself have provoked reactions that would have left their marks in our sources. If we accept ʿAlī's protest against the legality of the award as described from the Kufic side, it will be wholly inconsistent to treat ʿAmr b. al-ʿĀṣ' violation of the agreement as the heart of the matter, and ash-Shaʿbī must, therefore, concatenate this accusation with the protest against the warranty of the award.

Even though neither of the versions, then, consitutes a homogeneous whole they can hardly have come into existence without some kind of interconnection. Both carry nearly identical lists of those present, and their direct contradiction in respect of Saʿd b. Abī Waqqāṣ and ʿAbdallāh b. ʿUmar point in the same direction; it is, like-wise, remarkable that both have ʿAmr and Abū Mūsā make use of the same verses from the Quran[47] for the purpose of defaming each other when the meeting was shipwrecked. The crucial point, however, is this: The Kufic rendering describes the negative result as due to ʿAmr's deceit concerning the agreement, whereas Ṣāliḥ b. Kaysān and az-Zuhrī leave the impression that it was due to Abū Mūsā's incompetence at the conference table and, therefore, not to any fraudulence. Further according to ash-Shaʿbī's rendering, the two parties had in the *ṣulḥ* letter bound themselves to acquiesce in the arbitration award and not to revert to war, so only by representing the result of the arbitration as unlawful could ʿAlī's caliphate still be justified[48]. The only reasonable explanation of these absurd contradictions must thus be that the two accounts also on this point polemize against each other, and that the depiction in both cases rather depends on premeditated fabrications without any relation to the facts.

It is, indeed, remarkable how even the earliest accounts veil the events at Ṣiffīn and in Adhruḥ behind polemical constructions, and how difficult it is, especially to the Kufic version, to justify ʿAlī's conduct with the Umayyads and Khārijites. The Syrian version, both in ʿIyāḍ b. Khalīfa and az-Zuhrī, states that ʿAlī accepted arbitration without protest, and both Ṣāliḥ b. Kaysān and az-Zuhrī emphasize that ʿAlī failed to fulfil his obligation by staying away from the arbitration meeting, whereas Muʿāwiya arrived punctually. This statement, if correct, would in conjunction with the negative result of the arbitration imply that ʿAlī himself was wanting in will or ability to restore Islamic unity—as indeed accentuated by both renderings—and consequently justify Muʿāwiya in his receiving oath of the allegiance after the Adhruḥ meeting[49]. Again, ash-Shaʿbī tells that both Muʿāwiya and ʿAlī sealed the

47 viz. *sure* 7:174 *sq.*, and 62:5.

48 That the arbitration award appears to have caused defection among ʿAlī's adherents is quite logically veiled by ash-Shaʿbī in that he dates it to a time after an-Nahrawān (Tab. I. 3430; Caetani X, 187 *sq.*).

49 Cf. *AO* XXIII, 196.

arbitration agreement with the Caliph-seal[50], even though ʿAlī did not recognize his antagonists as believers and by drawing up the *ṣulḥ* message renounced his title of Caliph, the legitimacy of which Muʿāwiya called in question. But ash-Shaʿbī still maintains that ʿAlī had merely bowed to the majority's desire and that his *renunciatio tituli* did not affect his authority as Caliph; only after the battle at an-Nahrawān did he realize the hopelessness of his position and assented indirectly to Muʿāwiya's Caliphate[51]. So according to this account, the disintegration of ʿAlī's Caliphate cannot be ascribed to Muʿāwiya's activities, the religious unlawfulness of which ash-Shaʿbī consistently maintains, but to Khārijite opposition.

The consequences of the growing tradition round the ʿAmr figure can, quite naturally, be traced in the modifications that occur in the rendering of the *ṣulḥ* message. In ash-Shaʿbī it still says that the two parties are to resign themselves to the award passed by the two umpires on the basis of God's Book and the generally recognized *sunna,* By a comparison of this version of the agreement with the somewhat later one in the, incidentally, not very reliable Kufic traditionalist Jābir b. Yazīd al-Juʿfī (d. 128–32/746–50)[52] the differences will be shown up very strikingly. To a stipulation in ash-Shaʿbī to the effect that the two umpires are to enjoy personal security he adds a new clause: As long as they do not offend against the right guidance; if they fail to follow God's Book, the Islamic community shall revert to a state of war. The consequence of this version must be that the award does not bind ʿAlī if it be passed in an unlawful way; the shifting thus taking place presupposes not only knowledge that the umpires' decision failed to dispose of the quarrel but also, undoubtedly, of the apocryphal account of ʿAmr's treachery after the negotiations in Adhruḥ. Only by a modification of this kind can the Kufic tradition justify before its opponents that ʿAlī—in ash-Shaʿbī's words—has power to condemn the award as well as the two umpires' conduct, which have "delivered the believers from their responsibility"[53].

All circumstances thus seem to show that these events, which unquestionably concern a cross-roads in Islam's earliest history, are veiled by prosecution and defence of opposite opinions even in the earliest stages of the tradition. And it is the continuation of these proceedings that we observe in the secondary, Kufic tradition's shifting of the balance between Muʿāwiya and ʿAmr b. al-ʿĀṣ. It will hardly be possible to trace the prose tradition further back than to ash-

50 Accdg. to the text, both seals bear the legend "Muhammad, God's Prophet" (*Waq. Siff.*, 584).

51 Vaglieri II, 67; Bal.: *Muʿāw.*, no 143. As L. Veccia Vaglieri says, the tradition is no doubt false, most probably from ash-Shaʿbī's own hand.

52 *Waq. Siff.*, 578–82.

53 Bal. 534r–v (Caetani X, 83).

Sha'bī's, Ṣāliḥ b. Kaysān's, and az-Zuhrī's generation, and even these authors' material betrays a by no means inconsiderable tampering with the tradition. But in some of the leading poets from the decades round 700 we find occasional manifestations of different opinions of the kind that we have dealt with[54]. The poets of particular interest for our purpose—and whose stanzas have been preserved in such measure as to enable us to determine their general tenor with reasonable accuracy—are the Syrian Court poets al-Akhṭal (d. 710)[55] and Ka'b b. Ju'ayl (d. 690)[56], and the Iraqi an-Najāshī (d. after 669)[57], al-A'war ash-Shannī, Dhu-r-Rumma (d. ca. 729)[58] and al-Aswad b. al-Haytham.

The first four represent, as we shall see, extreme standpoints; the latter reveal less complex views, as seen, for instance, in a verse by Dhu-r-Rumma in honour of Bilāl b. Abī Burda b. Abī Mūsā al-Ash'arī[59]. The poet lauds Abū Mūsā for having on the Adhruḥ Day strengthened the religion when it faltered, and for having warded off the civil war already in progress—a conception which is undoubtedly incompatible with any idea of 'Amr's trickery in the prevalent Kufic presentation. al-Akhṭal in an enigmatic verse similarly intimates that Mu'āwiya intervened in the negotiations "when the two umpires did nothing but fear each other and err"[60]. This statement—its obscurity nothwithstanding —cannot by any stress of the imagination be harmonized with the Syrian-Medinese or with the Iraqian reading of the Adhruḥ negotiations. There is here no question of any deception during or after the negotiations, and the accusation against 'Amr must therefore appear to have originated at a comparatively late time.

---

54 We may in this connexion bypass the large number of poems that according to historians were contemporary; for one thing, these products are hardly of much interest as sources or as literature, and, for another, their authenticity is very often in dispute. This applies, e.g., to Mu'āwiya's poem in Bal. 500r (cf. Hishām b. 'Ammār ad-Dimashqī's comment; Caetani IX, 256); in 'Īsā b. Yazīd and al-Ya'qūbī an analogous stanza is ascribed to 'Amr b. al-'Āṣ, and presumably indicative of the shifting of the tradition. Similarly, there is hardly any reason for confidence in—at any rate the first part of—the stanza which Balādhurī (500r–01r; Caetani IX, 254) on the authority of al-Haytham b. 'Adī ascribes to al-Walīd b. 'Uqba b. Abī Mu'ayṭ; it conflicts with the next poem (also in Tab. I.3258), which alludes to the to all appearances false correspondence between 'Alī and Mu'āwiya, for it is met with for the first time in Abū Mikhnaf (cf. *AO* XXIII, 169). Elsewhere it is explicitly stated that poems are composed in the spirit of al-Ash'ath b. Qays (Brockelmann, 17); cf. also Lammens: *Omayyades*, 95 note 3, 168 note 5, and 274. On the following, see especially Lammens: *Mo'āwiya*, 252 *sqq.*; Nallino, 176 *sqq.*

55 Lammens: *Omayyades*, 211–68; *GAL* I, 43 *sqq.*; *(S)* I, 83 *sq.*; Nallino, 115 *sqq.*

56 *Ibid.*, 118, 178, 205, 239.

57 Schultess, 421 *sqq.*, 459 *sqq.*

58 *GAL* I, 58 *sq.*; *(S)* I, 87 *sqq.*; Nallino, 137 *sqq.*

59 Yāqūt I, 174 *sq.* (Caetani X, 56).

60 al-Akhṭal, 79 (Caetani X, 60).

Far more extreme and differentiated opinions are found in Ka'b b. Ju'ayl and an-Najāshī. Both of them present the conflict as national antitheses. Syrians and Iraqis detest each other's hegemony, as it says in b. Ju'ayl; 'Alī is the Iraqis' *Imām*, while "Hind's son (i.e. Mu'āwiya) pleases the Syrians", and he stresses the insuperable obstacles to mutual submission. He, unlike an-Najāshī, maintains that Mu'āwiya's rebellion is due not to personal ambitions, but solely to the fact that the Caliph protects 'Uthmān's murderers and fails to express a clear standpoint when the question is put to him[61]. Ka'b b. Ju'ayl's occasional glimpses from Ṣiffīn are of secondary interest[62], but his report concerning the Adhruḥ meeting: That when the umpires "discussed the legacy from Muhammad, his ('Amr's) deception gave Hind's son the leadership among the Qurayshites", a point of view in keeping with the Syrian prose tradition; the matter is decided at the conference table by 'Amr's stratagem, not by deception after the decision has been pronounced[63].

On turning to an-Najāshī's production we find his estimation to be in fair consonance with al-Jurjānī's and also to some extent with ash-Sha'bī's. In a great poem he urges Mu'āwiya "to forgo a cause that cannot be otherwise, for God has already declared that to be right which you endeavour to evade". The Iraqis and Hijazians stood united behind 'Alī who had already "put the fellowship of az-Zubayr and Ṭalḥa to flight, and the band of perjurers". The poem concludes with a manifestation of his indignation that the Syrians "have placed 'Alī and his adherents on an equality with the son of Hind"[64]. The same theme is subsequently taken up by an-Nahāsjī in phrases severely condemning "the Syrians for having sworn allegiance to you (Mu'āwiya)" against the Iraqis who have complied with 'Alī's earnest request "in a cause which will win glory for the righteously guided and which despises twaddle and nonsense"[65]. So the poet immediately reveals that he is entirely in line with the prose tradition in attaching great weight both to the legitimacy of 'Alī's election to the office of Caliph and to the belief that the support by the Iraqis and Hijazians is binding upon the Syrians too. He can thus quite logically—also in his explicit polemic against Ka'b b. Ju'ayl—entirely suppress Mu'āwiya's motives. The claim for vengeance for 'Uthmān is merely hinted at in a disparaging way,

61 Din., 170 *sq.*; *Kam.*, 184 *sq.* (where Muāwiya's motives, however, are bypassed) (Caetani IX, 256, 247; Buhl: *'Alī*, 60 *sq.*).—The same idea is found again in al-Akhṭal, 174 sq. (Caetani IX, 529 *sq.*).

62 Tab. I.3296–97; Din., 190 *sq.* = Bal. 513v–14r = Yāqūt III, 403 (in part); Din., 191–93 = Tab. I.3286–88 (Caetani IX, 446, 499 *sq.*, 487, 501, 440).

63 Bal. 523r = Yāqūt I, 174 *sq.* (Caetani X, 30, 56).

64 Din., 171; the first verses also in *Kam.*, 187 (Schultess, 463; Caetani IX, 247); cf. the poem from Ṣiffīn in Schultess, 464 *sq.*; Caetani IX, 449 note 3 to § 21. A similar evaluation is found in al-A'war ash-Shannī (Din., 162 *sq.*; Caetani IX, 166).

65 Bal. 500r–01r (della Vida, 455 *sq.*; Caetani IX, 255).

whereas the conflict assumes a national character. That he knew the Syrians' motives is apparent from a passage in which he denies that Shuraḥbīl b. as-Simṭ sided with Mu'āwiya for factual or religious reasons[66].

an-Najāshī's stanzas, like those of Ka'b b. Ju'ayl, are of little interest concerning the battle at Ṣiffīn; they are generally expressive of a uniform laudation of 'Alī and his comrades-in-arms and of a one-sided derision of the opposing party[67]. It is noteworthy that he nowhere mentions 'Amr's feints. His verses leave the impression with the reader that the Syrians were actually on the verge of flight[68], and in a brief stanza he has a particularly significant description of how the Syrians since the morning of the Ṣiffīn day fastened Qurans to their lances for the purpose of appealing to God's judgment—a version that is unmistakably different from and contradictory to the well-known Iraqian presentation of 'Amr's Quran stratagem[69].

There is no evidence in an-Najāshī on the subsequent events. An idea of how the Kufic side evaluated the arbitration negotiations can, however, be gleaned from, for instance, a poem by al-Aswad b. al-Haytham[70] in which he underlines that Abū Mūsā "did not consider it lawful to fail. He that failed was 'Amr. Oh, 'Amr, by forsaking the judgment you have proved the indignity of your life; may you be deprived of divine aid. He departed the Quran, he did not expound the verses, but contrarily remained in doubt when he was promised Egypt". This view of the Adhruḥ meeting is in fact entirely in line with what finds expression in the Kufic prose tradition of the following generation. 'Amr's denying his faith against the promise of Egypt is seen already here, and it is likewise stressed—as a natural consequence of the first action—that 'Amr failed in that he "forsook the judgment", that is: broke the agreements entered into on the conclusion of the negotiations; he is for this reason denied divine aid and thereby excluded from that covenant which binds the believers to each other in one unity. In other words, we have one more proof that the Iraqian tradition has at an early stage made 'Amr b. al-'Āṣ the prime mover in the rebellion against 'Alī's to-God-acceptable rule.

This poetry, belonging in the decades round the year 700, represents an evaluation of the years of conflict from 656 to 661, which, though revealing initial stages of a progressive traditional formation, does in many respects anticipate the earliest prose tradition in the first half of the 8th century. These circumstances must naturally give rise to the question whether the poetical tradition, which is generally of a slightly earlier date than both the Kufic and

66 b. al-Athīr III, 230 (Schultess, 463); cf. above pp. 33 *sq*.
67 Thus Din., 185, 198 (Schultess, 464; Caetani IX, 495, 505).
68 Schultess, 465 *sq*.; Caetani IX, 449 note to § 21.
69 Mas. IV, 378 (Schultess, 467; Caetani IX, 523); cf. *AO* XXIII, 183.
70 Yāqūt I, 174 *sq*. (Caetani X, 56).

the Syrian-Medinese transmission, was the model for the prose tradition, or whether both traditions should be regarded as shoots from the same stem, a common tradition that would, then, hardly be of a much later age than the events it depicts.

This approach is not without precedence in historical research. We know that the Scandinavian saga tradition is partly built over the skaldic poetry, and the same approach to the problems appears in B. G. Niebuhr's well-known, though quite untenable, hypothesis of an epic poetry underlying Titus Livius' presentation of Rome's earliest history[71]. It has in much the same way been asserted that the Islamic prose tradition drew extensively on the poetical transmission: "La poésie conserve les archives du peuple arabe ... Je n'ai cessé de montrer l'influence considérable exercée par la poésie sur l'historiographie arabe ...; tous (les chroniqueurs arabes) très empressés à se documenter dans les poètes arabes", says Lammens[72]. A few definite cases do exist where the late and secondary historical writing has developed and substantiated the poetical transmission by means of a combinational technique, but it will hardly be possible to maintain this conception categorically[73].

We may take it for granted that no poetry of an epic character is to be found in either the classical *ayyām al-ʿarab* tradition or the narratives with which we are here concerned[74]. Normally we know the poets' productions but fragmentarily through quotations by later historians, and even where they—as, for instance, al-Akhṭal's monumental, laudatory poem on the Umayyads—are available *in extenso* in the form of a *qaṣīda*, we find the presentations not epic, but commenting; not narrating, but morally evaluating. Often, no doubt, they are composed for particular occasions, though hardly contemporaneous; their presentation generally lacks in organic cohesion with past or subsequent events. In most instances they are merely allusions to the events dealt with, allusions that defy comprehension without knowledge of the prose tradition. Such is our position today, and such, too, was the position of historians in the Abbasid period; only those of that or the immediately following time, to whom the events might still be of topical interest, were able to add substance to hints thrown out by the poets. It would thus, if for no other reason, be irrational to assume that the prose transmission had come into existence by constructions over elements contributed by the poets; reversely, the poetical version must be dependent upon a tradition or recollection in coherent, epic form.

---

71 cf. e.g. E. Fueter, 467 *sq.*

72 Lammens: *Ommayyades*, 278 *sq.* with references; cf. pp. 95 note 3, 168 note 3, and 274; cf. also Margoliouth: *Lectures*, 59 *sqq.*

73 On such cases of construction, see above, p. 43; Caetani IX, 200. W. Caskel came to the same result concerning the *ayyām al-ʿarab* literature (Caskel, 66 *sqq.*).

74 Not until very late is historical writing in epic-poetical form met with on Islamic soil, and then rather owing to Persian influence; Margoliouth: *Lectures*, 65 *sq.*; Nallino, 258 *sq.*

This special fashioning of the poetical transmission seems to indicate that it cannot have been a direct model for the prose tradition, although the tendencies of both versions coincide in several of the instances dealt with in this work. Poetry, then, is scarcely a fundamental element in the traditionists' presentation. In most cases the historian will introduce poetry in order to utilize its static character primarily to support his own estimation rather than to carry on his narrative. In his dramatizing version, poetry may accomplish an important function, especially for the purpose of elucidating or motivating the actions of the *dramatis personae* (e.g. the psychological motivation of Mu'āwiya's summoning 'Amr and in elucidation of the latter's religious dilemma). The main point, however, is this: The historian's constructions defy any explanation based on information in the poetical works because both versions intermingle primary and secondary traits. There may be exceptions, and the traditionists may have borrowed certain details from the poets, but the most natural explanation is obtained by regarding the poetical as well as the prose transmission as developments of a common—presumably oral—tradition.

It is difficult to get any idea of in what mode this tradition existed. Posterity has—probably in exaggerated form—ascribed antiquarian interests[75] to Mu'āwiya, but that circumstance will hardly be of any use in establishing a connection. It is, however, of the greatest interest to observe the interrelation of the renaissance at the Umayyad Court of the classical Arabic poetry and the contemporaneous political poetry[76]. The agitatorial cogency of the poetry must undoubtedly be seen in the light of old Bedouin conceptions which attributed supernatural powers to the *rāwi* whose principal duty was to defend the tribe's honour or by his art to defame the adversary. The particular quality which the poetry thus acquired gave it unique possibilities as a factor in influencing public opinion, a fact that serves to explain its static and libelous form. It is then a product of the rulers' or their adversaries' official interpretation of the events.

There is no lack of evidence that both the Umayyads and their enemies made use of the gifts of the *ruwāt* for political ends. Mu'āwiya and his successors tried energetically to recruit panegyrists and agitators to counteract the Iraqian propaganda, and in emulation of their adversaries formed their own poetical party, *Shī'a*[77], to which Ka'b b. Ju'ayl and al-Akhṭal belonged. The Syrian rulers appear to have attached particular weight to the religious motivation of their caliphate, obviously because they were without their adversaries' asset: 'Alī's relationship with the Prophet. From one of these poets, 'Abdallāh b. Zabīr al-Asadī (d. 680), who belonged to the "Umayyads' *shī'a*", we learn that

75 Lammens: *Mo'āwia,* 354 *sqq.*; Abbott 9, *sqq.*

76 cf. Lammens: *Mo'āwia,* 252 *sqq.*; Nallino, ch. iii, *passim.*

77 Lammens: *Mo'āwia,* 264.

it is in reality Mu'āwiya to whom "asseveration of the religion"[78] is due, a statement of quite particular interest in that the propaganda thus acquires an object beyond the topical political aims. 'Abdallāh b. Zabīr is here undoubtedly alluding to the clash between 'Alī and Mu'āwiya. It was Mu'āwiya who overcame the *fitna* which had arisen at 'Uthmān's murder, and for which 'Alī indirectly shared the responsibility. It was Mu'āwiya who restored Islam's unity, the asseveration of the religion, as the poet puts it—an evaluation that is, incidentally, related to the one already met with in the prose tradition. To al-Akhṭal the Umayyads are likewise "God's Caliphs" who at Ṣiffīn received confirmation of God's support[79]. On the other hand, a slightly later Iraqian tradition asserts that the Prophet had predicted that 'Alī would come to shed Qurayshite blood for religion's sake[80].

So in this perspective poetry is raised to the politico-religious level and serves to motivate and defend the legitimacy of the Umayyad Caliphate against 'Alī's adherents in Iraq, or, *vice versa*, to throw suspicion on its title to suzerainty. It is therefore natural that the events which carried the Syrian Caliphate into power acquire a significance by far surpassing the antiquarian one. This phenomenon is very discernible in the Syrian and Iraqian poets. In Dhu-r-Rumma and al-Akhṭal we do not yet find any traces of the Syrian or Kufic prose tradition's version of 'Amr b. al-'Ās's deception in Adhruḥ, and an-Najāshī knows nothing of the report on 'Amr's exploitation of the Quran for his stratagem at Ṣiffīn. On this background it is noteworthy how 'Amr's share in and responsibility for the conflict assumes an increasing prominence, also in this branch of the tradition.

The formation of the tradition around 'Amr b. al-'Āṣ's Quran stratagem cannot be followed up in all its details. As we have seen, it has not yet materialized in an-Najāshī, and we cannot ascertain its existence in full display until the middle of the 8th century in such historians as Jābir b. Yazīd al-Ju'fī[81] and Abū Mikhnaf[82]. It is thus clearly due to a subsequent rationalization in the Kufic transmission, and the story of 'Amr's deception or trickery in Adhruḥ must, therefore, likewise be due solely to construction. This episode was absent in the earliest poets, but appears indirectly in al-Aswad b. al-Haytham's poetry whence it enters into 'Awāna b. 'Abd al-Ḥakam's, Abū Janāb al-

78 Lammens: *Mo'āwia*, 265.

79 *Idem: Omayyades*, 233.

80 Wensinck, 17.

81 *Waq. Siff.*, 546 *sq.*

82 Tab. I. 3329 (Caetani IX, 472). As mentioned above, this account is found also in az-Zuhrī, where it is presumably borrowed from the Kufic transmission.—It will appear from this review that I do not accede to L. Veccia Vaglieri's argumentation for the correctness of the episode (Vaglieri I, 24 *cum* note 2). The fact that most sources know the account cannot be decisive in the judging.

Kalbī's and, presumably, ash-Sha'bī's narrations. In contradistinction hereto we have from the Syrian side—in Ṣāliḥ b. Kaysān and az-Zuhrī—fairly contemporaneous, energetical protests against this version for the very reason that this event bore especially on the religious and moral aspects of the conflict. Both episodes, then, like the Kufic tradition's shift of the initiative in the Syrian rebellion from Mu'āwiya to 'Amr, are legendary, and must have arisen fairly early, probably in the decades about the year 700.

Once more it is no doubt Mu'āwiya's personal qualities underlying this process of adaptation: his *ḥilm*, as it comes to expression in his tolerance and opportunism, gradually assumes the character of passiveness, deficient competence or outright dependence upon 'Amr b. al-'Āṣ's astuteness. The perversion of Mu'āwiya's *ḥilm* into despicable cowardice before his enemies is observable already in the poets and in ash-Sha'bī[83], and contrasts his qualities with the chivalry *(futuwwa)* and the courage which the tradition in course of time ascribes to 'Alī[84]. And at the same time we see a qualitative, religious contrast being established between the two parties. It will appear from elements in the secondary accounts how Mu'āwiya's motives for his rebellion against 'Alī lose their religious substance as 'Amr b. al-'Āṣ's quite uninhibited worldliness penetrates into the tradition. In consequence hereof the conflict undergoes a complete change of character, and if Mu'āwiya's vengeance action could be proved to be merely a pretext, the legitimacy of his assumption of power would also become questionable.

Such shifts as we have been able to trace in the earliest transmission appear to be closely related to the formative process of the tradition itself, and it is difficult to find any consistent line of development. The actual events are veiled very early behind polemic constructions; in some of the poets and in Ṣāliḥ b. Kaysān, az-Zuhrī, and ash-Sha'bī we can still follow the reflexes of a discussion on the religious propriety of Mu'āwiya's conduct, on 'Alī's possible complicity in the caliph murder and on the justification of asserting that Mu'āwiya, unlike 'Alī, would be able to reestablish that *concordia omnium* which the *fitna* had wrecked. The later and secondary smearing or secularization of the Syrian governor's motives will then merely be the logical consequence of a development that had already taken place. Chronologically, the formation of the Arab tradition stretches over one or two generations. The earliest evidence of a discussion concerning 'Alī's Caliphate is found in such poets as Ka'b b. Ju'ayl and an-Najāshī, i.e. (presumably) in the late years of Mu'āwiya's reign. But already these poets' way of presenting the problems reveal a peculiar conglomerate of primary and secondary traits, which are

83 cf. Bal.: *Mu'āw.*, no. 132.

84 cf. Noeldeke, 28 *sqq.*; *AO* XXIII, 168 *sq.*

found again in the traditionists of the following generation, Ṣāliḥ b. Kaysān and ash-Shabī. The material at our disposal shows clearly that the conflicts issuing from 'Uthmān's murder were still of current interest after 'Alī's death and the establishment of the Umayyad Caliphate.

The genesis of historical tradition coincides temporally with the formation of the Shī'i opposition in the Eastern provinces until the first decades of the 8th century. The early Kufic tradition stresses the solidarity behind 'Alī's cause as the heart of the earliest Shī'ism[85], and the resistance and beginning risings against the Umayyads are, we think, attributable to the Iraqian Arab tribes' aversion to the resumption of the Medinian Caliphate's politics[86]. The first really serious Shī'i revolt occurred in 685–87. It was headed by the Kufian al-Mukhtār b. Abī 'Ubayd ath-Thakafī and not only anti-Umayyad, but also religious and social currents were here involved. Religiously, the Imamate was upon the death of 'Alī's and Fāṭima's sons Ḥasan and Ḥusayn transferred to their half-brother Muhammad b. Ḥanafiyya, and the *mahdī* idea—the divine guidance attributed to him—was thus incorporated into the Imamate. The revolt obtained social significance by an unprecedented occurrence: it was joined by *mawālī*, the non-Arab clients, i.e. converts without any religious or economic privileges[87].

This rebellion, too, was quelled, but the ramifications of this second civil war lasted until 692. However, behind it and behind the comparative quietness on the surface in Iraq under 'Abd al-Malik (685–705) and his heavy-handed governor al-Ḥajjāj b. Yūsuf there was ferment and intense propaganda on both sides. Politically, the decades are marked by reaction after the civil war, the stationing of Syrian troops in Iraq, and the arabization and centralization of the administration. It is exactly in this milieu that the formation of the historical tradition takes place; from the outset it bears the impress of violent discussions between Syrian and Iraqian points of view, which gradually leave the problems that had been predominant during the first civil war and turn to discussions concerning the politics and the justifications of the Umayyad Caliphate. The formation of the historical tradition consists above all in reflections of the political and religious conflicts of its own age, so there can be very little doubt that the tradition in itself was a product of the prevailing state of affairs.

85 an-Nawbakhtī, 15 *sqq.* (*RHR* 153, 194 *sqq.*); Tab. I.3350–51 (Caetani IX, 542). The religious veneration, however, hardly plays any part as yet, even though there may have been tentative approaches in that respect (cf. an-Nawbakhtī, 19 sq.; RHR 153, 199 *sq.*; Friedlaender: *b. Saba'* II, 27 *sqq.*; Hodgson in *E.I.*² I, 51 *sq.*); cf. also Moscati, esp. 255 *sqq.*

86 Wellhausen: *Opp. parteien*, 55–74.

87 an-Nawbakhtī 20 *sqq.* (*RHR* 153, 200 *sqq.*); della Vida in *E.I.*¹ III, 773 *sqq.*—On the *mahdī* concept, see D.B. MacDonald *ibid.* III, 120 *sqq.*

The most conspicuous feature in the historical tradition's genesis, then, is its touch of polemics. We have quite often observed the Syrian and Kufic poets endeavour to refute one another in mordant phrases, and, later, the Medinian and Kufic traditionists shape the transmission so that it will contradict the other party's version in chronology and facts. We know for certain that both Ṣāliḥ b. Kaysān and az-Zuhrī had relations with the Caliph's Court in Damascus. Ṣāliḥ b. Kaysān had apparently been attached to ʿUmar (II) b. ʿAbd al-ʿAzīz (717–20) by ties of personal friendship and as his children's teacher[88]. az-Zuhrī was likewise in contact with the Court, for Yazīd II (720–24) appointed him *qāḍī*, and Hishām (724–43) entrusted him with the education of his son[89]. From his pupil Muʿammar b. Rashīd (d. 771) we know that the rulers made him lend his name to false pro-Umayyad traditions[90]. To b. Rashīd this procedure discriminated in principle az-Zuhrī's authority; to our knowledge there is, however, nothing to contradict the assertion that he has at any rate wielded his pen to serve the Umayyad points of view.

Even the earliest tradition—the Kufic as well as the Medinese—is distinguished by its eclectic methods. Their rendering shows above all a partisan *opinio,* and methodically the shaping of the tradition is marked by harmonization and construction. We have often in all of them observed how the elements for their versions, true or false, are concatenated into a collective entity representing their particular points of view and bearing their name and authority[91]. az-Zuhrī accepts the Iraqian report of ʿAmr's Quran stratagem which he uses without reference to his source, and, like Ṣāliḥ b. Kaysān and ash-Shaʿbī, links up correct and apocryphal accounts of the arbitration meeting into one connected whole. Behind that work are both historical information through oral channels and constructions of details—especially around the figure of ʿAmr b. al-ʿĀṣ—of no factual interest to the historian, but with a deliberate function in the creation of public opinion at the transition from the 7th to the 8th century.

---

88 Sprenger: *Notes*, 208; della Vida 431, note 2.

89 cf. Horowitz: *Biographies*, 33 *sqq.*; Duri: *al-Zuhrī*, 11 *sq.* It is rather peculiar that the Syrian caliphs could apparently not make use of Syrian traditionists; that Medinese scholars could undertake the defence of the Umayyads may be a consequence of Medina's scepticism concerning the Iraqian opposition or view of it as being contrary to the interests of Ḥijāz.

90 Goldziher: *M.St.* II, 33 *sqq.*; *AO* XXVII, 99 *sqq.*

91 On az-Zuhrī, cf. Duri: *al-Zuhrī*, 8.

3. Secondary Stages of the Tradition of the Umayyad Era

The fragments on which we were able to draw in the preceding section for the purpose of determining the historical tradition's genesis indicated that even in its earliest stages the transmission of ʿAlī's Caliphate had been subject to decisive factual shifts in consequence of its inclusion into the topical political disputes during the decades around the year 700. This situation does not undergo any change in the last fifty years of Umayyad domination. The social and religious discords, of which we find the first seeds in al-Mukhtār's rebellion in 685, were deepened, primarily because society's beginning Islamization engendered serious difficulties. The Arab tribes in Iraq and Persia were partially assimilated, and the indigenous population was gradually converted, so that both the taxation on land in Arab possession and the poll-tax levied on *mawālī* constituted a religious and social discrimination, which could not be immediately set off within the framework of the military and aristocratic organization that the caliphal power had so far established. The Umayyads did, admittedly, succeed in devising taxational principles to solve this dilemma and to pave the way for a levelling of such problems as were raised by the old rules. However, the solution came too late to ward off the outbreak of latent ill-will towards the Syrian Caliphate.

Such changes as the extremist groups *(ghulāt, rāfiḍa)* underwent in the opening decades of the 8th century were to prove decisive factors in the Shīʿi oppositional movements. According to the tradition Muhammad b. Ḥanafiyya's son Abū Hāshim before his death in 716 transferred his Imāmate claims to the Abbasid Muhammad b. ʿAlī[1]. Thus an important branch of the extremist

1 an-Nawbakhtī, 29 *sq.*, 42 *sq.*, 46 (*RHR* 153, 211 *sq.*; 154, 79 *sq.*, 83 *sq.*), S. Moscati s.v. Abū Hāshim in *E.I.*² I, 124 *sq.*—The tradition may, according to Moscati, be correct, although it is generally assumed to reflect the Abbasid attempt to legitimate, *post festum*, their assumption of power.—This resistance movement is named after Abū Hāshim, and not, as sometimes maintained by the tradition, after Muhammad's, ʿAlī's, and al-ʿAbbās's common ancestor; but in the transmission the designation is frequently employed, as we shall revert to below, to establish Banū Hāshim's unity against their opponents.—On the following, see Wellhausen: *Kingdom*, 492 *sqq.*; *Opp. parteien*, 93 *sqq.*; B. Lewis's survey of the modern view points in *E.I.*² I, 15 *sq.*

Shīʿism came under Abbasid leadership in the Hāshimiyya movement, which from about 718 organized intensive propaganda from Kufa against the Umayyads in Iraq and Persia, and at the same time Shīʿism adopted a number of religious or messianic concepts from *mawālī*. After an intensive propaganda the rebellious movement proper against the Umayyads was launched in Khurasān in 747 and already three years later brought about the fall of the Syrian Caliphate. In this connection it is likewise of the greatest significance that the primary aim of the Shīʿi and Hāshimite agitation was to establish the Prophet family's *(ahl al-bayt)* legitimate title to the caliphate and to lay claim to practical enforcement of Islam's ethical normæ. The opposition considered the Umayyad Caliphate irretrievably compromised; the Syrian Caliphate was identified with the Arab tribal community. It is stamped as a profane monarchy *(mulk)* with roots in the pre-Islamic heathenism *(jāhiliyya)*, and from a pietistic point of view entirely incompatible with Islam's fundamental ethical and religious principles[2].

The ideological clash of the victorious eastern provinces with their former opponents is known *ad nauseam* from the merciless persecution of the Umayyads in the *ḥadīth* transmission for having transformed Muhammad's theocratic society into a profane *mulk* and for having broken the religious continuity from the Prophet by usurping the power to the detriment of ʿAlī[3]. The latent *fitna* and the unredemeed expectations of the to-God-acceptable caliphate without internal dissension would therefore continually need interpretation in the light of actual conflicts, an interpretation which in the historical writing assumed forms of ever increasing bitterness. The decisive shift in the earliest tradition concerned the moral responsibility for Muʿāwiya's revolt. The initiative in the Syrian action was transferred to ʿAmr b. al-ʿĀṣ, which gave rise to a contrast with a strong religious touch between the two parties, and which made the justification of Muʿāwiya's conduct appear somewhat doubtful[4]. The consequences of this reshaping can, however, be followed up through the late Umayyad age in diverse forms.

In ʿAwāna b. ʿAbd al-Ḥakam al-Kalbī[5] this tendency is observable in full

2 *HT* 11:V, 466 *sq.*

3 cf. Goldziher: *M.St.* II, 31 *sqq*; Lammens: *Moʿāwiya*, 189 *sqq.*

4 It is conceivable, though, that pietistiscal circles have by these very constructions wanted to avoid a too categorical condemnation of Muʿāwiya, who belonged after all to the Prophet's *aṣḥāb*, or have wanted to avoid a breach of the orthodox community's continuity by rejecting the Umayyad dynasty as illegitimate.

5 On the latter, se Margoliouth: *Lectures*, 83; Saleh el Ali in *E.I.*² I, 760. Highly different versions of ʿAwāna's personal standpoint are given in the biographical sources; he is reported as pro-Umayyad, pro-ʿUthmān, or extremist Shīʿi (Alawid, member of a proto-Nuṣayrite sect). None of these epithets is confirmed by our material. That he is not Uthmanite is shown, e.g. by Bal.: *Muʿāw.*, no 55, whereas his attitude towards extremist Shīʿism is obscure. ʿAwāna is primarily anti-Umayyad.

operation. On one point his exposition is identical with ash-Sha'bī's: The caliph's letter delivered by Jarīr b. 'Abdallāh informs Mu'āwiya that he has received oath of allegiance from *Muhājirūn* and *Anṣār*. On another point he differs from ash-Sha'bī in that he entirely passes over the authoritative nature of the election, which bound also Mu'āwiya to submission, and merely refers to the fates of Ṭalḥa and az-Zubayr. By this curtailment 'Awāna's story entirely loses its point and, reversely, his version reveals that the discussion no longer turns on the religious scruples Mu'āwiya had expressed concerning 'Alī or his demand for the setting up of a *shūrā*. The tendentious adaptations here undertaken seem to be in perfect agreement with 'Awāna's silence in the matter of Mu'āwiya's motives. The latter hesitates to reply to Jarīr b. 'Abdallāh in order to gain time for summoning 'Amr, who advises him to win the Syrians over to his side by "fastening the blame for 'Uthmān's blood on 'Alī"[6]. The Syrian action thus becomes a mere pretext for denying obedience to 'Alī, and consequently unlawful.

In 'Awāna's exposition 'Amr b. al'Āṣ has become the central and leading figure. In Balādhurī we are given the Kufic rendering of the arbitration meeting in 'Awāna's name[7]. It is likewise striking that for the first time we find here accusations against both 'Amr and Mu'āwiya for having themselves failed 'Uthmān. According to 'Awāna, 'Abdallāh b. 'Abbās denies the accusations against 'Alī for complicity in the caliph murder because Mu'āwiya himself hesitated when the distressed caliph appealed to him for help, whereas 'Amr, who had participated in the agitation against 'Uthmān, had fled to Palestine in time[8]. There is hardly any reason to believe in this anecdote, which does not appear until the secondary stages of the tradition, and which is probably nothing but a product of the polemics against the Syrians for the purpose of substantiating their unwarranted assertions. The decisive point is that at this stage of the development of the tradition the true nature of the conflict evanesces completely; Mu'āwiya's and 'Amr's revolt is according to this version quite secular and obviously illegal.

It is indeed noteworthy that the shifts in the tradition so far observable have had rather slight bearing on the chronological system in the Iraqian transmission. The most important exception in this respect is that ash-Sha'bī and a long series of subsequent *muḥaddithūn* have dated the arbitration meeting to the time appointed in the *ṣulḥ* letter, and timed the 'Alī-Khārijte showdown to

---

6 Tab. I.3255–56 (Caetani IX, 234). It cannot be ruled out that Ṭabarī has performed an abridgement *(ikhtiṣār)* of the account, though it is not probable; cf. also *infra* p. 154.

7 Bal. 525v–27r; cf. Caetani X note 4 to p. 18 and p. 24.

8 Bal.: *Mu'āw.*, no 255. The same tradition appears in the contemporaneous Muhammad b. Sā'ib al-Kalbī (Tab. I.2985–86; Caetani VIII, 166 *sqq.*; cf. *AO* XXVII, 89 note 25) and is touched on also in 'Īsā b. Yazīd; cf. *infra* p. 61.

occur after that event. On the other hand, ash-Sha'bī, the secondary Iraqian, and the Syrian-Medinese tradition are all in agreement that the breach between 'Alī and Mu'āwiya did not happen until Jarīr b. 'Abdallāh sojourned in Syria, i.e. after the battle of the Camel. The earliest Iraqian transmission has scarcely any further information on a contact between Syria and Iraq before this time[9], and the introduction of 'Amr b. al-'Aṣ in the given context goes to confirm this consensus concerning the dating of the breach. On proceeding to Abū Mikhnaf's version, which is of a somewhat later date,—this scholar died presumably in 774[10]—we shall find a completely different exposition. This is where for the first time we meet with a report in anecdotal form which says that immediately after the caliph election al-Mughīra b. Shu'ba advised 'Alī to let Muawiya keep his governorship and to allocate the two *miṣr*, Kufa and Basra, to Ṭalḥa and az-Zubayr in order to pacify them, but the caliph turned down the proposal at the instance of 'Abdallāh b. 'Abbās[11]. Moreover, the caliph dispatches a messenger to Mu'āwiya for the purpose of obtaining his recognition; but the Syrian governor refused to comply, so the messenger returns with the statement that he "came from a people that asserts that you ('Alī) have murdered 'Uthmān, and that will not rest content until they have killed you in avengement for him"[12].

Abū Mikhnaf thus links up Mu'āwiya's action with the rising of the 'Uthmāniyya. Mu'āwiya immediately rejected the newly elected caliph's demand for *bay'a* and acted *ipso facto* illegally. This is quite in line with Abū Mikhnaf's statement: That when Ṭalḥa and az-Zubayr ask the caliph's permission to go on *'umra* (pilgrimage), 'Alī asks them whether they intend going to Iraq or to Syria[13]. Apart from this recording of the temporal and factual coincidence Abū Mikhnaf's concatenation of the two rebellions has not been carried further. No sooner had Ṭalḥa and az-Zubayr left Medina than they withdrew their *bay'a*, raised the demand of vengeance for 'Uthmān's blood, and seized Basra. According to Abū Mikhnaf, Mecca as well as Medina and Kufa remained loyal to 'Alī, whereas he stresses the two claimant's mutual conflict of authority and their attachment to the old circle of Exiles in Medina.

Abū Mikhnaf, on the other hand, knows nothing of Jarīr b. 'Abdallāh al-

---

9 cf., however, *infra* p. 56.

10 Rosenthal's dating of Abū Mikhnaf's death at about 223/837–38 (*Historiography*, 63) can hardly be correct. According to Ṭabarī (cf. Wellhausen: *Kingdom*, 246 *sq.*) he was a friend of Muhammad b. Sā'ib al-Kalbī's (d. 763); this is also consistent with the fact that Hishām b. Muhammad al-Kalbī (d. 819/21) quotes him directly, and that he himself quotes ash-Sha'bī from al-Mujālid b. Sa'īd (d. 752/53) and Muhammad b. Ishaq (d. 768). About Abū Mikhnaf, see H.A.R. Gibb in *E.I.*[2], I, 140 with references.

11 Bal. 466v (Caetani VIII, 330).

12 Bal. 467v–68r (Caetani IX, 19).

13 Bal. 472r (Caetani IX, 63).

Bajalī's mission to Syria. Instead, he brings a circumstantial exchange of notes, in many ways a mere repetition or an exacerbation of that clash of interests between the Prophet family and the Umayyads of which we have already been apprised through other Iraqian sources[14]. In his letter Muʿāwiya accuses the caliph of complicity in the murder of ʿUthmān on the grounds that he failed to take measures against the murderers, and that he sheltered them. Under menace of war he now demands that they be handed over. Muʿāwiya goes on to remind ʿAlī of his having shown his ill-will towards the caliph elected at the three former elections, and especially towards ʿUthmān, who least of all deserved it. In his reply ʿAlī denies any share in the responsibility for the caliph murder and contends that Muʿāwiya's vengeance claim is merely a pretext for the purpose of obtaining secular power. He reminds Muʿāwiya of Banū Hāshim's[15] services to and sufferings for Islam, and that he (ʿAlī) had been offered the caliphate already on the Prophet's death by Muʿāwiya's father, Abū Sufyān—an offer he had rejected for fear of being allied with people rooted in *jāhiliyya*.

Abū Mikhnaf thus places the breach between the two parties to a date already immediately after the caliph election, and this shift is carried through consistently. Even in al-Jurjānī we find statements about negotiations dated to the months of Rabīʿ I–II and Jumādā I–II, presumably 36 A.H., i.e. 28th August–23rd December 656; the chronology here is, however, rather doubtful[16]. The negotiations are directed by Quran readers *(qurrāʾ)* who have to interrupt the participants' bickerings in order to save the negotiations from complete failure. In consequence of this exposition the two armies must have faced each other already at this time, when ʿAlī was occupied by this showdown with the ʿUthmāniyya. This does not preclude the possibility of orientational negotiations having taken place, even though this information may have served also to show that Muʿāwiya raised his vengeance claim immediately after the caliph murder. The linking up of such negotiations with the events at Ṣiffīn does not carry

14 Bal. 494v–97r; cf. *Waq. Siff.*, 61 *sqq.* (Caetani IX, 253 *sq.*); *AO* XXIII, 167, 169 *sq.*

15 cf. *supra* p. 52, note 1.

16 *Waq. Siff.*, 211 sqq.; cf. b. al-Kathīr: *Bidāya*, 141v–42r (Caetani IX, 293, where, presumably, Muhammad b. Saʿd should be rectified as ʿUmar b. Saʿd (Saʿīd), who likewise is b. Kathīr's source of the subsequent tradition; on this ʿUmar b. Saʿīd, see *infra* p. 111). In b. Kathīr the whole account is thoroughly repudiated in that ʿUmar b. Saʿīd immediately afterwards in what is obviously an apocryphal tradition states that fearing the recognition of ʿAlī by the Quran readers Muʿāwiya tricks ʿAlī into leaving his strategically advantageous position at Ṣiffīn by pretending sabotage of the Iraqi camp at Euphrates (b. Kathīr: *Bidāya*, 142r; Caetani IX, 294 *sq.*). The compilators of an only slightly later date seem to have realized the chronological inconsistencies of the account. The above four months appear in b. al-Kathīr's rendering only, whereas Naṣr b. Muzāḥim has only the latter three, and Dīnawarī (181; Caetani IX, 283) only the former three.

conviction, and the circumstance that the time limit nearly coincides with the battle of the Camel indicates that we are dealing with a complete or partial artifice that represents a transitional stage between ash-Sha'bī's and Abū Mikhnaf's chronological systems.

This account of skirmishes and negotiations during the first six months of 'Alī's Caliphate is not found in Abū Mikhnaf in complete form, probably because it was difficult to harmonize it with his detailed presentation of the caliph's preparations for war, or because it anticipated the diplomatic activity in his version. In a short transmission he merely tells of 'Alī's attempts immediately before Ṣiffin to persuade Mu'āwiya to abandon his project on the grounds that it was in fact due to impious lust for power and to lack of piety. The negotiations are dated by Abū Mikhnaf to Dhu-l-Ḥijja, i.e. May–June 657[17]. The chronological shift of the breach is thus quite consistently effected in Abū Mikhnaf, and his passing over of Jarīr b. 'Abdallāh's mission to Damascus must be deliberate.

There is, then, no reason to believe in Abū Mikhnaf's dating or in the circumstantial notes presented by him. We know the earliest sources to be correct in their dating of the breach to a time after the battle of the Camel[18]; it appears, moreover, from his account that he was aware of the presumably rather late discussion between the orthodox parties and the Shī'a on 'Alī's half-hearted attitude to the first caliphs and on his tittle to the caliphate[19]. As *terminus post quem* for this redating of the breach we are able to fix with certainty the time for the second civil war, for Abū Mikhnaf says that on receiving Mu'āwiya's rejection of *bay'a* after the caliph election 'Alī prophesied the fall of Medina. This *praedictum post eventum* must no doubt refer to the massacre at al-Ḥarra in 683 when Yazīd I's Syrian troops defeated the Medinians, who had supported 'Abdallāh b. az-Zubayr's rebellion[20]. After these events Medina lost its political influence for ever, a fact implying that the consequences of this defeat at al-Ḥarra were foreseeable at the time when Abū Mikhnaf shaped his tradition.

On confronting Abū Mikhnaf's version—a distinctly secondary one—with the Syrian-Medinese tradition in Ṣāliḥ b. Kaysān and az-Zuhrī the polemic element already observed in the formation of tradition once more stands out clearly[21]. Ṣāliḥ b. Kaysān concedes that Mu'āwiya rejected 'Alī's demand for *bay'a* immediately after the caliph election in an anecdotal form reminiscent of Abū Mikhnaf's, and it can hardly have come into existence without knowledge

17 Tab. I.3270–72 (Caetani IX, 274 *sqq.*).
18 cf. *supra* p. 37.
19 cf. Noeldeke, 32 *sq.*; Buhl: *'Alī*, 13 *sqq.*, 22 *sqq.*
20 cf. *AO* XXIII, 166 *sqq.*, 170 *sq.*
21 On the following, see *ibid.*, 168–74.

of the latter's version. He maintains, however, that the actual breach did not occur until "six months or more" after the election, i.e. after the battle of the Camel when Muʿāwiya sets up his vengeance claims and receives homage as *Amīr*. This dating, which does not occur in az-Zuhrī or in Abu-l-Faraj Bar Hebraeus, is rather puzzling unless we assume that Ṣāliḥ b. Kaysān was acquainted with Abū Mikhnaf's version.

Ṣāliḥ b. Kaysān's judgment of the ʿUthmāniyya's rising cannot be ascertained. But on proceeding to az-Zuhrī we are enabled to extend our pursuance of the chronological inconsistencies. He is in agreement with Abū Mikhnaf that Ṭalḥa and az-Zubayr repudiated their *bayʿa* when they had left Medina, but according to az-Zuhrī the two rebels did not leave the town until four months after the caliph election. They thought of going to Syria, but on learning that Muʿāwiya himself contemplated blood vengeance they preferred Basra. On this point az-Zuhrī's rendering is at variance with Abū Mikhnaf's; he disso-ciates himself clearly from the latter's identification of the ʿUthmāniyya's and Muʿāwiya's revolts—he can hardly have approved of the former[22]; Muʿāwiya nursed his own plans, and a four months' interval is created between the formal repudiation of ʿAlī and the ʿUthmāniyya's departure from Medina.

It is practically inconceivable that the Syrian-Medinese tradition should have been formulated without knowledge of the Kufic one, or, conversely, that Abū Mikhnaf was out of touch with Ṣāliḥ b. Kaysān and az-Zuhrī. The connection observed is, we think, most likely a manifestation of mutual polemics in line with what we have already ascertained. Such chronological discrepancies as we have established will thus serve as a reasonable explanation of why Ṣāliḥ b. Kaysān and az-Zuhrī do not challenge the assertion that Muʿāwiya immediately and formally disapproved of ʿAlī's election, though they vigorously assert that his demand for blood vengeance and wish for a new caliph election had no relation to the ʿUthmāniyya's revolt and was not put forward until this rebellion had been crushed. It is obviously to this interpretation that Abū Mikhnaf raises objection. He maintains ʿAmr b. al-ʿĀṣ's responsibility for the Syrian revolt, but by means of the reports on Muʿāwiya's refusing to recognize ʿAlī and on ʿUthmān's blood-stained *qamīṣ*[23] he puts the breach ahead to the summer of 656. On the other hand, he replaces the account of

22 az-Zuhrī distinguishes between the two rebels; he makes ʿAlī establish that despite their common belonging to Banū ʿAbd al-Muṭṭalib, ʿAbdallāh b. az-Zubayr was the one who caused the dissension. ʿAlī and az-Zubayr are reconciled; the fact that the battle of the Camel did take place nevertheless was due to b. az-Zubayr's intervention and Ṭalḥa's refusal to submit to the Quran's decision as proposed by ʿAlī (Tab. I.3184–87; Caetani IX, 136 *sq.*). These viewpoints come very near to the later ʿUthmāniyya and Muʿtazilite opinions; cf. *infra* pp. 72, 112.

23 Agh. XV, 71–72 (from ash-Shaʿbī; Caetani VIII, 305 *sq.*; cf. *AO* XXIII, 166 with note 5).

Jarīr b. ʿAbdallāh's mission with the circumstantial and highly doubtful exchange of notes.

This fundamental shifting of the chronological course in Abū Mikhnaf as compared with the earlier Iraqian tradition must naturally give rise to the question: Why does it occur at just this stage in the traditional development? This alteration is obviously secondary in relation to the mythogenesis around ʿAmr b. al-ʿĀṣ, even though hardly much later chronologically. From the material available to us Abū Mikhnaf has unreservedly accepted the condemnation of ʿAmr; the narratives of the Quran stratagem and the violation of the arbitration award occur in full display in his version[24]. Even this creation of the legendary figure tends, as mentioned above, to make Muʿāwiya's religious motives subject to suspicion, and Abū Mikhnaf goes still a step further. By raising the question of Muʿāwiya's removal from the governorship of Syria every doubt of Abū Mikhnaf's motivation disappears; his exposition makes it clear that Muʿāwiya, if ʿAlī were to remove him from his office, would organize a rising against him in order to revenge "his kinsman's blood".

This modification, then, implies that Muʿāwiya's official programme has been nothing but a pretence to disguise his personal ambitions—a line that Abū Mikhnaf carries through with consistency. Whereas al-Jurjānī in his account of the negotiations prior to Ṣiffīn still principally fastens upon the religious aspects of the conflict—justification of the vengeance and legality of ʿAlī's election—Abū Mikhnaf emphasizes that ʿAlī's title to the caliphate surpasses that of anybody else, including that of Muʿāwiya, by virtue of his services, his religion, his early conversion to the Islamic faith, and his kinship with the Prophet. This line of thought is developed further on subsequent occasions. When by his Quran stratagem ʿAmr called for arbitration, ʿAlī warned his troops no to accept it because one could not trust "people that are not identified with the faith". It is also worthy of mention that Abū Mikhnaf makes ʿAlī warn ʿAmr before the arbitration hearing. ʿAmr knows very well who is in the right in the dispute, and he has made himself an enemy of God in order to gain "a paltry wordly profit"[25].

Abū Mikhnaf's veneration for ʿAlī goes to prove that his points of view belong in the Shīʿi opposition in Kufa against the Umayyads. The decisive points in this connection are, however, first, that Muʿāwiya's motives are being completely secularized, and, secondly, that his ambitions aiming at the caliphate are deemed illegal. Muʿāwiya and ʿAmr are not identified with the faith, and in that exchange of notes which in Abū Mikhnaf replaces Jarīr b. ʿAbdallāh's mission the Umayyads are sarcastically characterized as "people who had barely

---

24 Tab. I.3329–30, 3354–56, 3358–60 (Caetani IX, 472 *sq.*; X, 18 *sqq.*, 22 *sqq.*).

25 Tab. I.3357–58 (Caetani X, 22).—This anecdote, which presupposes knowledge of the account of ʿAmr's deceit, is naturally also apocryphal.

left *jāhiliyya*". This identification of the Syrian Caliphate with the pre-Islamic heathenism is of the utmost significance because it proves that the opposition deemed the Umayyad Caliphate to be illegal. It appears from Abū Mikhnaf's exposition that Abū Sufyān and Mu'āwiya are looked upon as *ṭulaqā'*[26], "freedmen" in Islam, who are rooted in heathenism; who are in no respect of the same status as the faithful; and who can have no title whatsoever to the caliphate. Moreover, Abū Mikhnaf makes a point of demonstrating that Mu'āwiya attained to power solely by the use of unlawful means towards Islam. Immediately after, and in consequence of, the result that 'Amr b. al-'Āṣ achieved by his deceit in respect of the arbitration award, Abū Mikhnaf makes Mu'āwiya receive the oath of allegiance as caliph in Syria[27].

Abū Mikhnaf's identification of the Umayyad Caliphate with *jāhiliyya* and his denial of its legality are thus in complete consonance with the views found in the Shī'i opposition during the last generation of the Syrian period. There is every reason to fasten upon the circumstance that his historiographical agitation against the Umayyads goes to the heart of the matter. Mu'āwiya and his successors appear to have found it profitable—*per fas et nefas*—to stress the Syrian Caliphate's Arab qualities and, especially, the *ḥilm* attributed to them or utilized by themselves in their agitation[28]. Tolerance and calm deliberation prior to every action are manifestations of those qualities which the Arabs comprise under this designation, and which they held in so very high esteem. In this connection it is to be construed as a contrast to *jāhiliyya*: cruelty or brute force. In al-Akhṭal and other panegyrists we meet with this quality as a standing attribute to the Umayyad rulers. However, a somewhat later author remarks in exasperation that "good deeds, which they never did, are ascribed to them. Glory rises in this world as the merits of good deeds in the Hereafter. And more than this. Such men have been honoured with every anonymous characteristic, the originator of which remains unknown[29]. This terminology has thus already acquired an odious ring, and Abū Mikhnaf exploits the distinctive Arab stamp with which the propaganda surrounded the Umayyad Caliphate to deny its legitimacy in Islam.

The violent reaction against the Umayyads and, on the other hand, the veneration for 'Alī, of which Abū Mikhnaf is the spokesman, bear witness to his narrowly Kufic horizon, corresponding to his family's and his tribe's (Banū Azd) traditions. His paternal grandfather Mikhnaf b. Sulaym al-Azdī, who had participated in the wars of conquest in Persia, is lauded for his devo-

26 On this concept, see Buhl: *'Alī*, 12.
27 Tab. I.3396 (Caetani X, 214).
28 Lammens: *Mo'āwia*, 66–108; cf. *HT* 11: V, 465 *sqq*.
29 Lammens: *Mo'āwia*, 89 *sq*., 189 *sq*.

tion to ʿAlī, on whose side he fought against the rebels[29a]. Abū Mikhnaf makes no secret of his liking for ʿAlī; his description of the battle at Siffin builds in part upon his own tribe's transmission, and he laments the degradation suffered by Kufa[30] in the Umayyad period. In other passages we can, moreover, observe ʿAbdallāh b. ʿAbbās beginning his function as ʿAlī's loyal mentor, though without having as yet in any way obtained a dominating position by the side of ʿAlī. It is, for instance, b. ʿAbbās who in Abū Mikhnaf's apocryphal introductory tradition warns the caliph not to entrust Ṭalḥa and az-Zubayr with the two *miṣr*, and not to let Muʿāwiya retain his governorship. On the other hand, it evidently taxes Abū Mikhnaf's ingenuity that b. ʿAbbās in 38 A.H. left ʿAlī and abandoned his governorship in Basra. b. ʿAbbās' defection must presumably be ascribed to conclusions drawn by him from the arbitration award[31], conclusions shared by many other people. Abū Mikhnaf was not capable of entirely veiling the fact: he makes b. ʿAbbās plead to ʿAlī that he did not wish to compromise himself before God by shedding the blood of his fellow-believers; but he would use the money which the tradition—in its argument for his defection—had accused him of having appropriated in Basra, for distribution among needy believers[32].

Behind this building up of legends around b. ʿAbbās we perceive a deliberate purpose or an attempt to rehabilitate his conduct, which cannot have been accidental at this stage. On comparing this feature with Abū Mikhnaf's judgment of the Umayyad dynasty's raison d'être and his unreserved veneration for ʿAlī we must assume that his views are identical with those of the Hāshimite opposition, which had its centre in Kufa, and which during this period headed the Shīʿi resistance against the Umayyads. Abū Mikhnaf's interpretation of the *fitna* is thus plainly stamped with the anti-Umayyad currents among the Arabian tribes in Kufa, and they are at the same time a product of the situation then prevailing. His opinions are hardly an isolated phenomenon; we shall meet with related or still more extreme views in other Shīʿi traditionists.

Such a version is found in, for instance, ʿĪsā b. Yazīd b. Daʾb al-Kinānī (ca. 750), who is still more emphatic than Abū Mikhnaf in his exposition of the religious contrast between ʿAlī and Muʿāwiya. The demand for blood vengeance is explicitly stamped as a cover for secular ambitions; neither Muʿāwiya nor ʿAmr has any moral right to intervene as ʿUthmān's champions seeing that the former left him in the lurch when the caliph appealed for his help against the rebels, and the latter "left him in powerlessness and fled". It is noteworthy,

29a cf. Brockelmann, 18 *sq.*; the traditions transmitted on his and his family's authority entirely agree with this picture; Caetani III, 261, 268, 652; IX 144 with note 1 to § 155.

30 cf. Duri: *The Iraq School.*

31 Vaglieri I, 75 sqq.; *idem* in *E.I.*[2] I, 40.

32 Bal. 450v–53v (Caetani X, 198 *sqq.*).

though quite logical, that ʿĪsā b. Yazīd draws the consequences of the account of ʿAmr's agreement with Muʿāwiya in that he has the latter make light of the justification of the vengeance claim and call on ʿAmr to reach out his hand in token of homage[33]. The traditionist thus ascribes to the alliance the form of a normal *bayʿa* expressly to demonstrate the illegality of the action. This version, which appears to have had a certain propagation far into Abbasid times[34], rests upon the already well-known elements, here merely pushed to extremes. b. Yazīd, who belongs to the same observance as Abū Mikhnaf, likewise tries to prove b. ʿAbbās's loyalty to ʿAlī by an obviously apocryphal anecdote of how ʿAmr during the battle at Ṣiffīn makes a vain attempt to entice b. ʿAbbās away from the caliph[35]. This traditionist merely adapts the viewpoints to a more vulgar and extremist formulation[36].

What has been said here about ʿĪsā b. Yazīd applies more or less to the already mentioned Jābir b. Yazīd al-Juʿfī (d. 126–32/746–50), whose version of the *ṣulḥ* letter reveals his Shīʿi sympathies[37]. His traditional material is transmitted but extremely fragmentarily, and what is available deals solely with the encounters at Ṣiffīn. Before the battle he has Muʿāwiya impress on his troops in a *khuṭba* that either party had come to defend their country and to conquer that of the enemy; in addition, he tempts them with the riches of Iraq[38]. A later apocryphal tradition says that ʿAlī warned the Syrians against God's punishment, and that with his own hands he slew more than 500 enemies under invocation of a Prophet tradition that established ʿAlī's infallibility *(ʿiṣma)* and his right to chastise with his sword[39].

Generally speaking, Jābir b. Yazīd represents the same extremist tendency as ʿĪsa b. Yazīd, and likewise accepts b. ʿAbbās's position by the side of ʿAlī[40]. However, he furnishes a new feature in that he, unlike all earlier traditionists dealt with in this work, endeavours to link the tradition with eyewitnesses in

33 Bal. 498r–99v (Caetani IX, 240–42); cf. also the defence of ʿAlī's showdown with Ṭalḥa by means of a false Prophet tradition (*Agh.* XXI, 163; Mas. IV, 321–23; Caetani X, 407 and IX, 170 *sq.*). On the *bayʿa*, see E. Tyan in *E.I.*² I, 1113.

34 As already mentioned, the account is found in Balādhurī, but also al-Yaʿqūbī (II, 214–17; cf. della Vida, 456 and Caetani IX, 242 note 1 to § 329) uses it, and in pro-Umayyad version it appears in ʿAbdallāh b. al-Mubārak (Bal.: *Muʿāw.*, no 256; cf. *AO* XXVII, 113.).

35 Bal. 507v–08v (Caetani IX, 485).

36 This version is, incidentally, condemned as false already in the 9th century by the—himself not too reliable—pro-Umayyad traditionist Hishām b. ʿAmmār ad-Dimashqī (d. 858/60); Bal.: *Muʿāw.*, no 199; cf. Caetani IX, 256, 485.

37 cf. *supra* p. 42.

38 b. al-Kathīr: *Bidāya*, 142v–43v (Caetani IX, 537 sq.) and Caetani IX corr. e agg., xxxv to p. 493; cf. also b. Ḥajār I.1007–09, no 2493 (Caetani IX, 608).

39 b. al-Kathīr: *Bidāya*, 144r–v (Caetani IX, 538).

40 b. ʿAbbās appears in his version together with other members of Banū ʿAbd al-Muṭṭalib as a *ṣulḥ* letter witness; *Waq. Siff.*, 586; cf. also Brockelmann, 14 *sq.*

order to lend colour to his conception. The account of ʻAlī's valour is attributed to Numayr al-Anṣārī, while some other accounts—Muʻāwiya's *khuṭba* and the *ṣulḥ* letter—are ascribed to Abū Jaʻfar al-Baqīr, Zaid b. al-Ḥasan, Muhammad b. ʻAlī, and Muhammad b. ʻAbd al-Muṭṭalib without any attempts to fill in the interval between the eyewitnesses and himself. Similar tendencies are ascertainable in a report on the disposition of the two armies at Ṣiffīn, known also from a parallel version by Hishām b. Muhammad al-Kalbī, though here without al-Juʻfī's *isnād*[41]. It is undoubtedly well motivated, therefore, that a later historian, b. al-Kathīr, passes strictures on one of these traditions for being untrustworthy from a formal point of view; he says: "*isnād ḍaʻīf waḥadīth munkar*", the *isnād* is weak and the tradition reprehensible[42]. al-Juʻfī's attempts to lend eyewitness authority to his accounts thus turn out to be extremely maladroit. Nevertheless, his line of procedure is of fundamental interest in so far as we here observe tentative attempts to endue the *ʻilm al-akhbār* that he employs with a formally and religiously justified warranty, which the earlier scholars had not utilized

In ʻAwāna we can still find collective traditions cast in the same mould as the one which the earliest traditionists had made use of; though tendentious in their formulation they are yet expressive of the *opinio* of the scholar or his milieu. Abū Mikhnaf generally works in a corresponding way; where he employs *isnāds* at all, they are as a rule short and reach back no farther than to his authorities, ash-Shaʻbī or others. In one passage Abū Mikhnaf emphasizes that what he states "from Mujāhid, Saqʻab, and others is in line with the tradition's *consensus*"[43]. But when we reach the closing years of the 8th century, it becomes normal to endue the tradition with *isnād*; the pro-Syrian traditionist ʻAbdallāh b. al-Mubārak (d. 797) characterizes it as "part of the religion"[44]. Underlying these formal changes of the transmission's framework is no doubt a profound modification of the concept of tradition, of which we have parallels also in the legal tradition. In 128 A.H. (746) an official committee is set up for the purpose of codifying *sunan* and *siyar*, approved practice and rules, but the following

41 b. al-Kathīr: *Bidāya*, 142v–43r (Caetani IX, 537 *sq.*).

42 *Idem: Bidāya*, 144r–v (Caetani IX, 539). On this terminology, see Goldziher: *M.St.* II, 144, 251; Schacht: *Origins*, 36. Cf. also the lawyer, Abū Ḥanīfa's judgment on al-Juʻfī (Rosenthal: *Historiography*, 438); al-Juʻfī belonged to a Shīʻi school advocating a Prophet-allegorical Quran exegesis in ʻAlī's favour; Goldziher: *M.St.* II, 112 *sq.*; Friedlaender: *Heterodoxies*, 23 *sq.*, 86 *sq.*

43 Duri: *The Iraq School.* In a corresponding manner Sayf b. ʻUmar (d. 796) speaks of the authors' *siyar* (approved practice).

44 Schacht: *Origins*, 37 note 1; cf. Goldziher: *M.St.* II, 141; *AO* XXVII, 113 *sqq.*—These pietistical currents, which lead to the application of the circumstantial *isnād*, may well be assumed to have been influenced by Jewish forms of tradition; cf. J. Horowitz in *Der Islam* VII, 39 *sqq*, where the argumentation can hardly be binding.

generations draw up rules applying to the formal demands to be made on a legally valid tradition[45]. This disciplinatory process of the tradition must be construed as expressive of the need in the pietisic circles of Islam for a religiously authoritative transmission, *inter alia* in substitution for such administrative and legal rules as the Umayyad Caliphate had established, and the justification of which was now being denied.

In many cases the tradition's growth in the Umayyad period can no longer be reconstructed in its details. This is particularly true of the Syrian-Medinese version whose development cannot be pursued in quite the same manner as the Kufic tradition. However, in those instances where this process can still be followed we find as its most characteristic methodological feature that the expositions are tailored to the same prearranged pattern. The conflict concerning the justification of the Syrian Caliphate is the primary element, whereas the historical writing is considered merely as the most expedient means of expression. By virtue of daring and often quite ingenious constructions the historians create or fill in the framework delimited by a given standpoint, and the polemical element continues to play the all-dominating role in the historiographical debate around the *fitna*. The mythogenesis concerning ʿAmr b. al-ʿĀṣ and the later chronological shifts are countered adroitly by the Syrian-Medinese tradition, which cannot abandon its position. The material from either side, then, goes to prove that the schools deliberately discountenanced and refuted each other.

In respect of methods, the historiographical discussion in the late Umayyad period does not differ from such features as we have already observed in the genesis of tradition; but as regards facts, we perceive a marked sharpening of the Iraqian propaganda against the Umayyad Caliphate, entirely in line with the extremist views of the Hāshimiyya movement. It is no longer a dispute on the justification of Muʿāwiya's action or ʿAlī's personal attitude to the caliph murder: In the last generation of the Umayyad era the conflict simply turns on the legitimacy of the Syrian Caliphate, which was challenged by the Shīʿi opposition. Were it possible to prove that Muʿāwiya's motivation of his actions was false and that his and Amr's conduct towards their opponents was dishonest, the Syrian Caliphate would *ipso facto* lose its raison d'être, and its existence be due to unlawful usurpation. It is this process that furnishes the occasion and the substance for the mythogenesis around ʿAmr b. al-ʿĀṣ. In Abū Mikhnaf this line leads to identification of the Umayyads with the pre-Islamic heathenism and to the incipient religious veneration of ʿAlī, that is: the same features which in ʿĪsā b. Yazīd and al-Juʿfī occur in vulgar Shīʿi shape.

45 Margoliouth: *Mohammedanism*, 91 *sqq.*; Schacht: *Origins*, 36 *sqq.* and *passim.*

PART II

THE FIRST CENTURY OF THE ABBASID ERA

1. Introduction

The Umayyad period's attempts to meet the beginning islamization of the social system and to set up norms satisfying Islam's fundamental principles were to all appearances too tardy to ward off the effects of the the latent ill will in Iraq and Persia against the reigning rulers. In 750 the Syrian caliphate was overthrown and succeeded by the Abbasids, who had headed the Shīʿi opposition since about 718. However, this change of dynasty did not bring such clarification of the state of conflict as might have been expected. The antagonisms were merely led into other channels. The islamization process was, admittedly, accomplished during the following generations, but the vertical cleavage between Arabs and *mawālī* was replaced by political and social clashes of interest. Diversion of the trade routes in the course of the 8th century—diversions that made the new seat of the caliphs, Baghdad, into an international centre—, accumulation of capital, and the elaboration of credit and credit institutions were creating an immense economic and political concentration in the caliphate's eastern provinces[1]. The growth of the Islamic-Mesopotamian urban society brought about social distinctions between the orthodox urban patriciate of the eastern provinces and the poor groups of population in town and country, though this situation cannot be said to have come to a head until the 9th or 10th century[2]. The interval between this state of affairs and the conflicts of the late Umayyad era saw a long and still enigmatic development, and it was only in the course of this period that the political and religious formation of parties adjusted itself to the changed conditions. The social structure at the transition to the Abbasid era was indeed in the melting pot, but even so it is above all the consolidation of the new caliphate and the ensuing conflicts that leave their mark on the first two or three generations of the Abbasid age.

---

1 cf. *HT* 11:VI, 685 *sqq.* with references.

2 Even in the early Abbasid era much social unrest in the poor regions of the caliphate—northern Mesopotamia, North Africa, South Arabia—seems to have come to expression in Khārijite sympathies. Not until the end of the 9th or the beginning of the 10th century was Khārijism definetely replaced by extremist Shīʿism (Ismāʿīlism); cf. below p. 134.

It is not unlikely, then, that elements of this social reorganization process may have entered into the earliest Abbasid period's clashes of interest; but the real dilemma concerning the new dynasty's consolidation was rather bound up with its revolutionary past, which might easily have compromised it in the eyes of the orthodox majority—the expanding urban patriciate, the bureaucracy, and the scholars. As mentioned above, one branch of the extremist Shīʿi oppositional movement against the Umayyads had been systematically organized under Abbasid leadership, the coalition that led to the overthrow of the Umayyads. Its collapse immediately after 750 was not surprising. From the outset the Abbasids insisted on adopting the legitimacy principle as well as the theocratic idea into Islam, though the new rulers belonged to only a collateral branch of the Prophet family, and it was indeed to be expected that *al-ghulāt* summed up the deep disappointment at the Abbasid usurpation of the caliph office, to which they considered the Alids entitled by right. The coalition broke down, and the emancipation of Shīʿism issued already in 762 in the first serious anti-Abbasid rebellion under Alid auspices. The dissolution of this misalliance is reflected in a letter quoted by Ṭabarī from the Alid Muhammad b. ʿAbdallāh to al-Manṣūr, in which he explicitly cites Ali's dignity of *waṣī* (the Prophet's testamentary executor) and declares that none but his descendants can lay claim to the caliphate, an assertion which al-Manṣūr of course rejects categorically[3]. This exchange of letters is presumably no more than a precision in fictive formulation of the two cardinal points of view under al-Manṣūr. The Abbasids never abandoned their legitimacy claim, and even though they dared at no time disavow ʿAlī openly they gained their object in practice by representing him as a protégé of their ancestor, ʿAbdallāh b. ʿAbbās. This procedure, however, also meant that the Abbasids—apparently under al-Manṣūr—had to refrain from using such Shīʿi agitatorial means as they had done in the days of the revolution[4].

Besides preserving the unity of Banū Hāshim (although in a somewhat modified form) the orthodox tradition maintained the Abbasids' religious merits by virtue of their fight against the Umayyads' ungodly rule. It was indeed a feature of their policy to identify themselves with the religious opposition to the Syrian rulers and with the orthodox precepts, *ijmāʿ al-umma,* which Shīʿism could not invoke because its membership remained a minority, but which demanded all Islam's loyalty to their enforcer[5]. The new rulers, in harmony with these ideas, endeavoured to justify themselves by presenting their caliphate as the new era *(dawla)*, which according to the Prophet tradition was to replace the tyranny. As early as in the 9th century it seems to have been established

---

3 Weil II, 43–51; Gabrieli: *al-Maʿmūn.* 7 *sq.*

4 an-Nawbakhtī, 43 *(RHR* 154, 80*).*

5 cf. Goldziher: *M. St.* II, 98 *sqq.*

officially in the orthodox tradition that the rising against the Umayyads was organized under the Abbasid family's auspices in the year 100 A.H. immediately after the death of the only pious Umayyad caliph, 'Umar II[6].

So the modified political structure of the Abbasid era once more called for a historical and constitutional continuity. The debate concentrated on placing a distinction between the just, to-God-acceptable caliphate and the tyranny. All could agree in denouncing the Umayyads, whereas the judgment of the first four caliphs varied greatly. While Shī'ism with all means endeavoured to show that 'Alī was to be preferred to his three predecessors or sometimes even tried to stultify them[7], the orthodox tradition, indirectly, placed Abū Bakr, 'Umar, and (partly) 'Uthmān before 'Alī[8]. But in orthodox circles, too, the judgment of 'Uthmān varied according to circumstances. In the Medinese tradition is found evidence that Quraysh preferred 'Uthmān, the representative of the old aristocracy, and that 'Alī was to blame for the revolution, probably in order to exonerate the Medinians themselves[9]. In general the dispute had the effect that the orthodox transmission—incidentally the Medinese as well as the Iraqian—called attention to a report stating that the Prophet's signet ring, passed from caliph to caliph in token of its bearer's acting on his behalf until 'Uthmān lost it into a well in the seventh year of his reign[10], which thereby came to constitute the dividing line between the righteous caliphate and the tyranny.

In these many divergent views of 'Uthmān we find the principal focus of evidence that it was his violent death, or rather the justification of the murder and its consequences, which in the Abbasid era remained the constant bone of contention among the parties. At the transition to the 11th century al-Baghdādī could still divide up Islam according to the attitude adopted towards the events provoked by the murder. The conflict has no bearing on the religious status of the faithful as far as the *Sunna* is concerned; 'Alī's right to fight his enemies was well motivated, but his mistakes can be stamped neither as *kufr*, gross infidelity, nor, even, as *fisq*, sin, and the *Sunna* therefore recognizes the assertions of both parties as valid. The Khārijites denounce both the 'Uthmāniyya and Mu'āwiya as *kāfirūn* (or *kuffār*), whom 'Alī had a clear right to combat, but he himself turned *kāfir* by accepting the arbitration at Ṣiffīn. The Mu'tazila's

6 *HT* 11:V, 468.

7 Noeldeke, 28 *sq.*; Sarasin, 13 *sqq.*, 45, 47, 67.

8 Wensinck, 108; cf. p. 17. —It is presumably an extreme instance when b. Sa'd (II. 2. 38 *sq.*; Wensinck, 16) lets al-'Abbās suggest that oath of allegiance be sworn to 'Alī while Muhammad was lying on his deathbed, and lets 'Alī acknowledge al-'Abbās's rights.

9 b. Sa'd III. 1. 44; Bal. 467r–v (Caetani VII, 420; VIII, 331).

10 b. Sa'd I. 2. 161 *sqq.*; Bal: *Futūḥ*, 462; Tab. I. 2856–58 (Caetani VII, 387 *sq.*; Hitti-Murgotten II, 257); cf. Wensinck, 211 *sq.*; *AO* XXVII, 102.

framing of an intermediate stage between faith and infidelity implies that one of the two parties must be *fāsiq,* though which one cannot be determined with certainty. So evidence from neither party will be valid for judgment of its adversary[11]. Al-Baghdādī enirely bypasses the Shī'ism, probably because their standpoint was a foregone conclusion. Prophet traditions in favour of 'Alī or with threats of eternal perdition for resisting him are legion[12], and it appears, as traced above, already from the Kufic transmission that it regarded Mu'āwiya's opposition to the righteous caliph as immediately discriminating.

There is hardly any doubt that the concepts here dealt with gradually evanesced insofar as denunciations of this kind were used and abused on every occasion. It is, on the other hand, evident that if the attitude of the faithful to the events after 'Uthmān's murder can be classified as *kufr*, which automatically causes eternal punishment, or *fisq*, which deprives the believer of his *'adl* (verbatim: righteousness, religious habitus)[13], then the significance of the basic conflicts —irrespective of their immediate meaning—is raised to a religious level that makes the individual believer's standpoint into a grave matter of conscience. It is likewise evident that the historiographical argumentation was invariably more than a dispute concerning a buried past; the historical writing was simply an arsenal producing arms for the argumentation around the political conflicts, also in the Abbasid age.

11 Pellat: *Jāḥiẓ*, 186.

12 Typical are Mas. IV, 321 *sq.*; cf. b. al-Athīr IV, 32–33 (Caetani X, 407); cf. also *ibid.* X, 445 *sqq.*

13 On these concepts, see W. Björkman s.v. *kāfir* in *E. I.*[1] II, 662 *sqq.*, Th. W. Juynboll s.v. *'adl* in *E. I.*[2] I, 209 *sq.*

2. The Orthodox Tradition 750–800

In consequence of the changed political and social conditions in the earliest Abbasid period we must expect the inevitable historiographical debate to take new directions. Shī'ism and the spokesmen of the new regime were in accordance concerning denunciation of the fallen dynasty, whereas the problem of assigning responsibility for the Umayyads having been able to attain to the power at all gave rise to divergent opinions. If 'Alī's failure could be proved to be due to defection in critical situations on the part of his own adherents, Shī'ism would at the same time have forfeited its right to act on behalf of the Prophet family. Any such exposition would furthermore serve to justify the fact that it was the Abbasids who reaped the fruits: they would be seen as loyal to 'Alī and as taking a leading part in the fight against the unlawful caliphate. The predicament of the new rulers consisted first of all in that, unlike their predecessors and Shī'ism, they did not possess a historical tradition that had developed along with themselves. While the Abbasids had taken part in al-Hāshimiyya there had hardly been any acute need on this point, but under al-Manṣūr the rupture of the alliance with the Shi'ites prevented the Abbasids from employing the Shī'i propaganda material, and the ensuing void had to be filled in by other means. This is precisely the process observable in the building up of a pro-Abbasid tradition in the first generations after the change of dynasty.

The lack of historical tradition does not, however, in any way mean that the Abbasids were without independent standpoints. They, like the majority of Islam's religious and political party alignments, seem to have had their supporting party since the late Umayyad period, when they were beginning to assert themselves politically, in Mu'tazilism[1]. This movement—like Shī'ism and Khārijism—had a purely political origin and stemmed from the religious dilemma in defining its attitude to the *fitna* provoked by 'Uthmān's murder. A number of prominent Prophet Companions—Sa'd b. Abī Waqqāṣ, 'Abdallāh b. 'Umar, Muhammad b. Maslama, Usāma b. Zayd, Ṣuhayb b. Sinān, and Zayd b. Thābit—"segregated themselves *(i'tazalū)* from 'Alī and took up a

1 On the following, see H. S. Nyberg's fundamental article in *E. I.*[1] III, 850 *sqq*.

noncommittal attitude in that they would neither fight nor identify themselves with his cause, even though they had sworn allegiance to him and were well disposed towards him; they were known as al-Mu'tazila and became the originators of the later Mu'tazila" writes the heresiographer an-Nawbakhtī[2].

Mu'tazilism as a theological persuasion was framed in Basra in the last decades of the Umayyad period in contrast to other religious movements and was above all distinguished for its indeterminism and its call for rational thinking. But it seems that behind its subtle theological contemplations there were lurking politico-religious problems which still concerned the responsibility for the *fitna*. This applies especially to Ṭalḥa and az-Zubayr, who originally belonged to those *aṣḥāb* that had been unwilling to pay homage to 'Alī. The older Mu'tazilites were apparently rather vacillating as to the placing of the guilt or sin *(fisq)* which they recognized as ascribable to 'Alī, 'Ā'isha, Ṭalḥa or az-Zubayr, who had taken part in the battle of the Camel. The chief tendency, however, was to single out 'Ā'isha or, especially, Ṭalḥa as the really guilty one *(fassāq)*. az-Zubayr and 'Alī—both belonging to Banū 'Abd al-Muṭṭalib—thus became exponents of this proto-Mu'tazilism which at the same time and absolutely preferred 'Alī to 'Uthmān, while also recognizing Abū Bakr's and 'Umar's caliphates as legitimate, all in agreement with the result reached by the framers of the tradition.

The leading Mu'tazilites in the middle of the 8th century—'Amr b. 'Ubayd and Wāṣil b. 'Aṭā'—in consequence of the standpoint elaborated by themselves kept from the outset definitely aloof from the Umayyads and the extremist Shī'ism[3]. Their points of view seem to have been identical with those of the Abbasids, and we know that the Mu'tazilites in the Ḥijāz even supported the Hāshimiyya coalition in its fight against the Syrian caliphate[4]. It is, on the other hand, very difficult at this early stage to establish for certain to what extent the formation of these parties around the Abbasids was followed up by any development of a tradition to motivate its standpoint. In a few, though quite isolated, *muḥaddithūn* we observe points of view that seem to be in correspondence with those of the earliest Mu'tazilites. This applies with reasonable certainty to the Basrian scholar Abū Bakr al-Hudhalī (d. 784)—al-Manṣūr's boon companion *(nadīm)*—who on the basis of elements from both the Syrian-Medinese and the Kufic transmission or by constructions on the material available sought to give prominence to 'Alī and az-Zubayr, to denounce Mu'āwiya and 'Amr, and to discountenance Shī'ism[5]. The same standpoint

2 an-Nawbakhtī, 5 (*RHR* 153, 179 *sq.*). Wāqidī in Tab. I. 3072; contrary to b. Sa'd III. 1. 20 (Caetani VIII, 327; IX, 50); cf. *supra* pp. 11 *sq.*

3 cf. al-Khayyāṭ, no.s 100–04 (Traduction, 138 *sqq.*).

4 Buhl: *Aliderne*, 375, 385.

5 *AO* XXVII, 105 *sqq.*

is presumably represented by Muʿammar b. Rashīd (d. 771), who was likewise a Basrian by birth, though domiciled in Yemen[6]. His main contribution consisted in the transmission of the *maghāzī* tradition from az-Zuhrī, and his name is also connected with a few accounts of ʿUthmān's and ʿAlī's caliphates. This material, which consists principally in tendentious adaptations of az-Zuhrī's ideas, is likewise turned against the Umayyads and ʿAlī's adherents, and in this traditionist we meet for the first time with the symbolic story of how ʿUthmān lost the Prophet's signet ring. We do not know Muʿammar b. Rashīd's estimation of Ṭalḥa and az-Zubayr, but his sympathetic opinion of ʿAlī, whose preference to Ṭalḥa he brings out very clearly by an interpolation into az-Zuhrī's rendering of the caliph election, seems to indicate that he was Muʿtazilite. The same applies to his interest in Saʿd b. Abī Waqqāṣ and ʿAbdallāh b. ʿUmar, and his tendency to make Prophet Companions lend their names to his adaptations of az-Zuhrī's material.

Beyond al-Hudhalī and, perhaps, b. Rashīd it will hardly be feasible to establish any traditional formation round Muʿtazilism in this early period. Such evidence as can be gleaned from these traditionists is undoubtedly important for comprehension of the early Muʿtazilism's pro-Abbasid tendencies, and it is possible that the interest in az-Zuhrī[7], which can still be observed at the caliph court under Hārūn al-Rashīd, may have played a part in this connection. The epoch, however, is generally coloured by other tendencies, above all by the new rulers' showdown with Shīʿism. Although both al-Hudhalī and b. Rashīd are unmistakably anti-Shiite, and even if the prevailing trend in no way contradicts the programme of Muʿtazilism, this designation can hardly be applied to the framing of the Abbasid time's historical tradition.

It is in fact rarely Basrian or Medinese[8], but chiefly Kufian scholars who at this time are met with in the entourage of the Abbasids, and who are fashioning the anti-Shiite tradition. Also this part of the process of shaping the tradition is very obscure and can be followed only in indistinct outline. It is common knowledge that Kufic traditionists as, for instance, Muhammad b. as-Sāʾib al-Kalbī (d. 763) and his son Hishām b. Muhammad (d. 204 or 206 A.H./819

6 *AO* XXVII, 99 *sqq*.

7 Abbott, 24.—Muʿtazilism did not gain official recognition until under Hārūn's son, al-Maʾmūn, whereas he himself still persecuted this movement.

8 Among the Medinese it is reasonable to mention Muhammad b. Isḥāq (d. 768), who seems to have finished his *taʾrīkh al-khulafāʾ* at the Abbasid Court (Abbott, 87 *sqq*.). His version of the first civil war seems completely lost, apart from a single fragment (Bal. 502r; Caetani IX, 284 *sq*.). In this ʿAlī urges his opponents before Ṣiffīn to end the civil war; Muʿāwiya, however, demands the handing over of ʿUthmāns' murderers and confirmation of his governorship in order to recognize ʿAlī. Historically this fragment is important because it confirms indirectly the Syrian-Medinese version of Muʿāwiya's standpoint, but it affords no ground for a historiographical placing of b. Isḥāq.

or 821) carried on that Kufic tradition of which ʿAwāna, and, especially, Abū Mikhnaf had been representatives. Moreover, the unearthing of Balādhurī's *kitāb Ansāb al-Asrāf* has called attention to the fact that the traditional material available to Abū Mikhnaf—one of Balādhurī's chief authorities—has many points in common with the Baghdad historian Sayf b. ʿUmar's (d. 796) reports. The conclusion must then be that the Iraqian transmission had been fixed at the end of the Umayyad era[9]. And finally: on the basis of points of resemblance between the material found in the two al-Kalbīs and the somewhat later Medinese historians al-Wāqidī and b. Saʿd, Caetani draws the conclusion that the two former represent a transitional stage in the amalgamation of Medinese and Kufic tradition[10].

It is thus made clear that a process of amalgamation of the different lines of tradition is taking place, an observation that does not, however, satisfactorily characterize its individual stages. A comparison of Sayf b. ʿUmar's, Wāqidī's, and the somewhat later historians'—Dīnawarī and (in part) al-Yaʿqūbī—renderings will show that they must build extensively upon a common source, which in turn must rest upon Abū Mikhnaf's version[11]. This common account, the contents of which are reconstructible, thus—irrespective whether it was a unity or had come into being in stages—belongs temporally in the first generation of the Abbasid era, and is apparently identical with Muhammad b. as-Sā'ib's or, perhaps rather, his son's version of Abū Mikhnaf. Comparison of the ideas contained in the reconstructed source with the material of the al-Kalbis, and examinations of Dīnawarī's, al-Yaʿqūbī's, and Hishām b. Muhammad's particulars will render this assumption highly probable[12]. This reconstructed source and Hishām b. Muhammad's traditional material can thus, though with some reservation, be utilized as a unity; both rest upon Abū Mikhnaf, and our chief problem will then be to elucidate the development of the tradition from him and Muhammad b. as-Sā'ib ahead to the later stage.

Our knowledge of b. Sā'ib's traditional material is indeed very slight. In a long story about ʿUthmān's murder he—like subsequently al-Wāqidī—holds the Egyptian rebels responsible for the tragedy. He evidently makes a great point of proving that the Basrians, whose feelings are in favour of ʿUthmān, immediately respond to the distressed caliph's appeal for help while the Kufians remained neutral. In this way he explains how ʿĀ'isha, Ṭalḥa, and Zubayr can find support for their action of revenge in Basra after the murder. Muʿāwiya, despite ʿUthmān's urgent appeals, refrained from sending help for fear of coming into open conflict with the Prophet Companions whereas other

9 della Vida, 434 *sq.*, 443, 447 *sq.*, 451, 457.

10 Caetani III, 3 *sqq.*

11 On the following in general, see *AO* XXVII, 85 *sqq.*

12 *AO* XXVII, 92 *sqq.* and *infra* pp. 162, 169 *sqq.*

Syrians resolutely hurried to his rescue[13]. After a long interval Muhammad b. Sā'ib in a very precise narrative gives an account of the external circumstances round the arbitration meeting, which is stated to take place at Dūmat al-Jandal. On returning from Ṣiffīn to Kufa on the 20th Rabī' I, 37 A.H. (5th Sept., 657) 'Alī is for the following seven months engrossed in administrative business and the Khārijite opposition, and not until having received a reminder does he send a delegation headed by b. 'Abbās to the arbitration meeting, which was also attended by a number of prominent Arabs. They were in general of the same names as those presented by ash-Sha'bī, and the absence of Sa'd b. Abī Waqqāṣ is specifically stated[14]. There is, however, no direct evidence of Muhammad b. as-Sā'ib's attitude towards the arbitration; according to his dating of it he must, like Abū Mikhnaf and ash-Sha'bī, have set it for January-February, 658, and he must also have joined in the current Kufic reading of its outcome, for he makes b. 'Abbās warn 'Alī against sending Abū Mūsā as negotiator for fear of Mu'āwiya's and 'Amr's fraudulent intents[15].

So the basis for a safe determination of Muhammad b. as-Sā'ib's observance is slender[16]. We know by now that he harboured a personal antipathy against the Syrian "monarchy", and from a very early date took an active part in the campaign against it. He did, however, live to see both its fall and the Abbasids' rupture with the radical Shī'ism. The few traditions available seem to indicate a relationship with the current Kufic ideas, and also that he was more emphatic in his depiction of b. 'Abbās's collaboration with 'Alī and his dislike of the Umayyads. After the arbitration failure 'Alī regretted not having heeded b. 'Abbās's warning; "he sees the future as through a thin veil". al-Kalbī likewise strives to clear b. 'Abbās as regards the accusations of having misappropriated Basra's *bayt al-māl*, and entirely passes over his relations with Mu'āwiya during the last years of 'Alī's reign[17]. Here, then, we find for the first time

13 Tab. I. 2984–86 (Caetani VIII, 166 *sqq.*); cf. Bal.: *Mu'āw.*, no. 255, where he pursues a similar line of thought.

14 Bal. 523r (Caetani X, 32).

15 Bal. 524r (Caetani X, 34); cf. Caetani's note (*loc. cit.*) and *AO* XXVII, 93 *sq.*—This information may have arisen by a shifting of b. 'Abbās's warning to Abū Mūsā at the actual meeting.

16 *AO* XXVII, 93 *sq.*

17 Cf. *Ibid.* 94.—In Bal.: *Mu'āw.*, no. 35 he puts the accusations against Mu'āwiya into the mouth of b. 'Abbās. This corresponds with the *tafsīr* (exegesis) attributed to Muhammad b. as-Sā'ib, also known fragmentarily from Ṭabarī and b. Sa'd, which cites b. 'Abbās as final authority. (cf. Abbott, 45 *sqq.*). The fragments of legends from the Old Testament which are found here, are closely akin to Arab-Christian apocryphs from the same period—8th–9th cent.—,and in contrast to Nabia Abbott I am inclined to think that the citing of b. 'Abbās must be al-Kalbī's invention, even if some of the narratives serve to illuminate the Quran's accounts from the Old Testament, accounts which also b. 'Abbās may have known.

approaches in the historical tradition to justify the Abbasids for their own sake; no longer are they merely 'Alī's loyal supporters, but active and independent participants in the fight against the Syrians.

This tendency is gaining strength when we come to Muhammad b. as-Sā'ib's son Hishām, who already seems to have enjoyed al-Mahdī's favour on account of his anti-Umayyad traditions[18], and the anonymous tradition which we here with reservation identify with him. We can, generally speaking, take it that Hishām b. Muhammad has transmitted his father's account, but in addition hereto he supplies much other material; in particular he often cites Abū Mikhnaf, whose most important transmitter he is. It is generally extremely difficult to verify the reliability of his renderings[19], but there are instances where shifts are observable from Abū Mikhnaf to Hishām b. Muhammad or to the reconstructed common source.

The common source states that after the caliph election al-Mughīra b. Shu'ba advised 'Alī to keep 'Uthmān's governors—and particularly Mu'āwiya—in order to secure the loyalty of the provinces. However, when 'Alī hesitated, he withdrew this counsel and instead recommended that the governors be removed. Not even b. 'Abbās's explanation of the appropriateness of b. Shu'ba's first advice could shake 'Alī's pious stubbornness. We next hear of a number of appointments to governorships. None but Mu'āwiya rejects by force the man appointed by 'Alī, and he likewise rejects the caliph's request for *bay'a*. Finally this source states that 'Amr b. al-'Āṣ, who during the revolution against 'Uthmān had made off to Palestine, immediately after the murder set out for Syria, evidently for the purpose of siding with Mu'āwiya[20].

Ibn al-Kalbī goes on to repeat the essential points in Abū Mikhnaf's version of the course of events up to the arbitration meeting and the Khārijite rebellion, but to this main theme he adds a number of anecdotal details shedding light upon his own opinions. He repeats his father's account of b. 'Abbās's warning against employing Abū Mūsā as negotiator at the arbitration[21]; and after an-Nahrawān he makes Mu'āwiya's half-brother, 'Umāra b. 'Uqba b.

18 *GAL (S)* I., 211.

19 In one instance only is concrete verification possible, that is in the account of the 'Uthmāniyya's resistance against 'Alī in al-Raqqa (Tab. I. 3259–60 from Hishām b. Muhammad from Abū Mikhnaf; Bal. 502v–04v from Abū Mikhnaf and others; Caetani IX, 267, 287). In this instance agreement is almost complete; the fact that Ṭabarī in his rendering does not mention that the resistance is 'Uthmānite and does not specify the principal characters need not be due to Hishām b. Muhammad's abbreviation. This information is found also in al-Ya'qūbī (II, 217–19; Caetani IX, 263 *sq.*), who likewise seems to have known the latter's version of Abū Mikhnaf; cf. *infra* pp. 170 *sq.*

20 cf. *AO* XXVII, 88 *sq. cum* notes.

21 He adds an apocryphal prophecy of Abū Mūsā's failure. Ya'q. II, 221–22 (Caetani X, 35 *sq.*); cf. Mas. IV, 383 *sq.* and *infra* pp. 118, 170.

Abī Mu'ayṭ, inform him from Kufa that 'Alī had suppressed his own *qurrā'* and godly men *(nussāk)*; that the caliph's army and the inhabitants in the vicinity had been practically wiped out; and that violent diasgreements had broken out among 'Alī's adherents. Mu'āwiya's comment it to the effect that he ought perhaps to come to the rescue[22]. The anecdote is undoubtedly apocryphal, but its ironical point is of considerable interest because it illustrates clearly the pro-Abbasid tendency to emphasize how it was principally the discord within 'Alī's own ranks that paved the way for the illegitimate caliphate.

This tradition's—al-Kalbī's and that of the common source—partiality for the Abbasids is stronger and more detailed than his father's. The purge among 'Uthmān's governors has been given an unmistakably tendentious description, for the new names all belong to either Prophet Companions or al-'Abbās's sons, and its account of the appointments must rest on an arbitrary reshuffle of elements from the earlier transmission[23]. In quite a corresponding manner the story of al-Mughīra's advice to 'Alī must rest upon an adaptation of Abū Mikhnaf, who, unlike al-Kalbī and the common source, represents the advice as odious and as rejected unanimously by 'Alī and b. 'Abbās[24]. Abū Mikhnaf's version is still somewhat vacillating in its details, and knows nothing about 'Alī's appointments of governors. The formation of this tradition must thus be rooted in Abū Mikhnaf, but its further tendentious development must be ascribed to b. al-Kalbī himself.

Hishām b. Muhammad's transmission is strongly anti-Umayyad[25], but well disposed, even though occasionally somewhat forbearing, towards 'Alī, who (with all his pious fairness) is now being eclipsed by b. 'Abbās[26]. The most salient feature of this transmission is indeed its attempt to depict b. 'Abbās as the caliph's mentor and to make the latter's own adherents responsible for the Umayyad caliphate. The trend of this traditional development is thus primarily pro-Abbasid, quite an interesting and much more marked proof than hitherto of how the traditional elements of the Umayyad period are absorbed and modified according to the criterion set up by the new rulers. The principal elements

22 Bal. 542v–43r (Caetani X, 108 *sq.*).

23 *AO* XXVII, 91 *sq.* It is characteristic that none of the Abbasids is placed in exposed positions, such as Syria or Egypt.

24 cf. Abū Mikhnaf in Bal., 466v (Caetani VIII, 330).

25 Thus e.g. Bal., 587v (Caetani X, 354); Bal.; *Mu'āw.*, no.s 35, 215, 255 (where b. Abbās voices the condemnation).

26 The collection of fictitious letters and apophthegms rendered by Balādhurī from b. al-Kalbī (Caetani X, 444 *sqq.*) constantly emphasizes the caliph's piety. Also al-Ya'qūbī (II, 235 *sqq.*), al-Jāḥiẓ, and the author of *Nahj al-balāgha* have made use of the same material (cf. *infra*, p. 160).—Finally it is important that b. al-Kalbī maintains—in contrast to Abū Mikhnaf and his father—that b. 'Abbās respected 'Alī's demand for re-payment of Basra's money; we now see him completely cleared (Ya'q. II, 242; Caetani X, 205=423 *sq.*).

of this defence for the Abbasids are borrowed from the Kufic transmission, which thus at a surprisingly early date is being adapted to the new milieu, one reason being, presumably, that the rupture with the radical Shīʿism necessitated prompt building up of an official re-expounding of the *fitna*.

However, al-Kalbī's constructions are still no more than precursors of the extensive falsifications met with shortly before 800 in Sayf b. ʿUmar—fabrications whose historical absurdity was fully shown up by Wellhausen[27]. Still, the question remains concerning the placing of Sayf in this adaptational process: are his constructions devoid of meaning, or do they, too, indicate deliberate tendencies? Already Wellhausen established that the main object in Sayf b. ʿUmar's rendering was to demonstrate that ʿUthmān's murder was due to a rabid "proto"-Shiite sect, as-Sabaʾiyya, which for a time after the murder sabotaged the caliph election. It had really been ʿAlī's intention to punish the caliph's slayers, but he had to desist owing to lack of support (also in Medina) until with Kufic assistance he felt sufficiently strong: it was solely the sect's intervention that prevented a peaceful resolution of the conflict with Ṭalḥa and az-Zubayr before the battle of the Camel, and, consequently, punishment of the killers[28]. After the battle of the Camel as-Sabaʾiyya felt dissatisfied with the apportionment of the spoils and started intriguing behind ʿAlī's back. Sayf now evidently prusues the line from here into the budding Khārijism[29].

Sayf b. ʿUmar likewise fits ʿAlī's relations with Muʿāwiya into this framework. In the story of al-Mughīra b. Shuʿba's advice to ʿAlī he supplements b. ʿAbbās's grounds for the expediency of the first advice with a comment to the effect that ʿAlī ought to have left the place of the murder to evade all suspicion of complicity[30]. As matters stood now, Banū Umayya might charge him with being an accessory to the crime. The report on the allocation of governorships is elaborated by Sayf with accounts of the fate of each person involved; Sahl b. Ḥunayf—ʿAlī's designee for the replacement of Muʿāwiya—is intercepted by Muʿāwiya's horsemen, and in Ṣafar, 36 A.H., i.e. ult. July–ult. Aug. 656, the caliph is writing to him in vain. Not until the following month, Rabīʿ I, does Muʿāwiya dispatch a messenger to ʿAlī with his rejection of *bayʿa*. The messenger

27 Wellhausen: *Prolegomena*, 3–7; cf. Caetani VIII, 42 *sqq.*, 199 *sqq.*; IX, 5, 23, 86 *sq.* and *AO* XXVII, 97 *sq.*

28 Wellhausen: *Prolegomena*, 124 *sqq.* and passim; Friedlaender: *b. Sabaʾ*, 297 *sq.*; Caetani VIII, 42 *sqq.*

29 Tab. I. 3226–27 (Caetani IX, 199). The line leading to the Khārijites is indicated by Ṭabarī's remark I. 3230 (Caetani IX, 150 sq.; without *isnād*); cf. *infra* p. 152.—Sayf's version is, apart from a single fragment, exclusively transmitted by Ṭabarī, who follows it as his main source for his representation from the revolution against ʿUthmān to the battle of the Camel (Tab. I. 1844–3255; cf. *infra* p. 150).

30 Tab. I. 3081–83 (Caetani VIII, 337 *sq.*). Even before the murder Sayf has al-Mughīra advise ʿAlī to withdraw (Tab. I. 3019; Caetani VIII, 217).

states before the caliph that 60,000 Syrian *shaykhs* are crying because of 'Uthmān's *qamīṣ* which has been suspended on the *minbar* in Damascus; they have sworn chastity until they have avenged the murder on 'Alī. The caliph is taken by surprise at being the object for the vengeance; he assures the messenger that the murderers shall be punished, and only as-Saba'iyya's threats once more prevent him from that action[31].

By this exposition Sayf b. 'Umar succeeds in fitting Mu'āwiya's rebellion into his general view; the responsibility for the murderers' going unpunished and for the armed conflict lies solely with as-Saba'iyya and its adherents, whom Sayf finds primarily among the Bedouin *(ahl al-'Arab)*. We shall revert to these tribal antagonisms below, but it is obvious already now that in Sayf the course of events has been changed beyond recognition, and the real object of the conflict—the action of revenge for 'Uthmān—is lost sight of in a showdown with that heretical tribal barbarism which Sayf ascribes to as-Saba'iyya. At the same time the chronological structure of the rendering is rationalized accordingly. Mu'āwiya's breach with 'Alī is dated as in Ṣafar-Rabī' I, i.e. Aug.–Sept., 656, by which means Sayf manages to inspire Ṭalḥa and az-Zubayr with "courage to embark on the fight" while the caliph was engaged on Mu'āwiya's rebellion[32]. This corresponds perfectly well with Sayf's information that the suspension of 'Uthmān's *qamīṣ* in the mosque lasts for a whole year, exactly the time elapsing between the caliph murder and the encounter at Ṣiffīn[33]. We do not know Sayf's exposition beyond the battle of the Camel, but the accounts here referred to show that the picture he paints of tribal and sectarian conflicts must have come into being by tendentious alterations of the Kufic transmission, to a large extent, for instance, of Hishām b. Muhammad's and that of the anonymous common source, with which he has a great many details in common[34]. His exposition has nothing whatever to do with historical facts, but it rather reveals the problems with which Sayf's own contemporaries were occupied. It is possible that 'Abdallāh b. Saba', on whom Sayf b. 'Umar saddles the responsibility for the revolt against 'Uthmān and for the fact that the conflict was not settled in time, did live in the middle of the 7th century; but the sectarian teachings ascribed to him have hardly anything in common with the earliest *shī'at 'Alī* as we know it from the genuine sources. Sayf has it that b. Saba' or b. as-Sawdā', who according to his description is a Yemenite Jew identical with b. Saba', prophesies the Second Coming of 'Alī *(raj'a)*. By heretical interpretation of a Quran passage he asserts that every prophet has

31 Tab. I. 3087–91 (Caetani IX, 8–11).

32 Tab. I. 3091–92 (Caetani IX, 23 *sq.*).

33 Tab. I. 3255 (Caetani IX, 233 *sq.*).

34 *AO* XXVII, 84 *sqq.* This observation thus confirms, although rather indirectly, his already mentioned points of contact with Abū Mikhnaf.

his *waṣī*, Muhammad *in casu* ʿAlī; as Muhammad is the last prophet, so ʿAlī is the last *waṣi*, and ʿUthmān had by unwarranted means appropriated this authority, *waṣiyya*[35]. We need not go into details in order to realize that we are dealing with notions rooted in Persian and Jewish concepts, Metempsychosis and Messianism. Even if religious hysteria of this kind cannot be excluded in troubled times, there will be little reason to believe in Sayf's rendering. In the first place, these concepts can hardly have been absorbed into Shīʿism before the end of the 7th century, when the extremist *ghulāt* was fashioned as a social and religious resistance movement in the eastern provinces[36]. In the second place, the identity of b. Saba' with b. as-Sawdā', as postulated by Sayf, is extremely doubtful, and where the genuine sources tell that ʿAlī put one b. Saba' to death, they adduce grounds for this that differ entirely from those given by Sayf[37].

It is, finally, of importance that, on the basis of presumably genuine quotations from ash-Shaʿbī, b. Ṭāhir al-Baghdādī (d. 1038) asserts that b. Saba', from whom as-Saba'iyya has its name, and b. as-Sawdā' are not—as stated by Sayf—identical. The latter's prophesy is according to ash-Shaʿbī's statement in full conformity with the doctrines that Sayf b. ʿUmar attributes to as-Saba'iyya[38]; we must assume that it is from these very doctrines he derived the elements for his exposition of b. Saba''s teaching. The identification of b. Saba' with b. as-Sawdā' and the combination of this heretic persuasion with the rebellion against ʿUthmān with all its consequences can only depend upon Sayf's own constructions. The same applies to the postulated connection between the Arabian Bedouin and as-Saba'iyya. On the whole, then, we must assume that Sayf has reflected the radical Shīʿism of his own time back onto the first civil war by means of a series of venturous constructions; his drastic alterations were intended to make ʿAlī's own adherents, whom he identifies with *al-ghulāt*, responsible for the *fitna* and for having paralysed the caliph's freedom of action. We do not know for certain whether he also saddled as-Saba'iyya with the responsibility for the caliph's subsequent failure[39], though the suggestion that

35 Tab. I. 2941–44 (Caetani VIII, 49–51), from where b. al-Athīr, al-Miskawayhi, and presumably Maqrīzī have their accounts; Friedlaender: *b. Saba'*, 298 note 3. On the conceptions mentioned, see also Friedlaender, *passim*, and Buhl: *Aliderne*, 358 sqq., 374 *sqq*.

36 Friedlaender: *b. Saba'* II, 1 *sqq*.; S. Moscati, 257 *sqq*.; cf. *supra* p. 67.

37 Balādhurī's representation of him as an apostate is the more plausible one. The allegation of b. Saba''s Jewish extraction is due, no doubt, to a late construction, cf. Bal. 542r (della Vida, 495; Caetani X, 107), who with Abū Mikhnaf as source refers to him as an Arab. On b. Saba', see Friedlaender, *passim*; Moscati, 253 *sq*., 256, 264; Hodgson in *E. I.*² I, 51.

38 Friedlaender: b. Saba' II, 40 *sqq*. (translation I, 310 *sqq*.).

39 cf. infra p. 152. In the earliest tradition one of the Khārijite accusations against ʿAlī is his having omitted to take spoils at Basra. It is undoubtedly this very detail Sayf is utilizing to attach as-Saba'iyya's discontent after the battle of the Camel to the Khārijites.

the Khārijites grew out of the discontent prevailing after the battle of the Camel points in that direction. It thus appears that Sayf b. 'Umar's prejudice is rooted in his own environment at the end of the 8th century.

It does seem possible, however, to get yet a step nearer to Sayf's views. As mentioned above, he links up as-Saba'iyya with the Arabian Bedouin's revolt against 'Uthmān. This is hardly meant as an allusion to the antagonism between Syrian and Iraqian tribes[40]. According to this version b. Saba''s agitation does find a fertile soil in Kufa, and the movement is joined by Egypt too, whereas it finds no growing conditions in Syria. Sayf's intentions are especially observable in his accounts of the rebellion in Iraq against 'Uthmān. *Dhimmīs* and the believers complain of a certain Ḥakīm b. Jabala, "a robber in the shape of a soldier", who after the conquest of al-Fāris pillaged and exhorted contributions, in particular from *dhimmīs*. He was imprisoned by 'Uthmān's governor in Kufa, but with many others won over by b. Saba''s agitation[41]. Sayf thus achieves identification of as-Saba'iyya with the untamed Bedouin instincts in contrast to *dhimmīs*, the settled non-Moslem population and to the settled believers. His depiction of 'Abdallāh b. Saba''s activities in Egypt is on the same line. The Egyptians refuse to get mixed up with his heterodox ideas and do not accept them until he encourages them to a political revolt against b. al-'Āṣ, the Qurayshite who is exploiting them financially. b. Saba' overcomes their hesitation in rising against a man of Arab descent by suggesting that they motivate their rebellion by 'Amr's economic abuse; "you are the gateway of the Arabs and their dike—and we do not belong to the caliph's people"[42]. When 'Amr subsequently received the news of 'Uthmān's death, he declares that the gateway between Quraysh and Bedouin has been broken, and that "it will not be mended except with awls *(ashāfī)* that can separate the good guidance from the pit of evil and give man justice"[43]. It is obvious that in Sayf's mouth *ahl al-'Arab* is not a flattering designation but rather a derogatory label for simple-minded elements of the population who let themselves be exploited politically and religiously by propaganda for social reasons. Assuming this reading to be correct, we meet here for the first time with—albeit indirect—evidence in historical writing that the radical Shī'ism begins its infiltration into the lower classes as a social opposition to the orthodox rulers, though here reflected back onto a situation in which it does not belong.

The tradition mirrored by Sayf b. 'Umar's circumstantial constructions

40 Only the prophesy by al-Ḥarra in Sayf's version might be indication hereof ("*Yāla Muḍar! Yāla Qays*; Horsemen and Archers, your words will be repudiated by 4000 horses").

41 Tab. I. 2922–23 (Caetani VIII, 53 *sq.*).

42 *Kitāb al-Tamhid*, 74 *sq.* (Caetani VIII, 51 *sqq.*).

43 Tab. I. 3250–51 (Caetani IX, 235 *sq.*). A similar remark is found in the common source (b. al-Kalbī); *AO* XXVII, 89.

reveals on all points the settling of the first Abbasids with their revolutionary past, a coarsened continuation of such trends as were already observed in the al-Kalbīs. Sayf is obviously pro-Abbasid; he is well-disposed towards ʿAlī, but depicts him as powerless before the radical Shīʿism and therefore powerless, too, before his enemies. In his defence of the Abbasid cause Sayf b. ʿUmar's statement is carried through with a consistency that is quite unsual under the circumstances, with daring constructions over the Kufic sources at his disposal, and with a temperament and force that give his exposition a stamp of topical political agitation rather than of historical writing of lasting importance[44].

The growth of the Abbasid tradition in the first generations after the change of dynasty had thus been largely dependent upon traditional material from external, especially Kufic, sources. By borrowing from these a significant conception of the *fitna* is fashioned at a very early stage, with strong traces of the Abbasids' clash with the radical Shīʿism, and of the attempts to assign to these an active part in the fight against the Umayyads by the side of ʿAlī, where his own adherents had failed him[45]. That pragmatism which Wellhausen observed in Sayf b. ʿUmar thus grows organically into the consolidation of the Abbasid caliphate. If conceived as a link in the creation of public opinion pragmatism takes its place in the efforts of the new rulers to free themselves of their revolutionary origin and to adapt themselves to the beginning social shifts.

---

44 With the exception of Ṭabarī the Arabic historical writing seems to have been only very slightly influenced by Sayf's viewpoints and rarely quotes him, perhaps also because his approach to the problems was soon outdated. Already adh-Dhahabī denounces him as unreliable (Friedlaender: *b. Saba*ʾ I, 297). On one point, however, b. ʿAsākir seems to be influenced by Say'fs opinion inasmuch as he makes "ʿAbdallāh b. Saba"'s followers ...(to) the main reason for the conflict between the peoples" (b. ʿAsākir, 576, 586; Caetani VIII, 317); cf. also Friedlaender: *b. Saba*ʾ I, 298 note 3.

45 The reaction by Shīʿi historical writing to this challenge will be reverted to; see *infra* p. 108.—It is remarkable that even Abu-l-ʿAbbās, the first Abbasid caliph, in 749 endeavoured to compromise the Alids by identifying them *en bloc* with as-Saba'iyya; cf. Cl. Cahen in *Revue historique* CCXXX (1963) 333, note 1.

3. The Abbasid Tradition 800–850

In so far as the Abbasids appear to have attached great weight to their representation and enforcement of the Islamic society's orthodox *ijmāʿ*, so the historical writing during the second half of the 8th century must be described as orthodox, notwithstanding its being in fact a product of that period's violent struggles. Though Sayf b. ʿUmar's historical writing very likely furnished the clearest picture of the Abbasids' showdown with Shīʿism, it remained an intermezzo that left very few traces in the historical writing of the following generations. Even in the first decades of the 9th century his points of view had to give way to new lines of direction.

In 796—at the time of Sayf b. ʿUmar's death—the Medinese traditionist al-Wāqidī (d. 823) had, deep in debt, to leave Medina for Baghdad, where, first, the vizir Yaḥyā b. Khālid al-Barmakī, and later al-Maʾmūn supported him and rewarded him with a *qāḍī* office[1]. al-Wāqidī thus followed in Muhammad b. Isḥāq's footsteps, for he, too, was since his Medinese days revered for his knowledge of the Prophet tradition and seems to have devoted himself to "profane-historical" works[2] after his arrival at Baghdad. To us, however, it is most often impossible to determine with any show of verisimilitude from which period of his autorship stem such historical traditions as we know from subsequent quotations. Narratives concerning ʿAlī or other Prophet Companions may very well derive from *sīra* or *maghāzī* works aiming at illustrating their personal qualities and services, or from one of Wāqidī's topographical works for the purpose of elucidating the local activities of the person concerned; in either case without any chronological cohesion. Wāqidī's traditional material must therefore be treated with greater reservation than that of other scholars. As regards the Prophet tradition, both his and his disciple Muhammad b.

1 *GAL (S)* I, 207.—On Wāqidī, see b. Khall. no. 655 (de Slane IV, 61 *sqq.*); Horowitz: Biographies, 501 *sqq.*; *idem* in *E. I.*[1] IV, 1195 *sq.*

2 Wāqidī's historical work covers at any rate the period up to 179 A.H./795–96 when the last known quotation appears (Horowitz: *Biographies*, 516). So in contrast to Horowitz I should be inclined to think that this work (*taʾrīkh al-kabīr*) was finished after Wāqidī's arrival at Baghdad; it rests, as we shall see later, to a great extent on a study of sources, which could hardly be done in Medina.

Sa'd's (d. 845) subject-matter appears to depend almost exclusively upon local Medinese[3] tradition, and in their account of the patriarchal caliphate they likewise draw mostly on local sources[4]. Their interest in the clash between 'Alī and Mu'āwiya seems however to have been considerably lesser, so the available traditions handed down concerning this are far less circumstantial and evidently of a more varying provenance. Here, too, they frequently refer to Medinese authorities such as Abū Bakr b. Abī Ṣabra (end of 8th century), 'Abdallāh b. Ja'far b. 'Abd-ar-Raḥmān b. al-Miswar (d. 786/87), and Mūsā b. Ya'qūb (data unknown). Nevertheless, their transmission is based predominantly on sources of Kufic origin, and their Medinese provenance serves to elaborate their particular points of view.

As already mentioned, Wāqidī's version of 'Alī's measures after the caliph election—his conversations with al-Mughīra b. Shu'ba, and the story of 'Amr's flight to Palestine—seems to stem from an early Abbasid report, presumably al-Kalbī's despite the Medinese *isnād* with which it is invested, and although he has recounted it in the form of b. 'Abbās' recollection[5]. It is in the same way immediately clear that al-Wāqidī's account of 'Amr b. al-'Āṣ's consultation with his sons on his attitude to the situation that has arisen in consequence of 'Alī's election must be culled from Iraqian sources, although here, too, he refers to a Medinese informant, Mūsā b. Ya'qūb[6]; the same report is found nowhere else but in *Waq'at Ṣiffīn* from Kufic sources. In both versions 'Abdallāh b. 'Amr states that the Prophet as well as the first two caliphs died satisfied with 'Amr, whereas 'Amr's other son stresses that by virtue of his prominent position his father ought to assert himself. In contrast to the Kufic version, that of al-Wāqidī is at certain points distinctly rationalized. 'Amr's behaviour here differs entirely from what is said in the Kufic version, where the consultation was provoked by Mu'āwiya's request to 'Amr to come, whereas here he acts *sua sponte* because he is dissatisfied with the election of 'Alī, and because he knows that the Syrian governor agitated for vengeance directed towards the caliph. When he arrives at Damascus, Mu'āwiya ignores him—again in contrast to the Kufic version—until he himself offers his assistance. 'Amr knows perfectly well that they "will have to fight a man who can refer to his early conversion, his services, and his ties of kinship with the Prophet, whereas we desire this world", even though in 'Amr's opinion 'Alī rather exploits his

3 See e.g. Wāqidī-Wellhausen, *passim*; cf. however my remarks in *AO* XXVI (1962), 220*sq.*

4 See e.g. the account of 'Uthmān's murder, Caetani VIII, 141–94; Wellhausen: *Prolegomena*, 113 *sqq.*

5 Tab. I. 3083–85, 2965–68 (Caetani VIII, 338 *sq.*, 145 *sq.*); on sources and *isnāds*, see *AO* XXVII, 93.

6 Tab. I. 3252–54 (Caetani IX, 236); cf. *Waq. Siff.*, 38 *sqq.* and 'Īsā b. Yazīd in Bal. 498r–99v (Caetani IX, 240 *sqq.*).

religious prestige. However, ʿAmr makes his choice simply because he finds it convenient to join the Syrians. Wāqidī's adaptations are thus quite consistent inasmuch as they are entirely in keeping with his dating of the breach between the two parties to a time immediately after the caliph election. In this respect, then, he merely adheres to the line which Abbasid tradition had laid down from the outset, and which it had taken over from Abū Mikhnaf.

The story of ʿAmr's Quran stratagem at Ṣiffīn is adopted by Wāqidī from a Ḥijāzi source, from az-Zuhrī through Muʿammar b. Rashīd's pro-Abbasid adaptation[7]. But the account of the Adhruḥ negotiations stems no doubt from Kufic sources; Wāqidī repeats Abū Mikhnaf's version verbatim, the first part correctly with ash-Shaʿbī as informant, the second part with a purely Medinese chain of transmitters[8]. The first *isnād* is probably correct, at any rate in its last links; but it is indeed remarkable that Wāqidī (and after him b. Saʿd)—as well as Ṭabarī and Balādhurī—quotes the Kufic report in the same form, a fact seeming to indicate that he actually borrowed it from either Abū Mikhnaf or one of his pupils, and, if so, most likely from Hishām b. Muhammad, whom Balādhurī quotes as an intermediate link. If this reading is correct, Wāqidī's *isnād* must be due to a falsification.

It is, finally, significant that Wāqidī as well as Muhammad b. Saʿd knows nothing whatever about a meeting at Dūmat al-Jandal; they unreservedly place the arbitration at Adhruḥ in Shaʿbān, 38 A.H., i.e. January, 659[9]. Concerning this point al-Wāqidī builds upon az-Zuhrī's account, and seeing that he must certainly have known the Kufic chronology there is hardly any reason to doubt that the late and approximately correct dating of the Adhruḥ meeting and the elimination of Dūmat al-Jandal must have been set down deliberately. This

7 b. Saʿd IV. 2. 3–4 (Caetani IX, 531); on the adaptation of this tradition, see *AO* XXVII, 100 *sq*.

8 b. Saʿd IV. 2. 4–5 (cf. Caetani X, corr. e agg., xxv and pp. 21 and 40). The first part (IV. 2. 4. 9–14) is quoted from al-Manṣūr b. Abi-l-Aswad, from Mujālid b. Saʿīd, from ash-Shaʿbī, where the two earliest links are well known; the second part cites a Medinese *isnād* which Wāqidī has occasionally employed in his *kitāb al-maghāzī*; cf. Waqidī-Wellhausen, 112, 284, 308, and in part 55.

9 Wāqidī in Ṭabarī I. 3360, 3406–07; b. Saʿd III. 1. 21 (Caetani X, 18, 221, 53). In his report on the arbitration agreement at Ṣiffīn b. Saʿd does, admittedly, fix the time of the meeting for "the beginning of next year" (i.e. 37 A.H.) and does not mention any postponement. The chronological contradiction thus appearing in b. Saʿd has undoubtedly its most simple and correct explanation in the sources employed; his account seems also here to rest on Wāqidī, who in turn draws on az-Zuhrī. According to the latter the meeting was fixed for Dūmat al-Jandal in Ramaḍān 37 A.H., with allowance for postponement. There seems hardly any reason, therefore, with della Vida (487 *sq*.) to assume that Wāqidī and b. Saʿd should in this case operate with the solar year; cf. also Caetani X, corr. e agg., xxv and Vaglieri I, 80 *sq*., 85 note 2.

brings both Wāqidī and his pupil into contrast with the Kufic transmission[10]; 'Alī's clash with the Khārijites at an-Nahrawān is thus made to occur—still perfectly correct—before the arbitration meeting, a circumstance which also b. Sa'd expressly mentions in his summary of the events of these years[11]. We know neither al-Wāqidī's nor b. Sa'd's estimation of the Khārijites' rebellion beyond an isolated anecdote in which b. Sa'd parabolically has 'Alī denounce them[12]. It is anyhow obvious that they dissociate themselves from the current Iraqian view and from the last generation's evaluation, but no immediate explanation can be gleaned from the text itself.

There is generally no doubt that despite his invocation of Medinese informants and certain significant sprinklings from az-Zuhrī, al-Wāqidī was greatly dependent upon Kufic sources. The accounts here dealt with are incomprehensible without our assuming a connection with either the Kufic or the earliest Abbasid circle of traditions, which in turn draw on the Kufic one. The case for the latter possibility consists in the fact that Wāqidī is acquainted with traditional material that does not appear until found in that common source which we have already identified with b. al-Kalbī, whereas the Iraqian transmission before al-Wāqidī carries only very sporadic quotations from Medinese authorities in its depiction of the events of these years. These observations constitute an indirect confirmation of the impression that Wāqidī did not prepare this material thoroughly until after his arrival at Baghdad, and that he worked under the influence of the views of his Iraqian environment.

In al-Wāqidī it is more difficult than in numerous other authors to find a principal line in the conception of the *fitna*; the incoherent transmission offers no definite clues, even though our knowledge of his material indicates that on several important points he represents a re-appraisal as compared with his predecessors. He, too, dates the breach between 'Alī and Mu'āwiya to a time immediately after the caliph election[13], but in contrast to the Kufic tradition Wāqidī dates the Khārijite rising, the battle at an-Nahrawān, and 'Amr b. al-'Āṣ's conquest of Egypt[14] to the months before the Adhruḥ meeting, in Sha'bān, 38 A.H. The significance of this chronology is not quite clear because we lack details of Wāqidī's view of 'Alī's relations with his army at Ṣiffīn and of the Khārijites. The fact that he utilizes Mu'ammar b. Rashīd's version of the Quran stratagem would indicate a wish on his part to emphasize the

10 cf. e.g. Abū Mikhnaf in Tab. I. 3360–62, 3363–69 and Muhammad b. as-Sā'ib al-Kalbī in Bal., 523v (Caetani X, 77 *sq.*, 80 *sqq.*, 32).

11 b. Sa'd III. 1. 21 (Caetani X, 109, cf. 53).

12 Bal. 456r (Caetani X, 408).

13 It is, however, somewhat doubtful whether he intended postulating a connection between the rebellion of Mu'āwiya and that of the 'Uthmāniyya.

14 cf. Tab. I. 3406–07 (Caetani X, 221).

disunion within 'Alī's troops and that this makes it necessary for the caliph to accept the arbitration. The same indication is seen in another passage where Wāqidī asserts that the Prophet companion Abū Mūsā was personally blameless as regards the outcome of the arbitration meeting, whereas the responsibility[15] lay with those who had appointed or sent him, i.e. an intimation that a group in 'Alī's own army had forced him to employ Abū Mūsā as an umpire.

On the other hand, the material at our disposal shows clearly that al-Wāqidī joined whole-heartedly in the traditional condemnation of the Umayyads and their adherents. Mechanically he repeats the allegation of Mu'āwiya's worldliness; he makes him claim being God's Representative, and confutes it by establishing that Mu'āwiya "is the last of the people and rules by usurpation".[16] Elsewhere he insinuates in a malicious anecdote that Mu'āwiya—like his father Abū Sufyān—had procured his power through bribery.[17] The one properly responsible for "conditions of society" is, however, 'Amr b. al-'Āṣ; it was he who had agitated against 'Uthmān, but preferred to stay away; who had taken the initiative in the collaboration with the Syrian governor; and who by his Quran stratagem and fraud had again proved that he "shunned no means".

Wāqidī appears above all to have made a point of establishing that the Prophet Companions, including 'Alī, were non-participants in the caliph murder[18]. 'Uthmān fell a victim to his administrative errors[19], and the responsibility for the murder lay with the Egyptian rebels whereas the Basrians and Kufians are excluded[20]. Wāqidī remarks that the Arabs were unanimous in electing 'Alī, whose religious prestige he fully recognizes; he does, however, stress the fact that a few of the most prominent Prophet Companions, among which Sa'd b. Abī Waqqāṣ and b. 'Umar, "stayed away"[21]. The importance of the neutral Companions had formerly been touched on by Wāqidī; Sa'd b. Abī Waqqāṣ occasionally lends his name to the Medinese Helpers' efforts to keep away from the revolution against 'Uthmān[22], a point to which he reverts

15 b. Sa'd IV. 2. 5.=b. al-Athīr III, 278 *sq.* (Caetani X, corr. e agg., xxv and p. 40); this account here assumes the character of an elaboration of the Kufic tradition's information regarding b. 'Abbās's comments on Abū Mūsā's conduct.

16 Bal.: Mu'āw., no. 20.—Abū Mikhnaf tells a somewhat similar anecdote about 'Alī (Abu-l-Faraj al-Iṣfahānī: *Maqātil aṭ-Ṭālibiyyīn*, 14 (Caetani X, 414).

17 Bal.: *Mu'āw.*, no. 329.

18 Characteristically, he leaves out Sayf's information (Tab. I. 3249–50; cf. b. 'Asākir, 647 *sq.*; Caetani IX, 235; VIII, 241 *sq.*) on 'Amr's remark that everybody staying in Medina at the time of the murder will incur co-responsibility, an allusion to 'Alī and the Prophet Companions.

19 Tab. I. 2968, 2981 (Caetani VIII, 146, 162).

20 Tab. I. 2979–80; b. Sa'd III. 1. 44–45 (Caetani VIII, 156 *sqq.*).

21 Tab. I. 3072 (Caetani VIII, 327). The tradition, in the form of Sa'd b. Abī Waqqāṣ's recollection, is most likely due to an adaptation of Abū Mikhnaf.

22 e.g. b. Sa'd III. 1. 50 (Caetani VIII, 166).

several times. True, Sa'd was present at the arbitration hearing, but his attitude was one of frigid neutrality, whereas b. 'Umar regretted his presence and went on a pilgrimage to Bayt al-Maqdis (Jerusalem)[23]; both statements are so far unknown to the Arabic tradition and consequently no doubt products of Wāqidī's tendency.

Even though Wāqidī thus attaches particular weight to the conduct of the neutral Prophet Companions, it is nevertheless difficult to explain his points of view on the grounds of specifically Medinese opinions. That his exposition in the available form is not Shiite—though admittedly pro-'Alī—appears not only from his chronological system, but also from his sympathetic dealing with the Abbasids. He consistently describes 'Abdallāh b. 'Abbās as 'Alī's loyal mentor, and of quite particular significance is Wāqidī's full account of how Umar at the setting up of pension-registers *(dīwān)* lets the Prophet's nearest relations, Banū Hāshim, i.e. also the Abbasids, precede everybody else. This is in contrast to the Shiite tradition, which favoured 'Alī, 'Ā'isha, Ḥasan, and Ḥusayn[24]. On the whole, Wāqidī's rendering represents a noticeable shift as compared with his predecessors; the strongly anti-Shiite attitude is replaced by a positive evaluation of 'Alī, and only the denunciation of the Umayyads continues unabated. Already Sarasin pointed out that Wāqidī's position may be explained by the fact that he was writing during al-Ma'mūn's (813–33) relatively pro-'Alī rule, and a comparison with Muhammad b. Isḥāq's *sīra* will show that he estimates 'Alī higher than does the latter as the Prophet's exemplary companion and successor[25]. It should be possible, however, to get still a step nearer to an identification of his views.

As briefly referred to above, the Abbasids had their own supporting party, Mu'tazilism, which had taken shape primarily in Basra, and which was distinguished politically for its sympathetic evaluation of 'Alī and az-Zubayr and for its vehement denunciation of the Umayyads and the extreme Shī'ism[26]. We have already observed reflections of the earliest Basrian Mu'tazilism in the historical transmission in such figures as Abū Bakr al-Hudhalī and, perhaps, Mu'ammar b. Rashīd. But this movement—although its views were compatible with the prevailing anti-Shiitic atmosphere—does not until Hārūn ar-Rashīd's death in 809 appear able to assert itself side by side with such traditionalists as Hishām b. Muhammad al-Kalbī or Sayf b. 'Umar. Along with the Basrian Rationalism Baghdad saw the formation of a Mu'tazilite school under leader-

23 Tab. I. 3353–54 (Caetani X, 21).

24 Bal.: *Futūḥ*, 449 *sqq.*; cf. the pro-Alid tradition *ibid.*, 454 *sqq.* (Hitti-Murgotten II, 240 *sqq.*, 247 *sqq.*); al-'Abbās, according to b. Sa'd, figures first on the dīwān-registers (Horowitz: *Biographies*, 521); cf. Sarasin, 21 *sqq.*

25 Sarasin, 24 *sq.*—Cf. b. Sa'd III. 1. 13 *sqq.* (Caetani X, 391 *sqq.*) and Noeldeke, 19.

26 cf. *supra* pp. 71 *sq.*

ship of the theologian Bishr b. al-Muʿtamir (d. between 210 and 226 A.H./825–840), who had been a pupil of Wāṣil b. ʿAṭā'. But in comparison with the Basrian wing, which was generally well disposed towards ʿAlī, Bishr b. Muʿtamir's persuasion was characterized further by pro-Alid points of view; he preferred ʿAlī to Abū Bakr, for which reason he was persecuted as late as by Hārūn ar-Rashīd[27]. This movement penetrated under al-Ma'mūn; it endeavoured to meet the Alid standpoint both religiously and politically, partly by plans for a dynastic arrangement of benefit to the Alids[28], partly, in 827, by adopting Muʿtazilism as official dogmatics.

On comparing the pro-Alid currents and the Muʿtazilite system with al-Wāqidī's points of view we shall find them to be in consonance in their main features. His anti-Umayyad tendency is unambiguous; he makes a point of establishing the Prophet Companions' and the Basrians' absolute innocence of the catastrophe at Medina and emphasizes that a number of leading Prophet Companions "stayed away" from the *fitna*, and finally, by his chronological system repudiates the Shiite interpretation of ʿAlī's relations with the Khārijites. Despite the reservation necessitated by the fragmentary transmission Wāqidī appears to have been in agreement with the official standpoint during al-Ma'mūn's first years. Whether he joined Muʿtazilism remains a moot question, but there is hardly any doubt that during his stay in the seat of the Caliph he advocated a reconciliation with the moderate Shīʿism. This conclusion is indirectly borne out in Muhammad b. Saʿd's statement that Wāqidī in his works signed away his Shiite confession from *taqīya*, fear that exempts a person from his religious conviction[29]. This information, which in consequence of b. Saʿd's relations as both a pupil of and a secretary to Wāqidī cannot be disallowed, sheds quite an interesting light on the latter's literary activities and on the conditions of the Medinese tradition in the zenith of the Abbasid era. Despite his Medinese schooling and prophet-biographical work his material reveals a pronounced dependence on the Iraqian tradition; only in so far as he seems to have combined his own true convictions with the official views at the Abbasid Court can we join Caetani in speaking of an amalgamation of the Medinese and the Iraqian transmission. Again, the conclusions here arrived at correspond well with our knowledge of the development of the jurisprudential tradition during the same period, for it, too, seems to be of Iraqian origin, and at a later stage[30] to have incorporated into its system such Medinese opinions as fitted in with the milieu.

---

27 H. S. Nyberg in *E. I.*[1] III, 853; A. N. Nader in *E. I.*[2] I, 1243.

28 Gabrieli: *al-Ma'mūn*, especially 29 *sqq.*

29 *GAL(S)* I, 207. This corresponds with the bibliographer an-Nadīm's mentioning that Wāqidī favourized Shīʿism, but tried harmonizing its view-points with the official ones; Horowitz: *Wāq.*, 43.

30 Schacht: *Origins*, 223.

al-Wāqidī's pupil Muhammad b. Sa'd (d. 845) in many respects continued in the channels marked out by his teacher. On the other hand, his principal work, the comprehensive *ṭabaqāt*, was quite differently arranged and written for purposes quite different from those of the historical writing with which we have dealt so far. b. Sa'd's work firmly establishes the historico-biographical genre to which we find approaches as early as in the *sīra* literature, and the chronologic-historical aspect is therefore secondary to other ones: the systematics of the several categories of Arab believers according to generations and religious qualities[31]. It cannot, as mentioned in a single passage (in Ṭabarī), be entirely ruled out that in the last years of his life b. Sa'd felt attracted to Ḥanbalism, the strictly orthodox traditionalism[32]. The disposition of his work and his intense interest in the classical Arab community—according to the tradition organized by 'Umar—the last remains of which were disappearing in his own time[33], present a case for this deduction. However, the fact that b. Sa'd, like his teacher, worked in Baghdad, where Ḥanbalism was persecuted by the authorities, and appears to have been a favourite at the caliphal court[34] does not point that way. And neither does his attitude as expressed in his *ṭabaqāt* concerning the *fitna* strengthen our confidence in this information; in most respects he elaborates or modifies the opinions of his teacher.

Seen from our angle, Muhammad b. Sa'd cannot claim quite the same interest as Wāqidī. In all essentials he repeats the main lines of the latter's version as regards the events and the chronological systematism, though mostly in quite brief summaries inserted in the historico-biographical construction of his work. His distinct attitudes generally come out only in the variant material, which mostly stems from other—and, incidentally, much varying—sources in which Wāqidī was not concerned. His accordance with Wāqidī lies primarily in his anti-Umayyad trend. The contract between Mu'āwiya and 'Amr is by him given an entirely new semblance in epistolary form drawn up by 'Amr's *mawlā* Wardān, whereby 'Amr's initiative is concretized; the two parties promise each other unconditional aid against 'Amr's being promised Egypt; "'Amr's aid is, by God, a lamed arm", as b. Sa'd makes 'Alī comment on this event[35]. On a line with Wāqidī's insinuation that Mu'āwiya procured his power through bribery, b. Sa'd—and here unlike his teacher—has it that the Syrian governor also used that method towards Abū Mūsā al-Ash'arī;

31 On this work and its placing, see Loth, 593 *sqq.*; Rosenthal: *Historiography*, 82 *sqq.*; also Horowitz: *Biographies*, 522 *sqq.* Already Wāqidī is credited with a *ṭabaqāt*-work (*ibid.*, 516 *sq.*).

32 Patton, 64. On Ḥanbalism, see *infra* p. 123 *sqq.*

33 Symbolical of the liquidation of the Arab privileges was the withdrawal of their share in the State pensions in 833.

34 On b. Sa'd, see Sachau in *Einl. z. b. Sa'd* III: 1, xxx *sqq.*; *GAL* I, 136; *(S)* I, 207 *sq.*

35 b. Sa'd IV.2.2–3 (Caetani IX, 238).

he suggests that though the latter rejected a promise of the governorship of Kufa and Basra, he did nevertheless act in collusion with Mu'āwiya[36].

Generally b. Sa'd's anti-Umayyad tendency is thus merely an elaboration of that of Wāqidī. It is, however, a new thing that he apparently weakens the latter's defence of the Prophet Companions and surpasses him in eulogizing 'Alī in his capacity of Caliph[37]. In a polemic against the Basrian tradition he makes, in an undoubtedly apocryphal tradition, 'Alī seize the treasury (*bayt al-māl)* after the caliph murder for the purpose of preventing the election of Ṭalḥa and forcing through that of himself[38]. The initiative thus passed from the Medinians, and b. Sa'd records distinctly that all the Prophet Companions present—Sa'd b. Abī Waqqāṣ being no exception—swear allegiance to 'Alī, so on this point he contradicts Wāqidī[39]. b. Sa'd makes a particularly thoroughgoing study of 'Alī's personality; in his traditions on this subject, which are normally borrowed from other sources than Wāqidī, are seen the first traces of a beginning 'Alī-legend in the orthodox tradition: predictions of his murder by b. Muljam, etc.[40]; but he also repudiates definitely the Shiite ideas of an Alid millennium by making his son Ḥasan deny Shī'ism's assertion of 'Alī's second Coming[41]. Even though b. Sa'd bestows considerably less space and study on 'Alī than on his predecessors[42]—especially 'Umar—he is very well disposed towards him; he sets off, for the first time in the orthodox transmission, the figure of martyrdom, even if occasionally at the cost of the Prophet Companions. On the whole, b. Sa'd's exposition represents rather an intensification of that of Wāqidī, without, however, abandoning his liking for the Abbasids. Rather than being a Ḥanbalite, he is thus the exponent of the official standpoint in a less varied form than that of his teacher.

Common to these two historians are: first, their Medinese background, which is subordinated to the pro-Abbasid version of the Kufic tradition; secondly, the more benignant atmosphere around the figure of 'Alī as compared with that of the preceding generation; and, thirdly, their positive evaluation of the Abbasids—the unity of Banū Hāshim is constantly stressed. Simultaneous and similar shifts are observable in the historical tradition in Basra. Its main trend, to which we shall revert below, appears to have been Uthmanite; but here, too, we may in several historians meet with opposing tendencies revealing

36 b. Sa'd IV.1.82–84 (Caetani X, 54 *sq.*).

37 cf. Sarasin, 25 *sqq.*, 61 65, 68.

38 Bal. 469v; cf. the Basrian account *ibid.*, 467r–v (Caetani VIII, 331).

39 b. Sa'd III.1.20-21 (Caetani IX, 50). Here b. Sa'd mentions the very names excepted in the earlier tradition; his contradiction must thus be deliberate.

40 b. Sa'd III.1.16–20 (Caetani X, 385 *sqq.*, 356 *sq.*); Sarasin, 28 *sq.*

41 b. Sa'd III.1.26 (Caetani X, 463).

42 cf. Sachau in *Einl. z. b. Sa'd* III:1, xxxv.

either an amalgamation of Kufic and Basrian tradition or mutual contradictions between the two schools[43]. This progressive shifting culminates in 'Alī b. Muhammad al-Madā'inī, where by virtue of his calibre it obtains its widest scope. We should not lose sight of the fact that al-Madā'inī had been *mawlā* of a branch of 'Abd Shams b. 'Abd Manāf, which belonged to his native town, Basra, as a subdivision of the Umayyads. Though originally educated as a theologian (by the Mu'tazilite Mu'ammar b. al-Ash'ath), al-Madā'inī devoted himself progressively to historical studies and, in addition, to an extensive autorship of letters *(adab)*. Among his works the monographical treatment of Basra's history and the *kitāb akhbār al-khulafā' al-kabīr*, which reached on to al-Mu'taṣim's Caliphate (833-42), appear to have been the most comprehensive. al-Madā'inī moved from his native town to Baghdad where he seems to have been especially attached to the polyhistor Isḥāq b. Ibrāhīm al-Mawṣilī, in whose house he died (225/840)[44].

al-Madā'inī represents such an advanced stage in the shaping of historical tradition and has culled his subject-matter from so many sources that it is difficult to obtain any immediate and clear survey of his material[45]. The lack of homogeneity of his sources will appear from the fact that side by side with such Basrian scholars as the 'Uthmānī Yazīd b. 'Iyāḍ b. Ju'duba (d. 775/76), the hardly very reliable Abū Bakr al-Hudhalī, Juwayriya b. Asmā' (d. 789/90), Suḥaym b. Ḥafṣ Abu-l-Yaqẓān (d. 805/06), the pro-Umayyad Maslama b. Muḥārib (d. ca. 765–85) and the likewise pro-Umayyad 'Abdallāh b. Mubārak (d. 797)[46] he quotes a great many Kufic traditionists, whether moderate like 'Awāna b. 'Abd al-Ḥakam or intensely Shiite like 'Īsā b. Yazīd and Bishr b. 'Āṣim (data unknown). al-Madā'inī thus absorbs the works, irrespective of tendencies, of the preceding generations, and utilizes them as authorities or as butts of his confutations[47].

Two features are particularly noteworthy: first, that al-Madā'inī, though of Basrian parentage and education, quotes traditionists of Uthmanite cast of mind, but never the Syrian-Medinese tradition from the Basrain school, where

43 cf. *infra* pp. 109 *sqq*. and *AO* XXVII, 98 sqq.

44 On al-Madā'inī's biography, see Brockelmann in *E.I.*[1] III, 87; Margoliouth: *Lectures*, 85 *sqq*.; Pellat: *Jāḥiẓ*, 143 *sqq*.—Statements as to the year of his death vary greatly, from 215 to 231 A.H.; we here follow Goitein's reasoning and choose 225 A.H. as the most plausible (Bal.: *Ans.* V, 14 sqq.).

45 The material is somewhat affected by its resting almost exclusively, especially as regards the earliest stages of the conflict, on the quotations in Ṭabarī's Annals of the pro-Alid 'Umar b. Shabba (d. 875). (On the latter, see *GAL* I, 137; *(S)*, 209; Lammens: *Omayyades*, 72 *sqq*., 157 *sqq*.). Balādhurī seems, on the other hand, to have used Madā'inī directly, occasionally even *ex vivo ore*; cf. *infra* p. 138.

46 On the last two, see *AO* XXVII, 105 *sqq*.

47 cf. *ibid.* XXVII, 117 sq., where it is ascertainable that al-Madā'inī has made use of Maslama b. Muḥārib and other pro-Umayyad scholars as a starting point for his polemics.

it had found sanctuary[48]. That he knew it is not contested; he quotes—albeit rarely—Yazīd b. 'Iyāḍ b. Ju'duba, one of the chief transmitters of this tradition, which immediately suggests that he deliberately dissociated himself from that movement. The second remarkable feature is that al-Madā'inī never quotes Abū Mikhnaf from the informant often used by both Balādhurī and Ṭabarī, and from whom Sayf b. 'Umar and Wāqidī likewise seem to have borrowed, namely Hishām b. Muhammad al-Kalbī, while, reversely, Balādhurī rarely records such traditions from Abū Mikhnaf as are quoted by al-Madā'inī. The explanation may conceivable be that passages in which al-Madā'inī invokes Abū Mikhnaf often referred to conditions in Basra and belonged in one of his works on this town from which Ṭabarī quotes them[49]. However, the explanation is rather that he considered b. al-Kalbī less reliable, or felt repelled by his tendency[50]. Both these peculiarities will come out clearly on comparing the chronological systematics of these traditionists. In al-Madā'inī we find for the first time an elaborate series of chronological data—culled from all the sources he utilizes—that will enable us to appraise his interpretation of 'Alī's caliphate and his placing in his own age. These data are:

1. 'Uthmān's murder: 18th Dhu-l-Ḥijja, 35 A.H. = 17the June, 656[51].
2. 'Alī marches from Medina against the rebels in Iraq at the end of Rabī' II, 36 A.H. = 27th Sept.–25th Oct., 656 (most likely in the latter part of October, 656)[52].
3. 'Alī's breach with Mu'āwiya after the battle of the Camel and Jarīr b. 'Abdallāh's mission, which bears no exact date[53].
4. 'Alī returns to Kufa from Ṣiffīn on the 20th Rabī' I (37 A.H.) = 5th Sept., 657, and remains there for seven months (i.e. until Shawwāl, 37 A.H. = 12th March–9th April, 658), when Mu'āwiya requests him to attend the appointed arbitration hearing[54].
5. Mu'āwiya sets out for Dūmat al-Jandal at the beginning of Ramaḍān, 37 A.H. = 12th Jan.–9th Feb., 658 (i.e. most likely in mid-January). 'Alī is prevented from attending on account of the Khārijite opposition, but sends b. 'Abbās and Abū Mūsā[55].

48 Only one single time in the period here dealt with does al-Madā'inī quote az-Zuhrī and in this instance with the outside traditionist 'Uthmān b. 'Abd ar-Raḥmān as-Sa'dī al-Waqqāṣī (d. 809) as intermediary; *Agh.* XI, 30–31 (Caetani VIII, 87 *sq.*).

49 One exception is Tab. I.3202–04, corresponding to Bal. 478r–79r, 483v–84r (Caetani IX, 144 *sq.*, 129 *sq.*, 145 *sq.*).

50 cf. his fellow-partisan al-Jāḥiẓ's assessment of b. al-Kalbī; Pellat: *Jāḥiẓ*, 141.

51 Tab. I.3067–68 (Caetani VIII, 324).

52 Tab. I.3139 (Caetani IX, 120).

53 Tab. I.3255–56 (Caetani IX, 234).

54 Bal. 523v–24r (Caetani X, 32 *sq.*).

55 *Ibid.*

6. When the arbitrators part, the Syrians swear allegiance to Mu'āwiya as their caliph in Dhu-l-Qa'da, 37 A.H. = 10th April – 9th May, 658[56].
7. When Muhammad b. Abī Bakr (son of the Caliph, and 'Alī's governor in Egypt) had been killed, b. 'Abbās made his way to Kufa to install Ziyād b. Abīhi as his deputy in Basra[57].
8. After the battle at an-Nahrawān, 'Abdallāh b. Ḥaḍramī tried to stir up a revolt in Basra on the initiative of Mu'āwiya[58].
9. b. 'Abbās suggests to 'Alī that Ziyād b. Abīhi be sent to al-Fāris to put down an insurrection there; on his return to Basra after the battle at an-Nahrawān 'Alī does so (39 A.H.)[59].
10. Madā'inī denies that b. 'Abbās headed the pilgrimage in 39 A.H.[60].
11. In the same year b. 'Abbās is said to be staying with al-Ḥasan b. 'Alī[61].
12. The murder of 'Alī takes place on the 11th Ramaḍān, 40 A.H. = 18th Jan., 661[62].

Like the tradition generally, al-Madā'inī dates 'Uthmān's murder to the 18th Dhu-l-Ḥijja, 35 A.H., and even though the dating of 'Alī's murder differs slightly from the one normally stated, the limits are fairly well established, but beyond these matters the agreements ceases. As regards the main features he reverts to the Kufic chronology of the late Umayyad version, though with several not inessential correctives, which enable us to gain an insight into his personal physiognomy. First of all, with 'Awāna as his source, he dates Mu-'āwiya's breach with the caliph subsequent to the battle of the Camel and Jarīr b. 'Abdallāh's mission to Damascus[63]. Again, Madā'inī, unlike the Syrian-Medinese tradition, does not recognize any interval between the caliph election and the Uthmanite rising[64], but on the contrary states that Ṭalḥa

56 Tab. II.199.

57 Tab. I.3414 (Caetani X, 152). This event is set down by al-Kindī, 30 (Caetani X, 213) for the 14th Ṣafar, 38 A.H. = 22nd July, 568; cf. Elia Bar Sinaya (Baethgen: *Fragmente*, 13 *sq.*; *versio*, 113).

58 Tab. I.3440 (Caetani X, 187 *sq.*); according to Bal., 530 (Caetani X, 77, 101) the battle took place on the 9th Ṣafar, 38 A.H. = 17th July, 658; this has probably been accepted by Madā'inī, who supplies no more than the relative dating.

59 Tab. I.3440 (Caetani X, 187 *sq.*).

60 Tab. I.3447–48 (Caetani X, 296).

61 Tab. II.11 (cf. Wellhausen: *Kingdom*, 111).

62 Tab. I. 3456 (Caetani X, 366).

63 The account of 'Uthmān's *qamīṣ* (Agh. XV, 71 sq.; Caetani VIII, 305 *sqq.*) cannot be placed chronologically in Madā'ini, through whom it has been transmitted to Abu-l-Faraj al-Iṣfahānī. It is most likely connected with Jarīr b. 'Abdallāh's mission, where it is found in Ṭabarī, as a background to the agitation in Syria.

64 cf. Wellhausen: *Prolegomena*, 135 *sqq.*

and az-Zubayr gave up the idea of seeking support in Syria. Madā'ini thus precludes any connection between the two revolutionary movements.

Similarly, al-Madā'inī follows the Kufic dating of the arbitration meeting to Ramaḍān, 39 A.H., at Dūmat al-Jandal, the time and place appointed in the *ṣulḥ* letter. In this respect his information is extraordinarily precise; it builds upon Muhammad b. as-Sā'ib al-Kalbī, according to whom Mu'āwiya arrived on time whereas 'Alī was occupied with administrative work and with the Khārijites' protest against the arbitration, for which reasons he did not send b. 'Abbās and Abū Mūsā until having received a reminder. Madā'ini supplements this account with another one from Abu-l-Faḍl at-Tanukhī, from an anonymous author, from Maymūn b. Mihrān, who had communicated it also to 'Umar b. 'Abd al-'Azīz. According to the latter, Mu'āwiya set out from Dūmat al-Jandal in Ramaḍān, 37 A.H., and dispatched a messenger to Kufa to remind the Caliph of his obligation. 'Alī replied that he could not appear in person because the Khārijites were claiming his attention, and their resistance was a more serious matter than the war against Syria; he would, however, send Abū Mūsā and, as his personal agent, b. 'Abbās. Factually, this version covers al-Kalbī completely except for the malicious remark on the gravity of the two revolutionary movements, which, though not found in any other source, fits well into Madā'inī's general chronology. His rendering of the negotiations at the arbitration meeting is—as pointed out already by Caetani—a simple and tendentious paraphrase over Abū Mikhnaf[65]. It once more distinctly motivates 'Alī's non-attendance by the grave situation in consequence of the Khārijite opposition. He does not allude to the battle at an-Nahrawān, but, on the contrary, accents the allegation that the rising had not yet taken place; according to his account of 'Amr's treachery, "a tumult broke out among those present, and the Khārijites rose in rebellion".

We have no knowledge of details concerning Madā'inī's attitude to the Khārijite revolt; moreover, his chronology as regards the last years of 'Alī's Caliphate is in general only relative. To all appearances he accepted the current dating of the battle at an-Nahrawān, i.e. Ṣafar, 38 A.H. = July, 658, and in a brief narrative—incidentally, from ash-Sha'bī—he states that "when 'Alī had killed them (the Khārijites) at an-Nahrawān, many took exception to him, and several of his adherents rebelled against him". In this connexion he mentions Banū Nājiya, the tribe of the rebel al-Khirrīt b. Rashīd; 'Abdallāh b. al-Ḥaḍramī's Syrian-inspired rising in Basra; al-Ahwāz's revolt against the imposition of *kharāj*, a revolt that spread to al-Fāris. Only b.'Abbās is explicitly

65 *'Iqd* II, 291–92 (Caetani X, 57 *sq.*). This is in keeping with the fact that the Khārijites, when despite their protests 'Alī sent b. 'Abbās and Abū Mūsā to Dūmat al-Jandal, elected their own Imām on the 10th (or 20th) Shawwāl, 37 A.H. = 11th (21st) March, 658 (Bal. 531r–32v; Tab. I. 3365; Caetani X, 102, 81).

excepted[66]. al-Madā'inī's chronological system is thus built up with strict consistency. Like the Kufic tradition of the late Umayyad era he summons the arbitration hearing for one single meeting, which in accordance with the *ṣulḥ* letter is held in Ramaḍān, 37 A.H., i.e. six months prior to the battle against the Khārijites. In al-Madā'inī these chronological shifts serve not only to clear 'Alī of accusations of violating the arbitration agreement, but also to lend causality to the course of events. 'Amr's treachery in Dūmat al-Jandal provoked something like a chain reaction: the Khārijite rebellion and the massacre at an-Nahrawān in turn cause defection of 'Alī. Hardly anywhere else were such shiftings carried through more consistently than in al-Madā'inī; in him every factual and chronological uncertainty was smoothed away; but by the same token he did also—no doubt on the strength of his authority—throw almost insuperable difficulties in the way of not only the following generations, but also of modern research[67].

This apparently logical unity in al-Madā'inī's exposition is no doubt bound up with his wish to isolate Mu'āwiya's rebellion from the Uthmanite vengeance action, and at the same time to explain the Khārijite rising in the light of the Syrian treachery. His application of elements from the early Shiite or pro-'Alī transmission obviously serves the discrimination of the Umayyads. The breach is, admittedly, dated subsequent to the battle of the Camel; but for a continuation Madā'ini chooses 'Īsā b. Yazīd's extremist Shiite account in explanation of the contract between 'Amr and Mu'āwiya, by which means the latter's personal ambitions are automatically exposed as the decisive incitement[68]. 'Amr's deception in Dūmat al-Jandal[69] is given the same background, and this line is completed so far when Mu'āwiya receives the Syrians' *bay'a* immediately after the arbitration meeting. The strongly tendentious twist in the treatment of Mu'āwiya's action—every vestige of the vengeance motive is deliberately eliminated—is entirely in consonance with all that Madā'inī has to tell about it. With Shaddād b. Aws—a Prophet Companion and a whole-hearted follower of 'Alī—as his mouthpiece, Madā'inī unconditionally prefers 'Alī to Mu'āwiya. Ali was converted, and emigrated to Mecca before Mu'āwiya; is out of a better family; is more courageous and sounder in heart—Mu'āwiya

66 Tab. I. 3440 (Caetani X, 187 *sq.*).

67 See e.g. the discussion in Yāqūt (I, 174 *sq.*; II, 628; Caetani X, 55 *sqq.*) on the placing of the arbitration.

68 Bal 498r–99 v (Caetani IX, 240 *sqq.*); cf. also Bal.: *Mu'āw.*, no.s 60,125, 256.

69 It is in keeping with this line that Madā'inī's depiction of Abū Mūsā is little flattering. When Kufa revolted against 'Uthmān, the town elected him governor (Agh. XI, 30 *sq.*; Caetani VIII, 87 *sq.*); on his arrival 'Alī immediately deposes him (Tab. I. 3139; Caetani IX, 120). His ingenuousness at the arbitration meeting is emphasized, and his collusion with Mu'āwiya is stated as a fact (*'Iqd, loc. cit.*). Later when Abū Mūsā pays homage to Mu'āwiya he explains away his earlier refusal of *bay'a* (Bal.: *Mu'āw.*, no 127).

is but a freedman in Islam and son of the leader of *al-Aḥzāb*[70]. Madā'inī thus equates the Umayyad caliphate with usurpation, and his denunciation of it surpasses by far that of the preceding generation.

Madā'inī reverts several times to the fateful consequences of 'Uthmān's murder, the inmost cause of the *fitna*[71]. Not that al-Madā'inī has any very high regard for this caliph: Abū Bakr as well as 'Umar and 'Alī are put above him, and even b. 'Abbās must yield to 'Alī: "The people has sworn allegiance to 'Alī, who is a better man than I am", he makes b. 'Abbās declare[72]. However, this is by no means to say that Madā'inī gives up his defence of b. 'Abbās or the Abbasids. On the contrary, he frequently stresses the unity of Banū Hāshim as against Banū Umayya; with 'Īsā b. Yazīd as his source he established b. 'Abbās's loyalty to the Caliph at Ṣiffīn when 'Amr tried to win him over;[73] as 'Alī's personal representative at the arbitration meeting he warns Abū Mūsā against 'Amr's cunning[74]; b. 'Abbās has no part whatever in al-Ḥasan's compromise with Mu'āwiya after 'Alī's death, and later—in 676—he refuses categorically the caliph's demand that he pay *bay'a* to Yazīd b. Mu'āwiya[75].

Consideration for b. 'Abbās has, characteristically, influenced Madā'inī's chronological system. On antedating the arbitration Madā'inī must either advance b. 'Abbās's breach with 'Alī or fill in the ensuing interval, and he naturally chooses the latter way out. He states that when Muhammad b. Abī Bakr had been killed in Egypt, b. 'Abbās made his way to 'Alī in Kufa and installed Ziyād b. Abīhi as his deputy in Basra. On the assumption of Madā'inī's accepting the prevalent dating of this murder—14th Ṣafar, 38 A.H. = 22nd July, 658—his idea must have been that b. 'Abbās had had no part in the massacre of the Khārijites at an-Nahrawān a few days earlier[76]. He further says that 'Abdallāh b. al-Ḥaḍramī's attempted rebellion in Basra took place during b. 'Abbās's absence from the town. A comparison of Madā'inī's account with Balādhurī's, which is presumably of Syrian origin[77], will show agreement that this event took place after the loss of Egypt and after the arbitration; but Madā'inī not only carries the latter more than one year back, but also moves the rebellion in Basra back to the summer of 658. And unlike Balādhurī's source, according to which b. 'Abbās had already then left Basra "annoyed with

70 Bal.: *Mu'āw.*, no.s 260, 270. *al-Aḥzāb* is the Meccan coalition in "the trench-war" against Medina in 5 A.H.

71 e.g. *ibid.* no. 303; cf. no. 52.

72 Bal.: *Mu'āw.*, no. 270; cf. no. 124.

73 Bal., 507v–08r (Caetani IX, 234).

74 *'Iqd., loc. cit.*

75 Wellhausen: *Kingdom*, 108 note 1.

76 This is the general allegation in the Arabic tradition; Vaglieri I, 76 *sqq.*

77 Bal. 558r–61r (Caetani X, 156 sqq., 159 *sqq.*); the account is anonymous, but no doubt from Wahb b. Jarīr. It is remarkable, too, that Madā'inī quite suppresses the latter's information that al-Ḥaḍramī's action was to support the 'Uthmāniyya in Basra.

'Alī" and been replaced by Ziyād b. Abīhi, Madā'inī maintains that b. 'Abbās was still standing by the side of 'Alī. Later he elaborates this point indirectly by his information that b. 'Abbās returned to Basra, from where he in 39 A.H. with 'Alī's consent dispatched Ziyād b. Abīhi to Fāris for the purpose of subduing the rebellion that had broken out after the an-Nahrawān battle[78]. Madā'inī does not deny that b. 'Abbās broke with 'Alī and left his governorship; he knows that in 39 A.H. he still stayed with al-Ḥasan, and that he was in Medina at the time of 'Alī's death[79]. By means of these ingenious constructions Madā'inī succeeds in staving off b. 'Abbās's breach with the caliph until 39 A.H. and to demonstrate that his flight from Basra had no connection whatever with the arbitration or with the battle at an-Nahrawān, when so many other men defected.

al-Madā'inī's chronological system thus reveals a twofold tendency: first, his exceptionally savage attack on Mu'āwiya and the Umayyads; secondly, his defence of b. 'Abbās and the Abbasids. He is at the same time very well disposed towards 'Alī; but the indisputably audacious constructions he has to undertake in order to save b. 'Abbās show decisively that his points of view must be akin to those of the rulers. In choosing and adapting his sources according to his requirements Madā'inī shows himself more consistent than perhaps any other author. The chief elements in his exposition suggest that he was influenced by the prevailing Mu'tazilism; nevertheless, his version of the *fitna* diverges in several respects both factually and chronologically from Wāqidī's. Madā'inī's selection of sources is far more heterogenous than his predecessor's. Wāqīdī, despite his Medinese background, was dependent on the pro-Abbasid interpretation of the Kufic transmission; Madā'inī avoids it and seeks his informants in traditions that are primarily anti-Umayyad irrespective of their observance. Madā'ini apparently makes a point of isolating Mu'āwiya's revolt; in contrast to Wāqidī, he reverts to the earliest Kufic chronology and dates the breach to a time after the battle of the Camel.

al-Madā'inī's strenuous efforts to exorcise any vestige of legality in Mu'āwiya's action and to demonstrate its absolute illegality stand out as a main feature of his historical writing. He does, admittedly, attempt to harmonize elements

78 Tab. I. 3440, partly = I. 3449 (Caetani X, 187 *sq.*, 264). Also here does Madā'inī contradict Balādhurī's source, in so far as Ziyād b. Abīhi in the latter is simply an ordinary governor in al-Fāris, which under his leadership experienced economic growth (Bal. (without *isnād*) MS Constantinop. 388r; cf. Bal. 563v–64v, Caetani X, 265 *sq.*, 165). In Abu-l-Qāsim (Tab. I. 3449; Caetani X, 264) it is 'Alī who designates Ziyād to this post after an-Nahrawān. Madā'inī is thus guilty of a double misstatement.

79 Tab. I. 3455–56; II. 11; cf. *Agh.* XI, 107 (Caetani X, 204 *sq.*; Wellhausen: *Kingdom*, 107 *sqq.*). This corresponds completely with Madā'inī's denying that b. 'Abbās headed any pilgrimage during 'Alī's caliphate (Tab. I. 3447–48; Caetani X, 296); for if this had been so, he could hardly have participated in the battle at Ṣiffīn or so loyally followed 'Alī since.

of the Kufic with the secondary Basrian transmission, but it should be borne in mind that his harmonization did not aim at any mechanical reproduction of the pro-ʿAlī feelings of certain circles. Madāʾinī's work consists largely in the study of sources, though without historical criticism, but with quite definite purposes in mind; the selection of sources is done deliberately, and the traditional elements change their hue under his pen. His personal background as well as his adaptation of the sources go to indicate that his discrimination of the Umayyads must have served a topical function in his own age, a presumption that is strengthened through other reports. As discussed below[80], towards the middle of the 9th century a rising interest in the Umayyads is observable in Iraq, which, like Ḥanbalism, should not be taken for an expression of any liking for the Syrian caliphate, but rather as an opposition to the official Muʿtazilism. Concerning Madāʾinī's position in this situation we know from al-Yāqūt that he—according to the context, *sua sponte*—warned the caliph against this movement and the way in which it manifested itself through popular veneration for Muawiya[81]. In Madāʾinī himself reflections from the opposition against the politics of the Abbasids are observable in his anti-Umayyad exposition, which revives the polemics against the Syrian-Medinese transmission[82]. His points of view reappear in a still more concrete shape in his direct refutation of the argumentation of the Muʿāwiya cult: he makes a certain Salama—a man of the Shiite Banū Kināna—challenge the justification of the good acts which the contemporaneous apocryphal tradition attributed to Muʿāwiya—a device for the sole purpose of combating the anti-Muʿtazilite opposition of his own age[83].

Both al-Wāqidī and al-Madāʾinī belong to the Muʿtazilite period of the Abbasid caliphate, and both seem to have been influenced by the official dogmatics, even though a development from the former to the latter is clearly discernible. To the Medinese al-Wāqidī the reappraisal of the *fitna* and the more conciliatory judgment of ʿAlī after the preceding generation's violent anti-Shīʿism seem to have been decisive; this line is continued in Muhammad b. Saʿd in whom side by side with the veneration for the classical Arab Empire we observe the first seeds of the shaping of a legendary ʿAlī-figure and the first germs of the merciless denunciation of the Umayyads, which are brought to full development in al-Madāʾinī. Two currents meet in these historians, one pro-ʿAlī, the other anti-Umayyad, but both with a common background in the same generation and both flexibly adapted to the requirements of the moment.

80 cf. *infra* pp. 123 *sqq*.

81 Margoliouth: *Lectures*, 86; Pellat: *Muʿāwiya*, 54.

82 cf. also *AO* XXVI, 117 *sq*.

83 Bal.: *Muʿāw*., no. 239 cum note and 240; the same tradition, which seems to have been rather widely spread, is found in the Khārijite al-Haytham b. ʿAdī. On the apocryphal Muʿāwiya-tradition, see *infra* pp. 128 *sq*.

4. Shiite Tradition 750–850

The Iraqian tradition in the first half of the 8th century had been framed as a manifestation of opposition against the Umayyad Caliphate. Within this framework we observe several nuances that in one way or another reflect special views of Shiite or shiitizing observance. In Abū Mikhnaf we meet to all appearances the standpoint of al-Hāshimiyya in whose version—as referred to above—the pro-Abbasid tradition took root in the second half of the 8th century. Shiite points of view in their purest form—i.e. historiographical propaganda in behalf of ʿAlī's successors and their title to the caliphate without regard to the interests of other parties—are, however, in evidence in the Umayyad era, too, although we may also there find reflections of Hāshimite ideas. Shiite points of view are observable in traditionists who by special preference amplified the religious wrong done to ʿAlī; the Shiite persuasion is distinguished for the first attempted description of ʿAlī's martyrdom, but beyond an intimation here and there we do not yet within the available material find such hagiographical elements as were later attached to his figure. This Shiite transmission is seen in characteristic form in ʿĪsā b. Yazīd and Jābir b. Yazīd al-Juʿfī who operate primarily with the contrasts between the worldly ambitions of the Syrians and the obviously religious merits of ʿAlī. Both authors represent an attitude to the problems that still belong in the conflicts of the Umayyad era. The change of dynasty notwithstanding, Shīʿism remained in opposition, though its opposition assumed a different direction. The question, then, is whether the Shiite tradition could be adapted to the new conditions.

A comprehensive study of the Shiite version of the *fitna* during this period will encounter several obstacles. For one thing, as an oppositional movement Shīʿism changed its character, and in the course of the 9th century became rather the focus of social discontent in all its aspects; and, for another, it very soon split up into a great many sects, each with its own separate standpoint; finally, and this applies especially to the extremist Shiite sects: the esoteric mysteriousness surrounding their doings may have required a dogmatic and exegetic literature, but cannot have promoted historical writing in the proper sense of the term. An intimation hereof is seen from the fact that although we observe attempts to forge legendary traits around the ʿAlī-figure in the 8th century, we find but few reflections of the extremist Shi'ism's eschatological concepts—the same ideas that we meet in a caricatured form in Sayf b. 'Umar. We are in this respect more or less dependent on the more moderate historians' selections from the Shiite transmission, and even though pro-'Alī narratives or anecdotes are available in a great number and with much varying cogency, we cannot expect to find expressions of radical Shiite views to any great extent—and even the moderate tradition can hardly be followed in more than a rough outline.

On turning to a traditionist like Naṣr b. Muzāḥim al-Minqarī (d. 212/827-28)[1], whom Brockelmann characterized as Shī'ism's earliest historian, we shall find both unmistakable Shiite views and an approach to the problems rather different from those with which Abū Mikhnaf operated. In his discussion of al-Minqarī Brockelmann emphasized that, as compared with him, Abū Mikhnaf went much farther in his harmonization of the individual renderings; that as a rule his exposition appears in a more concise and rational form than Naṣr b. Muzāḥim's. Brockelmann, however, takes it for granted that Naṣr's more sweeping exposition could not be due to his own supplementing the sources, which in principle cannot be rule out[2]. A study of his *Waq'at Ṣiffīn* will—as we shall revert to below—in many cases establish that he must have known Abū Mikhnaf or his informants; but in addition he brings a great many traditions unknown to Abū Mikhnaf, and which indeed gives his physiognomy its distinctive character. Naṣr b. Muzāḥim's material seems on the whole to have been borrowed from three main sources in the generation preceding his own, and through which the earlier transmission is quoted[3]: 'Umar b. Sa'īd b. Abī ṣ-Ṣa'īd al-Asadī, Muhammad b. 'Ubaydallāh al-Qurashī, and 'Amr b. Shamir. In consequence hereof his work falls into three main parts, which it will be expedient to treat separately.

'Umar b. Sa'īd appears to have obtained the principal part of his rendering from ash-Sha'bī through Numayr b. Wā'ila. This applies to the account of Jarīr b. 'Abdallāh al-Bajalī's mission and al-Ashtar's clash with him after his return, traditions that Abū Mikhnaf had suppressed[4]. This representation,

1 Brockelmann, 8 sq.; *GAL (S)* I, 214.—He, is despite Wüstenfeld's (*Geschichtsschreiber*, no. 37) and Brockelmann's assumption, thus a generation younger than Abū Mikhnaf.

2 Brockelmann, 19 *sqq.*—His reasoning is *inter alia* due to the fact that he has had access to only the earlier and inferior Beirut edition, which leaves out the *isnāds* of the individual renderings.

3 cf. *Waq. Siff.*, 3–5, where his main *isnād* is set down thus: Naṣr b. Muzāḥim, from 'Umar b. Sa'īd, from al-Ḥārith b. Hasira, from 'Abd ar-Raḥmān b. 'Ubayd b. Abi-l-Kunūd, and others, a series also frequently quoted by Abū Mikhnaf. There are no data concerning Naṣr's three chief informants.

4 *Waq. Siff.*, 32 *sqq.*, 67 *sq.* From ash-Sha'bī he likewise quotes (*ibid.*, 584–86) the *ṣulḥ*-letter in a form practically identical with Abū Mikhnaf's (Tab. I. 3336–38; Caetani IX, 478 sq.). He declares *per fas et nefas* to have it in a specially Kufic form from Sa'īd b. Abī Burda b. Abī Mūsā al-Ash'arī.

however, carries an additional tradition from "'Umar b. Sa'īd with his *isnād*", (presumably the general *isnād* in Naṣr's introduction), concerning Mu'āwiya's negotiations with 'Amr al-'Āṣ in a form akin to, even if hardly identical with, the one found in 'Īsā b. Yazīd[5]. In both cases the beginning consists in 'Amr's warning the Syrian governor because he is not 'Alī's equal; not in possession of his *hijra* and his pioneer status; is not, as 'Alī is, a Prophet Companion; not in possession of his *jihād* or jurisprudence; nor, as 'Ālī, favoured by luck and by God. Even though we here receive all the attributes ascribed by Shiite transmission to 'Alī, the resemblances are so weighty that there must exist some kind of relationship which proves b. Sa'īd's indebtedness to the Umayyad era's Shiite tradition; in him it is used as an annotating supplement to the old Kufic tradition[6].

The source material with which 'Umar b. Sa'īd operates is thus of a pronounced and one-sided Iraqian provenance. Unlike Abū Mikhnaf—and the pro-Abbasid version in b. al-Kalbī—but like ash-Sha'bī, he follows the earliest Kufic chronology: Mu'āwiya's breach with the Caliph is again dated to a time after the battle of the Camel. We do not know his view of the revolution against 'Uthmān, but it appears from his quotations that he stresses the conflict as concerning the justification of the caliph murder, whereby he again differs from the pro-Abbasid tradition. On the other hand, he also stresses that all except the Syrians had sworn allegiance to 'Alī before the battle of the Camel and thereby recognized his innocence of the caliph murder[7]. 'Alī and the Iraqians are therefore fully entitled to take up arms. God has allowed dissociation *(al-barā'a)* from separatists, who do not observe the divine revelation, and it is entirely lawful to combat a *fitna* of this description until those members *(khulaṭā')* that have violated the covenant submit and repent[8]. According to this version Mu'āwiya can hardly have any share in the Uthmanite revolt[9], but the election of *Muhājirūn* and *Anṣār*—which thus sanctions 'Alī's

5 *Waq. Siff.*, 42 *sq.*, 44 *sqq.*

6 To the same circle of sources belongs the historically very important account of an argument between the two parties after the arbitration agreement (*Ibid.*, 590–93; Vaglieri II, 88 *sqq.*).

7 *Waq. Siff.*, 32 *sqq.*, from ash-Sha'bī.

8 *Ibid.*, 590 *sqq.*—b. Sa'īd divides the contending parties into four separate groups: (1) 'Alī and the Kufians, (2) Ṭalḥa, az-Zubayr, and the Basrians, (3) Mu'āwiya and the Syrians, (4) and the neutrals in the Ḥijāz, to which group Abū Mūsā belongs and against whose equivocation he warns. (Tab. I. 3152; Caetani IX, 121 sq.). That Mu'āwiya's breach with 'Alī is dated to after the battle of the Camel is borne out by b. Sa'īd's mentioning that Qays b. Sa'īd is sent as *'amīl* to Egypt to replace Mu'āwiya's kinsman Muhammad b. Ḥudhayfa in connection with Jarīr's mission (*Waq. Siff.*, 143).

9 He indirectly dissociates himself also from the Basrians and the 'Uthmāniyya among them. The few Basrians who joined 'Alī are expressly listed by name; Waq. Siff., 130; cf. also the preceding note.

conduct and which, incidentally, is likened to a *shūrā*—is binding on him, too; "their choice is acceptable to God; the apostates shall be brought back to the fold and be punished by God".

A preliminary recapitulation of b. Saʿīd's points of view shows clearly that his horizon is narrowly Kufic. Contrary to the former pro-Abbasid tradition, he entirely passes over b. ʿAbbās's activities, and reverts to the earliest Kufic veneration for al-Ashtar, who occupies a very prominent position by the side of ʿAlī[10]. At the same time b. Saʿīd emphasizes Kufa's loyal collaboration with the Caliph. Seen in the light of the tendentious transformation in the late Umayyad era both of the conflict's chronology and of Muʿāwiya's motives, it is indeed remarkable that b. Saʿīd goes back to the primary Kufic version. The absurdity of the Syrian governor's vengeance action does admittedly stand out clearly against ʿAlī's innocence, but his motives do not disappear in any human lust for power inasmuch as b. Saʿīd continually reverts to the demand for blood vengeance in Muʿāwiya's argumentation, on the latest occasion in the circumstantial discussion between the two parties after the arbitration agreement at Ṣiffīn, though Muʿāwiya's behaviour as ʿUthmān's *walī* against ʿAlī is presented as illegal in the light of the latter's obvious right. ʿUmar b. Saʿīd thus makes a clear distinction as regards the elements in the resistance against the Caliph, but maintains the unity in his and Islam's front against the rebels. His rendering preserves its Shiite stamp by brushing aside all other considerations concerning ʿAlī's showdown with the unlawful opposition to his caliphate.

On one point, however, ʿUmar b. Saʿīd's version looks ahead inasmuch as he inserts a number of legendary features. His rendering is occasionally interrupted by religious or edifying anecdotes which undoubtedly serve a function in the whole as foretokens of coming combats or in elucidation of ʿAlī's religious prestige. He mentions, incidentally, that a funeral procession passed an-Nukhayla near Kufa while ʿAlī was camping there on his way to Ṣiffīn, and in the same breath he states on ʿAlī's authority that at an-Nukhayla was a burial place around which the Jews buried their dead. al-Ḥasan b. ʿAlī adds that it is supposed to be the prophet Hūd's grave: "when his people was disobedient to him, he came and died here". ʿAlī, however, knows better, corrects this statement and defines the tomb as being that of Yahūdā b. Isḥāq b. Ibrāhīm, the first-born of Jacob[11]. Yahūdā is here no doubt a generic term for the

10 He is the one who during the ʿUthmāniyya's revolt persuades ʿAlī to resort to Kufa, whose support he obtains for the Caliph in spite of Abū Mūsā's objections (Tab. I. 3152–54; Caetani IX, 122 *sq.*). Again, it is al-Ashtar who advises ʿAlī against sending Jarīr b. ʿAbdallāh as envoy because he considers him Muʿāwiya's henchman (*Waq. Siff.*, 32, 67 *sq.*; cf. also Naṣr in al-Kindī, 24; Caetani IX, 561 *sq.*), and he who most loyally supports ʿAlī at Ṣiffīn.

11 *Waq. Siff.*, 142.

Jews, or for one of the twelve tribes of Israel, who segregated themselves from Allah's original revelation to which Ibrāhīm, Isḥāq and Ya'qūb had submitted[12]. In other words, it is a re-emergence of the apostasy theme. At a later stage a Christian monk in Balīkh presents the Caliph with a book from 'Īsā (Jesus), in which are found prophecies on Muhammad's mission and the quarrel that was to arise after his death; a man—implying 'Alī—will pass at the Euphrates; he will represent the true cause and is assured of Paradise as well as all those who follow him[13]. Prior to this 'Umar b. Sa'īd has told us that at sunrise 70,000 men from Ẓahr al-Kūfa gathered in the camp at an-Nukhayla, so that the march thence to Ṣiffīn is paralleled with the Resurrection; "they enter Paradise without being called to account". Immediately below it says that 70,000 *sayyids* wept at the sight of 'Uthmān's *qamīṣ* in Damascus[14], whereby the contrast between the parties is completed.

This semi-hagiographic symbolism so ingeniously concatenated in the element of genuine Kufic tradition rounds off the impression of 'Umar b. Sa'īd's Shiite views. His version can hardly be characterized as radically Shiite, though it is no doubt typical of the Arabic historical writing of his time. We do not know his personal data, and the tradition carries practically no quotations from him apart from Naṣr b. Muzāḥim's work; according to the context his activities must belong in the decades around the year 800, the period that saw also Hishām b. Muhammad and Sayf b. 'Umar at work. A comparison of these versions will reveal how they contradict one another point by point, a matter to which we shall revert below[15]. For the present we shall merely note that the Shiite exposition—in contradistinction to the pro-Abbasid one—gives prominence not only to the religious aspects of 'Alī's line of action but also quite consistently justifies his conduct in a way that accentuates the unity in Islam's showdown with the unlawful forces. In 'Umar b. Sa'īd the apostates are identified with the 'Uthmāniyya and the Syrians, not with 'Alī's adherents. So, the Shiite tradition, too, knew how to adopt itself to the changed conditions.

Among Naṣr b. Muzāḥim's other informants Muhammad b. 'Ubaydallāh al-Qurashī's transmission does not seem to raise any special problems in this connexion inasmuch as he only appears in the capacity of transmitter of al-Jurjānī's material. The essential point is no doubt that we again meet with evidence of how the Shiite historians in the earliest Abbasid era resort to the traditional stages prior to Abū Mikhnaf. They look behind the Hāshimite historical writing, not in order to reach back to the true or only slightly re-

12 cf. the Quran, *sure* 2:133 *sqq.*

13 *Waq. Siff.*, 164 = b. al-Kathīr, 139v (Caetani IX, 292, from al-'Uranī (d. 695/96) a traditionist of doubtful reputation).

14 *Waq. Siff.*, 143.

15 See *infra* pp. 118 *sqq.*

touched sources, but in order to disengage themselves from any connexion with the new rulers. In al-Jurjānī the initiative to the revolt has, admittedly, passed from Mu'āwiya into the hands of 'Amr b. al-'Āṣ, but the decisive points are these: like ash-Sha'bī, he maintains that the outbreak of the conflict occurred after the battle of the Camel and describes it as an evident violation of the Caliph's lawful power[16]. The citing of this tradition, like 'Umar b. Sa'īd's writings, attests to a reaction in Shiite circles provoked by the pro-Abbasid tradition's blatant interpretation of the *fitna* and by the allegation that 'Alī's adherents by failing him were indirectly responsible for the Syrian Caliphate. The anti-Shiite historical writing compels the Shiite writers to insist on the conflict's religious character as the basis for their accentuation of Islam's unity against the renegates.

Any such line cannot be established with certainty in the case of Naṣr b. Muzāḥim's third informant, 'Amr b. Shamir, who also belongs in the second half of the 8th century. His principal source, the clumsily tendentious Jābir b. Yazīd al-Ju'fī, does to be sure call special attention to the solidarity of Banū 'Abd al-Muṭṭalib; but b. 'Abbās is entirely subordinated to 'Alī whose infallibility *('iṣma)* does not allow of any disintegration of his absolute authority. These elements have presumably still served a function in the Abbasid era, though they represent at the same time a far more vulgar-Shiite interpretation than the one found in the two other Shiite historians.

With this tendentious and unreliable version 'Amr b. Shamir combines a detailed description of the battle at Ṣiffīn, for which he chooses his starting point in the same sources as Abū Mikhnaf drew on. In so far as we may believe in Naṣr b. Muzāḥim's *isnāds*, they both build upon the old Iraqian *ruwāt*'s *ayyām* material with al-Qāsim b. Muhammad, Yazīd b. Mu'āwiya's *mawlā*, and others as joint transmitters[17]. These traditions lead us immediately to the question of how Naṣr b. Muzāḥim employs his material. The fact that his exposition is less concise than Abū Mikhnaf's does not, as mentioned above, preclude his having drawn on the latter, or that he added to the material on his own. In one passage only does he quote Abū Mikhnaf, namely concerning a detail in the narrative of the march to Ṣiffīn[18], but the dependence undoubtedly goes farther than that. A comparison of the two historians' fairly parallel descriptions of the preparations for the military showdown and certain details relating to the battles at Ṣiffīn will show that Naṣr b. Muzāḥim utilizes not only 'Amr b. Shamir, but additional particulars from other sources that were known also to Abū Mikhnaf, even though sometimes in a modified form.

Naṣr b. Muzāḥim's account of the Iraqian troops' formation, which he places

---

16 cf. *supra* pp. 31 *sqq.*
17 cf. *supra* pp. 26 *sq.*
18 *Waq. Siff.*, 165; cf. Abū Mikhnaf in Bal. 502v–04v (Caetani IX, 286).

at Kufa, whereas Abū Mikhnaf places it in the camp at an-Nukhayla, some distance from the town, is in almost verbatim correspondence with Abū Mikhnaf's version, merely with an addition to the effect that b. ʿAbbās and a number of Kufians mentioned by name: al-Aḥnaf b. Qays, Khālid b. al-Muʿammar, and ʿAmr b. Marjūm al-ʿAbdī immediately responded when they were summoned by the Caliph[19]. This list of names is no doubt culled from the immediately following schedule in Abū Mikhnaf on the allocation of commands, and the same applies to the replies attributed to the Kufians mentioned above; they are simply paraphrases over the Caliph's letter. All these particulars are presumably additions intended to prove the Kufians' high moral standard and their loyalty to ʿAlī. Something similar applies to a tradition according to which the inhabitants of al-Raqqa refuse ʿAlī's order to build a bridge across the Euphrates to enable him to cross the river.

The same tradition is found in al-Balādhurī in an apparently complete form, from which we learn that the opposition is due to the ʿUthmāniyya of the town, and that by the use of threats al-Ashtar forces the inhabitants to build the bridge. As both features are missing in Naṣr b. Muzāḥim, his account leaves the impression that ʿAlī had to cross the river at al-Manbij[20]. In this case he quotes the same source as Ṭabarī, namely al-Ḥajjāj b. Arṭā (or b. ʿAlī) from ʿAbdallāh b. ʿAmmār b. ʿAbd Yāghūth al-Bāriqī with ʿUmar b. Saʿīd as the intermediary where Abū Mikhnaf appears in Ṭabarī and Balāhdurī. Naṣr likewise follows Abū Mikhnaf's source, Khālid b. Qaṭān al-Ḥārithī[21], in his account of ʿAlī's activities after his having crossed the Euphrates. On the whole, then, there is a very close factual and chronological agreement with Abū Mikhnaf, whom he must therefore be supposed to have known, even though he quotes him in only one single passage.

The parallels in the two versions of Muʿāwiya's breach with ʿAlī are of fundamental interest. Although al-Minqarī, like ʿUmar b. Saʿīd and Muhammad b. ʿUbaydallāh, dates it after the battle of the Camel, he combines the account of Jarīr b. ʿAbdallāh's mission to Damascus with the circumstantial exchange of notes already known from Abū Mikhnaf, who substituted it for Jarīr's mission[22]. Even though Nasr cites two scholars, Ṣāliḥ b. Ṣadaqa and Muhammad b. ʿUbaydallāh, as immediate informants, we must nevertheless presume that on this point he gained his knowledge, directly or indirectly, from Abū Mikhnaf. This presumption is borne out by the fact that despite

19 *Waq. Siff.*, 130 *sqq.*; cf. Abū Mikhnaf's account in Bal., *loc. cit.* and Tab. I. 3259–60 (Caetani IX, 267).

20 *Waq. Siff.*, 169; cf. Abū Mikhnaf in Bal. *loc. cit.* and Tab. I. 3259–60 (Caetani IX, 267).

21 *Waq. Siff.*, 170 *sqq.*; cf. Tab. I. 3060–62 (Caetani IX, 267 *sqq.*).

22 *Waq. Siff.*, 61 *sqq.*; cf. Abū Mikhnaf in Bal. 494v–97r (Caetani IX, 253 *sq.*). Also his circumstantial *isnād* in which even a Persian name is found throws suspicion on the authenticity of the *isnād*.

his combination of primary and secondary elements from the Kufic transmission he also carries a reference to al-Mughīra b. Shu'ba's warning to 'Alī not to remove Mu'āwiya from his governorship in Syria and makes the Caliph reluctant to follow this advice because he could not be answerable to God for being supported by an erring man[23]. This information is likewise met with for the first time in Iraq historical writing in Abū Mikhnaf, here merely immediately after the caliph election; in Naṣr, however, it is inserted in connexion with Jarīr b. 'Abdallāh's sojourn in Syria, when Mu'āwiya by letter requests 'Alī to grant him Syria and Egypt as *jibāya* (sources of income from taxation). It is especially this parallel that decisively strengthens the probability of Naṣr's knowing and drawing on Abū Mikhnaf, even if he did not quote him, and it further shows how he combines and harmonizes elements from the Kufic tradition in order to serve his own purposes.

Naṣr b. Muzāḥim thus constitutes a focal point of the early Shiite historical writing and seems at the same time to have tried to obtain a comprehensive picture by including elements from Abū Mikhnaf. His working method, no less than that of the contemporaneous pro-Abbasid historical writers, is characterized by harmonization or—where his material does not cover his own views—by construction of details. Like that of his predecessors, his tendency is Shiite, though hardly of any extremist mould[24]. He, too, maintains definitely the earlier Kufic chronology, and especially his knowledge of Abū Mikhnaf's version of the Iraqian transmission goes to show that the discountenance of his views that had been taken over by the pro-Abbasid tradition must have been intentional. Paradoxically, he avails himself of Sayf b, 'Umar's authority in stating that immediately on having received information of the caliph murder 'Ā'isha asserts its unlawfulness[25]. The 'Uthmāniyya rising is naturally considered a violation of the lawful order and will draw down God's punishment; but it appears at the same time as an intermezzo that was passé with the battle of the Camel[26]. Naṣr also isolates Mu'āwiya in relation to the neutrals: Sa'd b. Abī Waqqāṣ, who turns down his proposal that a *shūrā* undertake a legal caliph election[27], as well as the Medinese and 'Abdallāh b. 'Umar, who distinctly dissociate themselves from the Syrians[28], whereas 'Alī on his part takes note of their standpoint[29]. Generally speaking, Naṣr b. Muzā-

23 *Waq. Siff.*, 58.—In the same connection Naṣr also places the anecdote that Mu'āwiya had clothed the *minbar* at Damascus with 'Uthmān's *qamīṣ* (cf. Abū Mikhnaf in *Agh.* XV, 71 *sq.*; Caetani VIII, 305 *sqq.*).

24 cf. Brockelmann, 9–14.

25 Tab. I. 3111–12 (Caetani IX, 33 *sq.*, 40 *sq.*).

26 *Waq. Siff.*, 18.

27 *Ibid.*, 79 *sqq.*; cf. Ya'q. II, 217 (Caetani IX, 263).

28 *Waq. Siff.*, 80 *sqq.*

29 *Ibid.*, 129.

ḥim's historical writing represents a more explicit formulation of Shī'ism's standpoint at the transition to the 9th century: 'Alī's religiously accentuated merit and his absolute independence of his surroundings are firmly maintained, no doubt in opposition to the pro-Abbasid tradition. In his capacity of independent traditionist he is of particular interest as a focus of Shiite historical writing of earlier generations; his own historical work was not confined to *Waq'at Ṣiffīn*, but comprised also a series of other works, all of them books of special interest to Shī'ism[30], and, finally, he seems to have held a central position as a ninth-century intermediate link of the Shiite transmission.

This circumspect reaction against the orthodox tradition in the decades around 800 are traceable in several variations, but always with the searchlight playing on the 'Alī-figure or on the wrong done to him. A reflection of this polemic—presumably turned against b. al-Kalbī—can be observed, for instance, in an isolated narrative by the otherwise quite unknown Abu-l-Qāsim b. Muhammad[31], according to which the Caliph informs b. 'Abbās of the vengeance action initiated by Ṭalḥa and az-Zubayr, "although, by God, we know that they themselves are the murderers". At the same time, 'Alī tells b. 'Abbās of al-Mughīra's advice, which he had turned down because he dared not "use hypocrisy in .... (his) religion", and al-Mughīra had realized that it would be better avoiding any stain on his government. b. 'Abbās's reference to a prophet tradition that admitted of deceit in war, is likewise rejected by the Caliph, and his cuosin bowed to his religious demand for propriety: "I find nothing easier than to obey you". This account follows Wāqidī's fairly closely, but its point is entirely reversed by slight retouchings. Once more, the Caliph's independence and b. 'Abbās's natural obedience to him are stressed, and, again, a sharp distinction is drawn between the 'Uthmāniyya and Mu'āwiya. Where 'Alī's strictly religous conduct had acquired a tinge of unwordly ingenuousness, Abu-l-Qāsim defends its justification.

So, despite its isolated transmission this account touches once more the crucial point in the Shiite argumentation. However, apart from the vulgar-Shiite fragments in al-Ju'fī's version, none of the historians here discussed can with any show of reason be regarded as extremist. It is characteristic of them that they separate Mu'āwiya's action from that of the 'Uthmāniyya, but, on the other hand, with the earliest Kufic tradition as their source insist that the illegality of his resistance to 'Alī does not lie in the demand for blood vengeance but in the fact that it is directed towards the blameless Caliph and the unanimous front surrounding him.

30 cf. *GAL (S)* I, 214.

31 Tab. I. 3085–86 (Caetani VIII, 339 *sq.*) = Mas. IV, 300–03; cf. Wāqidī in Tab. I. 3083–85 (Caetani IX, 338 *sq.*).

5. Survival of the Pro-Umayyad Tradition 750–850

It is, as frequently adduced, true that the Syrian tradition as found in Ṣāliḥ b. Kaysān's and az-Zuhrī's versions of the first civil war showed but very little viability and was suppressed very early by the Abbasid and Shiite tradition. Keeping for the present to the nucleus of the Syrian transmission we find it clearly established that the historians of the Abbasid era were not only aware of its existence, but must in some degree have known and utilized its points of view. This is apparent both because occasional traces of a progressive polemic are observable, and because it is quoted in other connexions by several outstanding historians of that period. On the whole it is solely to al-Balādhurī we owe our knowledge of the Syrian-Medinese tradition of the civil war in a fairly coherent form, whereas Ṭabarī confined himself to isolated fragments from az-Zuhrī.

az-Zuhrī is quoted more frequently than any other pro-Umayyad traditionist, possibly because his connection with the caliphal court could not compromise his position as Medinese legist and Prophet biographer. In any case the Medinese school of traditionists, al-Wāqidī and b. Sa'd, quoted him continuously—admittedly most frequently as a source of Prophet traditions of purely Medinese interest[1], but also occasionally as an authority for historical traditions—and normally, according to an exclusively Medinese *isnād*[2]. The Iraqian school of traditions, too, carries frequent quotations from az-Zuhrī, but then generally as a "profane historical" source; the Iraqians must likewise quite obviously have known Ṣāliḥ b. Kaysān and his opinions[3]. Both these tradition-

---

1 e.g. b. Sa'd III.1. 38, 44, 72, 118, 154 (Caetani VIII, 308, 310 (=VII, 420); IX, 408, 625 382).

2 b. Sa'd III.1. 52 (Caetani VIII, 188 *sq.*, cf. VII, 420). Most often Muhammad b. 'Abdallāh is the intermediate link between az-Zuhrī and Wāqidī. An exception from the local tradition is, however, b. Sa'd IV.2. 3–4 (Caetani IX, 531).

3 Ṭabarī e.g. cites him unrestrainedly on other and more neutral subjects from Islam's earliest history but in a strangely haphazard and not particularly convincing way; e.g. Tab. I. 2139–41, 2144–45 (with 'Īsā b. Yazīd as the connecting link!), 2214–15 (Caetani III, 87, 132, 280).—Once or twice genuine details from the Syrian-Medinese school are found in the pro-Umayyad 'Abdallāh b. al-Mubārak, who acts as transmitter of az-Zuhrī's version of Qays b. Sa'īd's governorship in Egypt; Tab. I. 3241–42, 3245–46, 3391–92 (Caetani IX, 316, 325 *sqq.*).

ists are peculiar in that their transmission seems to have been confined to a very narrow, but unusually homogeneous circle of scholars. Ṭabarī's and Balādhurī's *isnāds* enable us to list their authorities for the quotations from az-Zuhrī and, in the case of Balādhurī, from Ṣāliḥ b. Kaysān, and thereby obtain the following table:

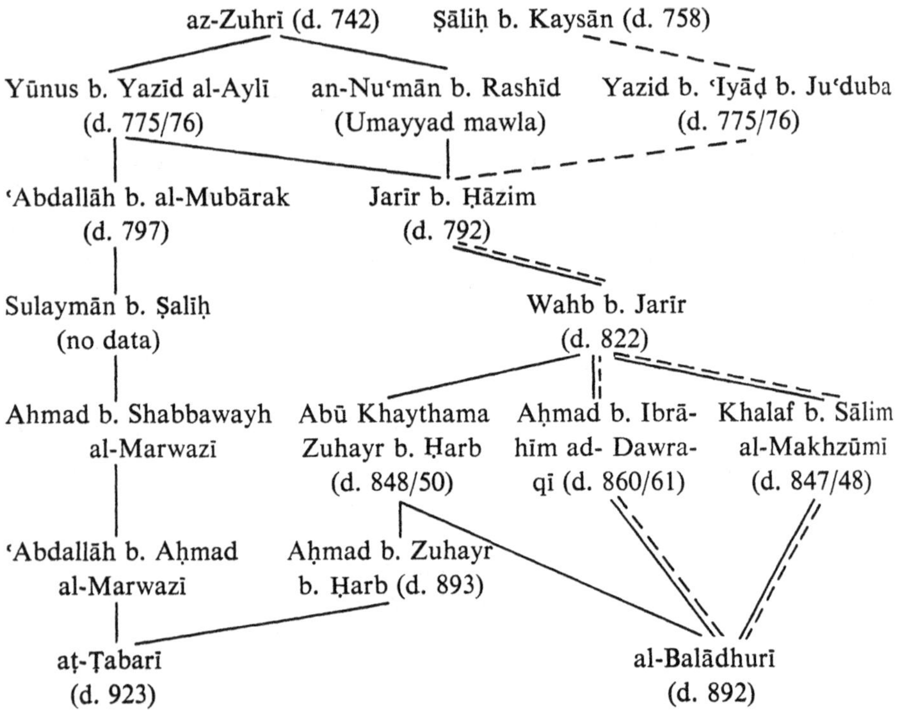

This table is really very firmly fixed. The main stem in the narratives generally follows these courses throughout, whereas the variant material falls entirely outside the system[4]. Except for the line from 'Abdallāh b. al-Mubārak (al-Marwazī) to Ṭabarī, which may have been specially attached to Merw in Persia, the continued existence of the Syrian-Medinese tradition must have been confined to this particular circle of scholars, who otherwise are but rarely quoted in the historical transmission, and the majority of whom belong in Basra. Yazīd b. 'Iyāḍ b. Ju'duba, who resided in the town and to whom we

4 b. 'Asākir likewise has often used az-Zuhrī via the usual channel, e.g. Caetani VIII, 231; of other historians only 'Umar b. Shabba (d. 875) seems to have known az-Zuhrī through other channels, e.g. *Agh.* IV, 185 *sq.*; XI, 30 *sq.* (Caetani VII, 349; VIII, 87), but so sporadically that no clear conclusion can be drawn.—On the variant material, see *AO* XXVII, 99 *sqq.*

are wholly indebted for our acquaintance with Ṣāliḥ b. Kaysān, Jarīr b. Ḥāzim and his son Wahb b. Jarīr were, like Yūnus b. Yazīd al-Aylī, held in high esteem as trustworthy traditionists. It is of considerable interest that the members of this circle—at any rate Jarīr b. Ḥāzim and Yūnus b. Yazīd—also seem to have occupied themselves with the Prophet tradition and the *maghāzī* tradition[5], which, as in the matters of Quranic exegesis and philology, set them at variance with Kufa, a variance that was very likely deliberate. The passing on to Basra of the Syrian-Medinese tradition must have taken place very early, presumably before the overthrow of the Umayyad Caliphate[6].

These considerations might lead to the inference that the scholars at Basra who handled the pro-Umayyad transmission were themselves sympathetic to the Syrian Caliphate, and it might be tempting to find support for any such idea primarily in the circumstance that b. Ju'duba and Jarīr b. Ḥāzim unreservedly adopted both az-Zuhrī's and Ṣāliḥ b. Kaysān's version fairly consecutively, as far as can be judged from Balādhurī's recension. The fact that one of the transmitters of this version was an Umayyad *mawlā*, an-Nu'mān b. Rashīd, might likewise seem to bear out any such assumption. It is, on the other hand, peculiar that such part of the tradition as we rediscover in Basra deals solely with the immediate consequences of 'Uthmān's murder; outside this period it contains hardly any reference to events on the authority of the Syrian-Medinese school, whereas both az-Zuhrī and Ṣāliḥ b. Kaysān, except for the civil war, are invariably quoted through local Medinese authorities in b. Sa'd, Balādhurī[7], and not particularly convincingly and very unsystematically in Ṭabarī[8]. Moreover, so far as can be judged from the works of Balādhurī, the Basra school does not seem to have dealt with Mu'āwiya's governorship or caliphate, and the few traditions on this subject known from b. Ju'duba do not indicate any liking for him. On the contrary, b. Ju'duba censures him

5 Rosenthal: *Historiography*, 323 *sq.*

6 In support hereof may be mentioned that az-Zuhrī had died in 742, but also that Yūnus b. Yazīd as well as b. Ju'duba and presumably Jarīr b. Ḥāzim have themselves witnessed the unsettled period, the fall of the Syrian Caliphate and the Abbasids' earliest conflict with Shī'ism at the beginning of the 760s, events in which Basra was involved. The same dating is also corroborated by one of the Umayyads' *mawālī* appearing among the transmitters of az-Zuhrī's account. On the later Basrian traditionists at the middle of the 9th century, see *infra* pp. 103 *sqq.*

7 e.g. b. Sa'd III.1.193, 249 *sqq.*, 258 *sq.*; III.2.31; Bal., 104, 266 (Caetani V, 110, 65, 57, 213, 69 *sq.*; IV, 138; III, 87; V, 365). Ṣāliḥ b. Kaysān appears in b. Sa'd as az-Zuhrī's pupil; on this cf. Sprenger: *Notes*, 208, 211.

8 See *supra* p. 109 note 3. Likewise in b. 'Asākir (341; Caetani III, 238 *sq.*), who gives an account of 'Alī's relations with Abū Bakr with the *isnād*: Yūnus b. Bukayr—Muhammad b. Isḥāq—Ṣāliḥ b. Kaysān—'Urwa—'Ā'isha, in which the two earliest links are no doubt false.

for his worldliness and for his unwarranted ambition to set up as God's representative[9].

It would be more correct, we think, to say that the Basra school was not pro-Umayyad, but Uthmanite in the sense that it joined in the accusations against 'Alī for complicity in the murder of 'Uthmān and was opposed to Shī'ism, in particular the Kufic branch. This assumption is in accordance with what we learn from other quarters concerning the town's political standpoint and its political, religious and cultural opposition to Shiite Kufa[10]. The tender beginnings of an Uthmanite party at Basra are already found shortly after the caliph murder; the town appears to have supported Ṭalḥa's and az-Zubayr's action and on later occasions to have objected to 'Alī; the sources indicate clearly that the 'Uthmāniyya's attitude was based on kinship or client relations with 'Uthmān[11]. The 'Uthmāniyya, however, proved to be extremely tenacious, most likely because of their disapproval of Shī'ism, though, again, disinclined to recognize the Umayyads to whom they showed no sympathy. The Basrian tradition often extols 'Āisha, Ṭalḥa, and, especially, az-Zubayr as exponents of the genuine resistance to 'Alī, and by the very citation of the Syrian-Medinese tradition the Basrians avoided the Kufic tradition's inclination to identify Mu'āwiya's revolt with that of the 'Uthmāniyya as we see it done particularly in the pro-Abbasid historical writing. However, during the life of the Syrian Caliphate Basra leaned on it because it was the only force able to restrain Shī'ism. After the overthrow of the Umayyads al-'Uthmāniyya gradually assumed other shapes, but still maintained 'Alī's complicity in the caliph murder and disallowance of the Prophet family's special title to the caliphat[12] as the dominant themes in the opposition against the pro-Alid tendencies.

Apart from the historians here discussed the Basrian tradition appears to have been passed on very fragmentarily[13]. As late as in works by the traditionist Maslama b. Muḥārib (ca. 765–85) who, it seems, belonged to the Basrian branch of the Umayyad family, we observe occasional reflections from a defence of Mu'āwiya and rancorous attacks on 'Alī, though he appears, paradoxically, to have reached his points of view primarily through tendentious adaptations of the Kufic transmission. In contrast hereto other Basrian his-

9 Bal.: *Mu'āw.*, no.s 20, 124, cf. 2, 148 and 340.—Similar expressions of dislike of Mu'āwiya are found in ad-Dawraqī; Bal. 429r–v (Caetani X, 404 *sq.*).

10 Basra's supporting a Shiite rising in 815 is presumably due to antagonism to the pro-Persian policy of al-Ma'mūn and Faḍl b. Sahl; cf. Pellat: *Jāḥiẓ*, 194 *sqq.*

11 az-Zuhrī in Tab. I. 3126–28; Abū Mikhnaf in Bal. 502v–04v and Wahb b. Jarīr (?) *ibid.* 558r–61r (Caetani IX, 56 *sqq.*, 287; X, 156 *sqq.*).

12 Goldziher: *M. St.* II, 119 *sqq.*; Lammens: *Mo'āwia*, 109 *sqq.*; Pellat: *Jāḥiẓ*, 188 *sqq.*

13 On the following, see *AO* XXVI, 98 *sqq.*

torians of the same period reveal a reaction to the pro-Umayyad transmission or attempts to harmonize it with extraneous elements, in most cases we must assume, of Kufic provenience, though still based on Uthmanite points of view. The Basrians no more than the Abbasids had any independent or local tradition to draw upon; the Syrian-Medinese might serve the special standpoint of the town, but the very reaction against this transmission seems once more to reveal that its leanings were not towards the Umayyads, but, if anything, toward the ʿUthmāniyya. Abū Bakr al-Hudhalī, a neither particularly notable nor trustworthy historian (d. 167/784), is far more strongly than any of the other writers here mentioned opposed to Muʿāwiya: "had he not dealt with people in a patient, generous and tolerant way, he would have been wiped off the face of the earth"[14]. On the other hand, he feels a certain veneration for az-Zubayr, who, incidentally, appears to have become a kind of Uthmanite patron saint of Basra[15]. Our material, as far as it goes, would thus indicate that Basrian historians of the first generations of the Abbasid era set up as spokesmen of Uthmanite views; we find neither pro-Abbasid nor Shīʾi tendencies in them. The maintenance of the Syrian-Medinese tradition on the *fitna* as well as the attempts to combine it with extraneous elements or even to transform Kufic tradition *ad hoc* points in this direction.

The Syrian-Medinese tradition was no doubt still known, even if rarely quoted, in Iraq in the 9th century, but it appears to have been limited to certain localities; outside Basra its transmission seems to have been haphazard, and even in the town itself to have taken place within a narrow party framework. In the decades up to 850, the culmination period of the official Muʿtazilism, the pro-Umayyad transmission probably no longer served—or rather: unilaterally or solely served—Uthmanite points of view. As in the preceding generations the Kufic and Medinese, so the Basrian tradition—apparently still in the last years of al-Maʾmūn's reign—is drawn toward Baghdad, the primary centre of that period's political, religious and cultural ferment. It is not, as was the material of the two other schools of tradition, subjected to any process of transformation, but is being handed down in its pure form, and is soon included in Balādhurī's historical writing.

The pro-Umayyad transmission was brought to Baghdad principally by such traditionists as Abū Khaythama Zuhayr b. Ḥarb (d. 848/50), his son Aḥmad b. Abī Khaythama (d. 893), and Aḥmad b. Ibrāhīm ad-Dawraqī (d. 860/61). We know for certain that the first and the last-mentioned were among the group of scholars who by al-Maʾmūn's orders were brought before the Muʿtazilite inquisition (*miḥna*) accused of being followers of Aḥmad b. Ḥanbal and the

---

14 Bal.: *Muʿāw.*, no. 330; Muʿāwiya's *ḥilm* is thus turned against himself.
15 Pellat: *Jāḥiẓ*, 107, 158 *sq.*

Ḥanbali opposition[16]. They yielded to pressure by the Court of Justice, and were then sent back from Sāmarrā', the Caliph's residence, to Baghdad to renounce and abjure their Ḥanbali persuasion publicy before the assembled *fuqahā'* and traditionists.

We have no particular knowledge of the mentioned three scholars' participation in the Ḥanbali movement. They are referred to occasionally in connexion with Imām Aḥmad and the principles of traditional criticism which he instituted. In the later historiographical literature (in as-Sakhāwī) they are mentioned with high esteem as his pupils[17]; reversely, their own judgments on untrustworthy traditionists bear the imprint of acrimony and sometimes of an almost pharisaical self-righteousness. As referred to above, the Basrian school of historians was, in contrast to other traditional schools, distinguished for its sobriety and for keeping comparatively aloof from the adaptional work going on elsewhere. The same phenomenon is ascertainable also as regards other disciplines within the Basrian *ḥadīth* school. The Basrian school itself did apparently not exercise any systematical criticism on traditions, presumably because its material was more strictly transmitted than that of other schools[18]. In the hands of the Ḥanbali movement, to which it reached through the above-mentioned scholars, it obtained particular importance, mainly perhaps because it entirely satisfied the technical requirements of the tradition by its sobriety and pure transmission. It did full justice to b. Ḥanbal's theoretical ideals and constituted for that reason alone a suitable point of departure for a systematism according to the lines of direction that he had laid down[19].

Furthermore, the material handed down on the authority of these scholars corresponded perfectly with the Ḥanbali points of view, the conservative attempt to reestablish the Islamic society according to the norms supposed to have been set up by the earliest community. The material transmitted on the authority of the above-mentioned three scholars is on the whole identical to the substance with which the Basrian school had operated; frequently the same accounts are transmitted by both Abū Khaythama and ad-Dawraqī. The material is thus narrowly confined to the period of conflict during 'Alī's Caliphate. However, this does not mean that they were more sympathetic to Syria than were their Basrian precursors or the Ḥanbali school generally. This is particularly well illustrated in ad-Dawraqī. He shares his fellow-townsmen's moderate veneration for az-Zubayr and states that 'Ā'isha's advice was not to make him caliph, but for the present appoint him commander *(amīr)* of the combatants

16 Patton, 64.—The information stems from Ṭabarī, who was himself opposed to Ḥanbalism. There is hardly any reason to doubt its correctness.

17 Rosenthal: *Historiography*, 362, 373 *sq.*, 440; cf. p. 55.

18 Pellat: *Jāḥiẓ*, 89.

19 On Ḥanbalism cf. *infra* pp. 121 *sqq.*

until the fight had been decided[20]. His ill-will towards Mu'āwiya is revealed in a tradition according to which 'Alī says that he "had not inspired to the caliphate were it not for fear that a man of Banū Umayya would again possess himself of it and play the fool with God's Book", an unmistakable post-rationalization[21].

The transmission of this material its too narrow to provide guidance for the interpretation of these historians' individual points of view[22]. The interpretation of their motives for calling attention to and making use of the pro-Syrian sources must therefore rest solely on whether they can be naturally inserted into the framework of Ḥanbalism. The applicability of this version must most likely be explained as an attempt to rehabilitate the legitimacy of the Umayyad Caliphate, even if hardly of the Umayyads themselves. By this means the continuity in the orthodox community that Aḥmad b. Ḥanbal had in view could be maintained: Mu'āwiya had not raised the rebellion against 'Alī from personal ambitions, but in order to assert that in his capacity of the victim's *walī* he was entitled to blood vengeance provided that the caliph murder was committed unlawfully. Moreover, the arbitral award was not illegal, as asserted by the Kufic transmission, and Mu'āwiya did not receive *bay'a* prior to the award.

To all this must be added one other aspect that undoubtedly played a vital part in the Ḥanbali argumentation. It was indeed through the application of the pro-Syrian transmission that they expressed their opposition to the prevailing Mu'tazilism and its attempts to combine pro-Abbasid and pro-'Alī viewpoints, a fact which, conversely, provides a likely explanation of the unbridled attacks that al-Madā'inī at this very time launched on the Umayyads. Provided that this reading is correct, the historiographical debate leads us into the violent ferment that took place in the middle of the 9th century between the official Mu'tazilism and the Ḥanbali opposition, the reaction of the orthodox and prosperous towns—Basra and Baghdad—against the Abbasids' attempts to shape the Islamic society in their own image.

20 Bal. 475 r (Caetani IX, 66).—This tradition may be an adaptation of the parallel Zuhrī tradition concerning Mu'āwiya. Correspondingly, Abū Khaythama (Bal. *loc. cit.*) makes the Basrians reprove Ṭalḥa for his share in 'Uthmān's murder, though without involving az-Zubayr.

21 Bal. 429r–v (Caetani X, 404 *sq.*).

22 The chronological continuity of the transmission is presumably a relative warranty of its completeness. On the other hand, we can have no definite knowledge of what other narratives they might have obtained from other sources.

6. Recapitulation

1.

The change of dynasty in 750 did not bring about a bridging of the antagonisms that had embittered the Umayyad era but, if anything, led them into new channels; neither did the framing of the historical tradition cease at that time. Confining ourselves for the present to the first two generations of the Abbasid Caliphate until Hārūn ar-Rashīd's death in 809 we see how this period is quite naturally marked by the new rulers' efforts to consolidate their power. The breach—presumably under al-Manṣūr—with the radical Shī'ism that had prepared their way to power is but one aspect of this process, though indubitably of far-reaching significance in that it reflects the necessity of assimilating the foundation of the caliphal authority with the orthodox majority and the leading social groups in the eastern provinces of the Empire. Among other problems incident to the period of consolidation were the centralization of the caliphal authority from the closing years of the 8th century, the build-up of the Abbasids' *khalīfat allāh*, and the immense growth of the bureaucracy.

In many respects the way for this centralization is prepared by picking up the threads leading back to the political and literary traditions of the Sassanian era, a procedure that did apparently not yet cause any clash between the Mesopotamian-Islamic theocracy and the anti-Persian tendencies. The tradition from Sassanian Persia is observable in the budding literature on political theory, which also, at any rate from the 9th century, incorporated elements of the Arab historical transmission into its didactic considerations. This state-theoretical tradition, the first approaches towards which took place already in the late Umayyad era, was created by the central administration's civil servants, but it does not seem to have been inspired by the Abbasid Caliphs themselves[1]. We can, however, still follow the early Abbasids' interest in the Arabian tradition and find that a number of the period's outstanding traditionists worked under the court's auspicies. This applies, *inter alia*, to Muhammad b. Isḥāq and b. al-Kalbī. The Persian tendencies in the administration and the literature

1 Gibb, 62 *sqq*.

related to it are but very faintly reflected in the historical writing of this period and can hardly have exercised any appreciable influence on the historians' discussions of the problems, and no attempt is made to involve the Persians in the conflicts provoked by the *fitna*[2]. In the shaping of historical traditions and in the debates which it reflects the main interest is focused on the responsibility for the *fitna* and for the Umayyad Caliphate. The decisive incitement must still be sought in the Abbasid Caliphate's attitude to its revolutionary origin and to Shī'ism.

One apparent feature of the branches of tradition with which we are operating here is a certain one-sideness. Our knowledge of the historical transmission of this period is limited to the pro-Abbasid, the moderate Shiite and the Uthmanite, whereas neither the extremist Shī'ism nor Khārijism is represented, apart from a few and widely scattered fragments. A detailed collocation is therefore impracticable for the purpose of obtaining insight into how the Khārijite opposition is gradually relegated to the outer provinces of the caliphate, or is displaced by the radical Shī'ism. Possibly, as intimated above, no extremist Shiite historical tradition of any considerable extent ever did exist, and the same may, more or less, apply to Khārijism in the Abbasid era. That orthodox or moderate Shī'i authors invariably stood aloof from Khārijism seems evident from the interest they devoted on subjects of particular significance to this oppositional group. Cases in point are found in such works as "*kitāb an-Nahrawān*" which are ascribed to Abū Miknaf, Naṣr b. Muzāḥim, and al-Madā'inī[3]. The attitude of the first mentioned to the Khārijite tradition has already been commented on; concerning Naṣr b. Muzāḥim and al-Madā'ini, although we did not know the attitude of either to Khārijism, their writings are, if anything, of a polemic nature, too.

It is likely that the split of Khārijism into minor sects that found their followers mainly in the empire's outlying—and often unprosperous—provinces, and that the fanaticism generally characterizing these movements rather discouraged any development of the historical tradition. On the whole, such late works of this observance, as we know so far, build upon 'Abdallah b. Yazīd al-Fazārī's transmission. This is true of the south Arabian version in its theological adaptation found in Abū Sa'īd al-Qalhātī in the 11th century[4] as well as of the much later expositions in al-Barrādī (second half of the 14th century) and ash-Shammākhī (d. 1521). Both authors are from al-Maghrib, and their works were prepared in more favourable economic and cultural conditions

2 Attempts to parallel the Persians with the Arabs round the 'Alī-figure are not met with until in ad-Dīnawarī. Correspondingly, al-Ya'qūbī tries to establish a family connection between the Prophet family and the Sassanids; cf. *HT* 11: V, 471 note 2.

3 Vaglieri I, 14.

4 On the dating, see M. Kafāfī in *B. Fac. Ar.* XIV: 2, 30 *sq.*

than were available in the earlier Abbasid era. Of Khārijite historians proper during this period the only ones definitely known seem to be Khālid b. Sa'īd (d. 806)[5] and the disreputable al-Haytham b. 'Adī aṭ-Ṭā'ī (d. 822/23)[6]. Despite the latter's immense production the stories transmitted on his authority are confined to either anecdotes or fragments of very doubtfyl value, which in no way contradict the epithets—mendacious, talebearer—fixed upon him by his contemporaries[7]. Although religious considerations may to a great extent have barred the passage of quotations from Khārijite authors into the historial literature known to us, there is hardly reason to think that any special historical writing of Khārijite observance—apart from that of al-Haytham b. 'Adī, who seems to have dealt with many other subjects—did exist in this period.

The tradition from the earliest Abbasid era thus moves within a rather narrow and one-sided framework and cannot be expected to give a complete picture of the conflicting views of those days. Turning to the pro-Abbasid and the moderate Shiite transmission we find that the former made a great point of establishing 'Abdallah b. 'Abbās's achievement at 'Alī's side as his mentor, and also that the Caliph's lack of success was occasioned by his own adherents who failed, above all by enforcing the arbitration agreement at Ṣiffīn, and his *renunciatio tituli* on the same occasion. The former feature is met with very early in the tradition, in Hishām b. Muhammad al-Kalbī, and the latter is carried to its logical conclusion in Sayf b. 'Umar under Hārūn ar-Rashīd; these two main points in the pro-Abbasid argumentation are very closely bound up with each other.

The Kufic transmission reveals already from the Umayyad era attempts to create a factual contrast between 'Alī's chivalry and pure, religiously motived conduct and Mu'āwiya's *ḥilm*; the procrastinating opportunism could without marked strain be interpreted as lacking competence, cowardice, or guile and

5 Vaglieri II, 3 *sq.*—One reflection of polemics is no doubt found in a tradition according to which al-Ashtar, Yazīd b. Qays, and Shabath b. Rib'ī were among those who continued the fight after the Quran stratagem at Ṣiffīn. b. al-Kalbī states (Tab. I. 3274–76; Caetani IX, 431 *sqq.*) that 'Alī, when »weapons were desisted from at Ṣiffīn«, sent four men, among which Yazīd b. Qays and Shabath b. Rib'ī, to Mu'āwiya »to urge him to make an agreement that can re-unite us and our community«. Shabath b. Rib'ī even offers to hand over the caliph murderers ('Ammār b. Yāsir) to Mu'āwiya. Hishām b. Muhammad's version is presumably an adaptation of a tradition in Abū Mikhnaf concerning negotiations before the battle (cf. *supra* p. 56).

6 On the latter, see b. Khall., no. 634 (deSlane III, 633 *sqq.*); Margoliouth: *Lectures*, 95 *sq.*; Rosenthal: *Historiography*, 63, 65.

7 Verified fragments of his *kitāb al-khāwarij* are found only in b. al-Kathīr: *Bidāya*, 149r, 151r, and Bal. 533r–34r, 543r–v (Caetani IX, 539 *sq.*; X, 104 *sq.*, 109), perhaps also an apocryphal prophesy of Abū Mūsā's failure known likewise from b. al-Kalbī (Ya'q. II, 222; cf. *supra* p. 76, note 21) and in al-Barrādī (Vaglieri II, 12 *sq.*), both citing Suwayd b. Ghafala al-Ju'fī (d. 695/96); cf. Caetani X, 35 *sq.* and *infra* p. 170.

set off against ʿAlī's probity. In Shiite historical writing the contrast is as a matter of course unconditionally positive, and this applies likewise to the Abbasid era where it is met with several times in Naṣr b. Muzāḥim's historical writing[8]. In the pro-Abbasid tradition, however, the Caliph's integrity assumed indirectly the character of unreflective integrity or doctrinaire rigidity. The irrationality of ʿAlī's persisting in his religious *normæ* in the face of illegal adversaries is pointed out already by al-Kalbī, and repeated by subsequent historians, but refuted by Shīʿi scholars. That this was a main point in the pro-Abbasid tradition is attested to by the fact that it makes b. ʿAbbās act as the far-sighted and sober *deus ex machina* in situations where ʿAlī had behaved unwisely, unrealistically, or too honestly; "b. ʿAbbās...sees the future as through a thin veil", is b. al-Kalbī's comment *post festum* to his warnings against the Syrians' aims at the arbitration. As the very contrast to his depiction of ʿAlī's good intentions and b. ʿAbbās's positive influence Sayf b. ʿUmar deliberately saddles an extremist proto-Shīʿism—as-Saba'iyya, the reflected image of rabid Shīʿism in his own time—with the responsibility for the outbreak of the *fitna*, and in its ranks Khārijism takes root.

The Shīʿi historians' reaction to these accusations has been referred to above. We can occasionally ascertain in details how they dissociate themselves from the opposite party's attempts to depict ʿAlī as b. ʿAbbās's protégé or reduce him to a state of pupilage before his own adherents, and how they defend the justification of his probity. In the Kufic tradition, as represented by ʿUmar b. Saʿīd and Naṣr b. Muzāḥim, ʿAbdallāh b. ʿAbbās, though never openly criticized, plays but an insignificant part and is replaced by a united front behind ʿAlī against the illegal resistance. Confronted with Sayf b. ʿUmar's massive attack on the Iman conceptions of Shīʿism, which in his rendering merely hindered ʿAlī in following his inmost intentions, Shiite historians maintained consistently that the Prophet's family passed on his divine revelation. The Prophet-predictions *post eventum* of ʿAlī's merits are met with for the first time in ʿUmar b. Saʿīd as a fixed element in his argumentation. By virtue of his religious prestige and the veneration surrounding his person ʿAlī is exalted above the *fitna*, and the main credit for the fight against the apostates is concentrated round Kufa, the Shīʿi tradition's firmest bastion. This is where ʿAlī finds his sincerest adherents against ʿUthmāniyya and Muʿāwiya, and the fact that the Kufians subsequently support the arbitration scheme at Ṣiffīn does not mean that they failed him, but that they acted in conformity with the Prophet's example. Naṣr b. Muzāḥim, in contrast to Abū Mikhnaf, points to the Ḥudaybiyya treaty as the model for ʿAlī's renunciation of his title of caliph. So, attack as well as defence in this historiographic exchange of views turned on the cardinal

8 cf. Brockelmann, 9 *sqq.*

point in the programme of Shīʿism: The justification of its assertion that ʿAlī's descendants passed on the divine revelation. If the Abbasid tradition were to yield on this point, the legitimacy of the orthodox caliphate would crumble away.

Both the pro-Abbasid and the moderate Shīʿi transmission—though with varying emphasis—use the claim for blood vengeance as the motive in Muʿāwiya's argumentation, whereas the vulgar Shīʿi adaptation, as found in ʿĪsā b. Yazīd and al-Juʿfī, hardly appears in these traditions. But while the Shīʿi version in ʿUmar b. Saʿīd and Naṣr b. Muzāḥim tries to attest to the absurdity in Muʿāwiya's accusations against ʿAlī by pointing out that *Muhājirūn* and *Anṣār* by electing him caliph have recognized his innocence, the pro-Abbasid tradition revives Abū Mikhnaf's assertion that from the outset Muʿāwiya's demand for blood vengeance was sheer pretence, in addition to which it accuses him and ʿAmr b. al-ʿĀṣ of having failed the murdered caliph. A concatenation of this postulate with the attack on Shīʿism from this branch of tradition makes it clear that by its defection Shīʿism had automatically incurred a heavy responsibility for admitting not only illegal but even criminal elements to the caliphal power.

Carried to its logical conclusion this subtle debate turned on the justification of the Prophet family's pretensions and the Abbasid Caliphate's legitimacy. The dualistic argumentation presumably also serves to explain either party's choice of sources. The pro-Abbasid tradition, which had been built up with surprising firmness and strength in the second half of the 8th century, borrowed its material principally from Abū Mikhnaf. By means of venturesome constructions it subjected the elements to a re-casting according to its immediate requirements, a procedure that reached its full development in Sayf b. ʿUmar's historical writing. On the whole there is a case for assuming that b. al-Kalbī, whose opinions we have in several instances been able to trace, played a leading part in framing the Abbasid interpretations of the *fitna*, and that he must have exerted quite a decisive influence on the historians of his own time and the immediate future. The historical pragmatism in Sayf, on which Wellhausen shed light, thus applies to this transmission in its entirety; its adaptation of the tradition exceeds by far that of the contemporaneous Shīʿi transmission in the form in which we find it in Naṣr b. Muzāḥim, and it has indubitably its place in the new dynasty's tempestuous propaganda for its raison d'être. The moderate Shīʿi tradition, however, avoided Abū Mikhnaf, even though Naṣr presumably made use of him without quoting his works specifically. It did, on the contrary, revert to the earlier elements of the Kufic transmission. The somewhat paradoxical consequence of this process is this: The Kufic version of the *fitna* is no longer confronted with the pro-Umayyad one, whereas its earliest elements—ash-Shaʿbī and the secondary al-Jurjānī—are confronted with the later, secondary or tertiary layers in the tradition. In this way only was it possible to adapt the Kufic transmission to the new state of affairs in the second half of the 8th century.

2

On approaching the early decades of the 9th century we find this situation undergoing a rapid and sweeping change when Mu'talizilism makes its entry politically and religiously under al-Ma'mūn. This movement had since the late Umayyad era apparently been the supporting party of the Abbasids, and even though the anti-Shiite reaction did not appreciably alter this situation, there is hardly any question of a noticeable framing of a Mu'tazilite tradition before al-Ma'mūn. The turning point did not arrive until the Mu'tazilite school in Baghdad advocated a reconciliation with the moderate Shī'ism. The placability towards 'Alī observable in the leading historians of this period also finds its expression in a corresponding and progressive condemnation of the Umayyads. Even al-Wāqidī founds his (primarily pro-Alid) points of view on the preceding generation's pro-Abbasid material and merely brings it up to date. This version, however, is completely abandoned already by al-Madā'inī, who collects a scattered and far from homogeneous material. Still, none of the historians make use of the contemporaneous Shiite literature or, apart from Muhammad b. Sa'd, advocate religious veneration for the 'Alī figure; the rapprochement is, then, rather pro-'Alī; it is not Shiite but proceeds along other channels. The main stress in their argumentation—as well as in Mu'tazilism altogether—lies primarily in the endeavour of the rulers to bring about an understanding with the moderate Shī'ism under Abbasid auspices. We cannot rule out the possibility that social factors and the radicalization of the extremist Shī'ism have been contributory to this process, which may as well be explained by the Abbasids' anxiety to emphasize that religious continuity and unity of which they claimed to be the representatives and enforcers. These two possibilities can hardly be considered mutually contradictory or exclusive, and at any rate, Mu'tazilism is again instrumental in bringing the Abbasid Caliphate's endeavours to identify itself with and control Islam's religious and political institutions into the foreground.

There exists, on the other hand, an unquestionably intimate connexion between al-Ma'mūn's and his immediate successors' attempts to make the caliphal power the common denominator of the orthodox precepts of the Islamic society and adapt its dogmatic development to the basic views of the Abbasids, and the reaction growing up under Aḥmad b. Ḥanbal's (d. 855) leadership. Mu'tazilism, as referred to above, represents to all appearances the specific points of view of the Abbasids; theologically it is characterized by its rationalism and severe criticism of the tradition-bound orthodoxy. In contrast to the latter's unmerciful, antropomorphic concept of God, Mu'tazilism postulated man's free will and the distinction between the nature of God and His word. Methodologically Mu'tazilism differs clearly from the classical Arabic theology's fundamental dependence upon the Prophet tradition in its employment of the Hellenic *Logos* doctrine and conceptions of substance and accident in a metaphorical Quran exegesis. The speculative theology of Mu'tazilism thus goes to the core of the Islamic theocracy: the doctrine of predestination and indeterminism, *ḥadīth* science and rationalism are confronted as irreconcilable antitheses[9]. To Aḥmad b. Ḥanbal the combat simply turned on the justification and existence of Islamic traditionalism as a basic religious principle, and so these encounters could hardly fail leaving their marks also on contemporaneous historical writing.

The Mu'tazilites' attack on the Islamic tradition struck of course also at the historical writing[10]. From their fundamental points of view they naturally took exception to the traditionists' accumulation of individual and incoherent data. Like their classical model—Aristotle—they threw doubt on whether history could actually be considered a science: it was no empirical science but dealt with widely diffused individual data that did not lend themselves to re-examination by rational means. And as regard the completed product, it was in their eyes on a level no higher than that of compilation, a mechanical rendering of narratives by other authors. Only insofar as the historian undertook a classification and assessment of his data as constituents of a comprehensive perspective in order to arrive at a general explanation or interpretation of the causes and correlations of the events did history acquire the character of a practical science. The Mu'tazilite criticism of the prevailing work on the Islamic tradition would of course be warranted on the precondition that a philosophical contemplation of history is the highest object for every occupation with past times, but it miscarried completely because no such precondition had ever existed in Islam, and was indeed foreign to the nature of Islam. Arabic historical writing was not lacking in conceptual content, and the didactic element had always, even if normally implicitly, been very much apparent, but the demands adduced by Mu'tazilism implied in practice that historical writing be detached from its religious foundation and its political function: a process of readjustment that would hardly have been feasible in the prevailing conditions.

The dogmatic attack on the Arab traditionalism launched by the Mu'tazilites thus struck as principle at the life nerve in the construction of the Islamic com-

9 Goldziher: *Islam*, 61–102; H. S. Nyberg in *E.I.*[1] III, 850 *sqq*.
10 al-Khayyāṭ, no.s 103–04 (Traduction, 143 *sqq*.); Mahdi, 137 *sqq*.

munity[11]. Nothing but the Quran could, according to the Mu'tazilite doctrine, give the Muslims the absolutely authoritative guidance, and the rationalists accepted the tradition merely as far as it was not at variance with the commandments of the Quran or had acquired common recognition. It is safe to say that the stock of traditions such as it existed in the 9th century must have been an easy target for rational criticism; but, again, the criticism seems to have incited the Arabic traditionists themselves to formulate clearer than heretofore the fundamental demands to the framework of the transmission[12], and at the next remove to lay down the alignment of a traditional criticism for the purpose of ridding the tradition of its unauthentic elements. Among the jurists ash-Shāfi'ī (d. 820) was the one who first and most decisively retorted to the Mu'tazilite attack on the raison d'être and authencity of the legal tradition by formulating definitively the demand that in order to claim legal validity the tradition must be traceable to the Prophet or his Companions. ash-Shāfi'ī's jurisprudence may thus be said to have submitted to the criticism, but it did not, and could not, prevent false traditions, nor prevent authentic narratives from being reflected back to the Prophet or his entourage. This dilemma was dealt with in the next generation by his pupil Aḥmad b. Ḥanbal in that he combined systematics of Shāfi'ite observance with traditional criticism, as yet perhaps rather imperfectly, but for all that a new-broken ground of paramount scope, new ground that by the very virtue of its leading principle revived the power of resistance of Islamic traditionalism[13].

Aḥmad b. Ḥanbal's doctrine, which, incidentally, he never managed to commit to writing, in many respects supplements and develops the principles in ash-Shāfi'ī's jurisprudence in its attempts to reconstruct or realize the basic ideas of the orthodox Islamic community before the *fitna* broke its unity. On the basis of the store of traditions and all critical facilities at his disposal he undoubtedly from his inmost conviction strived to recreate the framework within which the Prophet and the earliest caliphs had established Islam, and in consequence hereof turned sharply against every innovation. Keeping to such

---

11 On the following, see particularly Schacht: *Origins*, 40, 44 *sqq.*, 258 *sq.*

12 On the other hand, the factual contents *(matn)* of the tradition was never submitted to principial examination, except in such cases as could serve to elucidate the external shape of the tradition, and, consequently, to control its genuity.

13 It is no doubt correct that b. Ḥanbal's criticism of tradition proved in practice insufficient and far from perfect, and that his pupils exercised a more refined critical technique. Nevertheless, censuring him as a jurist Goldziher (*Litt.*, 477 sqq.) appears too vehement; the point is that his ideas broke new ground in the development of Islam. On Aḥmad b. Ḥanbal and Ḥanbalism, see Patton, *passim*; H. Laoust in *E.I.*[2] I, 272 *sqq.*; *idem*: *Ḥanbalisme*, 67–128.

aspects of b. Ḥanbal's doctrines as are of special interest in this connexion[14] we find the most significant of the new features to be his endeavours to raise Islam above the *fitna*, which since ʿUthmān's death had split it into irreconcilably hostile camps. His polemic is directed primarily against the Muʿtazila, Khārijiyya and extremist Shīʿa, who all issued from the first civil war. He attaches particularly great weight to the continuity in Islam effected through the Quraysh Caliphate, "which no person has the right to oppose". The sequel must be that the legitimacy of the Umayyad Caliphate was not to be denied[15], from which again follows that unlike the majority of his contemporaries, he did not repudiate the Syrian or the pro-Umayyad transmission (even though he had hardly any liking for the Syrian rulers), but places either on an equal footing with the orthodox and moderate Shiite ones.

In the contemporaneous *ḥadīth* doctrine—as we find it applied in b. Saʿd's and other authors' *ṭabaqāt* collections—it is primarily the individual traditionist's personal opinions that determine the evaluation of his trustworthiness, i.e. the tendency of the narratives or the narrator rather than his scholarly precision Although b. Ḥanbal does not clearly abandon these views, he appears to be less interested in the party-directed standpoints than his predecessors had been. Syrian or pro-Syrian traditionists—e.g. az-Zuhrī—are not, as in other authors, condemned for having served the Umayyads in the capacity of public officers, and even if doubts concerning the religious standpoint of the person in question still play some part in his assessment, it is evidently the traditionist's personal truthfulness and the transmission's extrinsic data he considers decisive as regards their applicability[16]. This basic outlook serves to explain why b. Ḥanbal in the purely historical sections of his jurisprudence follows az-Zuhrī as his chief informant though never, in noteworthy contrast to the Basrian tradition, as the ultimate authorithy but merely as the chief transmitter of eyewitness accounts, i.e. to all appearances unauthentic adaptations from the Syrian-Medinese transmission[17]. From a strictly objective point of view his criticism of the tradition also in this respect suffers from serious defects,

14 b. Ḥanbal's main effort naturally applied to the fight against the Mutʿtazilite dogmatics and dialectics; he himself was consistent in maintaining the antropomorphic concept of God. On the other hand, he also dissociated himself from the Persianizing tendencies of his time; in his eyes the final consequences of this movement were anti-Islamic.

15 The fact that Muʿāwiya and his son Yazīd had after all belonged to the Prophet's Companions and Followers may also have been of importance in this connexion; a categorical denouncement might incur dangerous consequences; cf. *AO* XXVII, 110, 114 *sqq.*

16 as-Sakhāwī mentions that Aḥmad b. Ḥanbal wrote a book on »*Names* and *Patronymics*« (Rosenthal: *Historiography*, 370 *sq.*; cf. pp. 263, 271, 440). This work, which was transmitted by his son Ṣāliḥ, probably has its place and function in the biographical criticism exercised by b. Ḥanbal.

17 cf. Goldziher: *Litt.*, 474.

even though he himself was hardly able to see through the mechanism in the falsification of tradition that had taken place. However, the cardinal point remains: By raising his formal and factual demands and by his fanatical fight against Mu'tazilism Aḥmad b. Ḥanbal had retorted to the anti-Islamic principles of rationalism and had paved the way for a renewal of traditional scholarship in all its ramifications.

A severer criticism of the traditional material is found in his pupils. His son 'Abdallāh Abu 'r-Raḥmān b. Aḥmad (d. 903/04), who edited his jurisprudence, proved a more rigid critic of such traditional material than his father, who had accepted it despite reservation concerning the trustworthiness of the transmission; the historians among his pupils—Abū Khaythama Zuhayr b. Ḥarb, ad-Dawraqī, and b. Abī Khaythama—did likewise exercise greater moderation. We have been able to observe how the Syrian-Medinese transmission, which in the early Abbasid era was handled by a narrow Uthmanite school in Basra, is being taken over in the second quarter of the 9th century by these historians, who carry it to Baghdad, the centre of political discussion. This transmission was distinguished especially for its exceptionally pure and homogeneous handling, so in that respect it met the requirements laid down by b. Ḥanbal. On one point only do these historians deviate from their teacher's fundamental directions: To judge by the material available, they never attempt to carry the verification of their information back to eyewitnesses, but maintain consistently az-Zuhrī's and Ṣāliḥ b. Kaysān's authority as final; on the other hand, their names never occur in connexion with the false Zuhrī-tradition found in Mu'ammar b. Rashīd and his pupil 'Abd ar-Razzāq and which appears to have been known in Baghdad at that time. This difference between the methodology of b. Ḥanbal and that of his pupils is noteworthy, and there can be very little doubt that it was conscious. In this respect the historians here referred to are, like the jurists among his pupils, more Ḥanbalite than b. Ḥanbal himself.

On the other hand, b. Ḥanbal's pupils never modify his principal object: to regenerate Islam according to the norms set up by the Prophet and the earliest community. On this point, too, the Syrian-Medinese tradition appears to have a significant function in the Ḥanbalite historian's argumentation. In the first place, in the nature of things, it established the Umayyad Caliphate's position as a legitimate and necessary link in the continuity of Islam; secondly, it could, as was the case in the Umayyad era, be used in terms of opposition against the Kufic interpretation of the *fitna*; and, thirdly, in consequence hereof it dissociated itself from Mu'tazilism's pro-'Alī tendencies and rationalism. As ascertained above, al-Madā'inī differs from al-Wāqidī and Muhammad b. Sa'd in that he reverts once more to the primary chronology of the Kufic transmission, and also in that he lays more stress on Mu'āwiya's wordly motives. This conglomerate of elements of very diverse origin and age cannot with any show of reason be construed as solely destined to meet Shiite points of view; al-Madā'inī's purpose was no doubt to meet also Ḥanbalism's interpretation of the *fitna*. His chronologic systematism does admittedly correspond to that of the Ḥanbalite historians both as regards Mu'āwiya's breach with the Caliph and the distinction between the actions of the 'Uthmāniyya and those of Mu'āwiya; but his fierce accusations against the Syrian governor obtain quite particular weight by the very fact that they are launched within this framework. In other words, al-Madā'inī probably polemizes against the Ḥanbali historians on that same level which they themselves had chosen.

In the pro-Alid and the Mu'tazilite historical writing a perceptible shifting takes place from al-Wāqidī to al-Madā'inī, from the former's attempts to reconcile Alid and Abbasid points of view to the latter's temperamental condemnation of Mu'āwiya. The significance of this development should not be underrated because it proves in a most striking way that the Ḥanbalite opposition must have been so widespread and so cogent in the towns of the eastern provinces that the rulers, no doubt rightly, construed it as a serious menace to their politics. This conclusion is quite in harmony with the measures that the government took in order to counteract Ḥanbalism, *inter alia*, by setting up an inquisition *(miḥna)*; among its victims were Aḥmad b. Ḥanbal, Abū Khaythama, and ad-Dawraqī. In its entire range the violent ferment, into which the historical writing, too, gives us some insight, concerned the orthodox urban patriciate's fight against the attempts of the Abbasids to force upon the Islamic society persuasions alien to it, and which thus once again involved the essence of the caliphate's programme during this period.

3.

One of the characteristic traits of the early Abbasid period is the attraction exerted by Baghdad on the contemporary intellectual milieu, in which respect the historical writing is no exception. A number of outstanding Kufic, Basrian, and Medinese scholars, whose education had been acquired in their native towns or on study tours, forgathered in Baghdad where, more or less, they were to work under influence of the town's leading circles, either at the caliphal court or in the oppositional groups. A parallel course is ascertainable within the spheres of politics and economy. The Abbasid Caliphate reached its most impressive development in the political field, and in economic and social respects we can trace the same tendency to concentration in Iraq, whereas some other of the caliphate's provinces—Syria and Egypt—appear to remain in an economic decline. The Iraqi towns witness the emergence of a prosperous social middle class, which in the capacity of bankers and purveyors had connections with the caliphal court. But the economic expansion also resulted in a growing gap between the leading urban patriciate and the lower classes in towns and country, a gap which in the course of the 9th century amounted to a latent conflict between the orthodoxy and the extremist Shī'ism, eventually crystallizing in Ismā'īlism, a movement in which the dislike of the orthodox classes was gradually concentrated.

The political and intellectual trends in the central provinces of the caliphate in the 9th century are clearly interrelated. When al-Jāḥiz, Mu'tazilism's most prominent spokesman, in his no doubt officially inspired writings pleads for the cause of rationalism, it is not so much to the narrow academical circle as to the prosperous middle classes with intellectual ambitions that he appeals; and when he criticizes the anti-Mu'tazilite opposition it is above all the Islamic tradition's hold over the society that he attacks. The crux of these controversies still turned on the caliphate's right to consider itself as being above the law and all the attendant dangers that this experiment might create a gap between itself and the orthodox majority, whose support it had from the very beginning tried to gain, and which it could hardly dispense with. This clash of interests, observed already in al-Madā'inī's historical writing and in the Ḥanbalites, proved to be of a far-reaching nature. In al-Madā'inī we have found a further suggestion of polemics against pro-Umayyad tendencies on a less elevated level, and the same applies more or less to al-Jāḥiẓ (d. 869).

In his polemic writings from the 830's and 840's al-Jāḥiẓ operates with three distinct groups of that age: Mu'tazilism, which he himself professed; Shu'ūbism (the Persianizing movements); and, finally, what he designates "the Raw Youth Party" *(an-Nābita)*[18]. In his description this *an-Nābita* is identified with the conservative anthropomorphism in Islam and politically stigmatized as adherents of the Umayyads, whom his mordant pen represents as religious scoundrels of the worst kind. al-Jāḥiẓ gives no detailed definition of which groups—social or geographical—he has in mind, but we know from other writings of his that socially he distinguishes between an intellectual élite and the common herd. We know, too, that he somewhat arrogantly emphasizes that the enlightened scholastic, by which term he understands that circle of rationalistic scholars to which he belonged, ought to guide the ignorant; and we know, finally, that he deeply regretted that, on the contrary, the common man preferred to be led astray by the "anthropomorphists", who to him represented the conservative and narrow-minded Islamic traditionalism[19]. For all their one-sidedness Jāḥiẓ's lines of demarcation provide a clear illustration of the opposition that the Abbasids encountered in orthodox circles; it is indubitably this very opposition that finds expression in the popular pro-Umayyad cur-

18 Jāḥiẓ: *Nābita*, 302–25.

19 Najīm, 208 *sqq.*

rents emerging in this period. In his polemic he likens—presumably in a somewhat exaggerated manner—the pro-Umayyad trends and the cult of Mu'āwiya's *faḍā'il*, the peculiar quality possessed by the Prophet's *aṣḥāb* and *tābi'ūn*, to the extremist Shī'ism's cult of 'Alī. His broadsides are aimed primarily at the worldliness of the Umayyads, especially of Mu'āwiya. al-Jāḥiẓ thus ranges himself alongside al-Madā'inī; he emphasizes that they called down *kufr*, infidelity, upon themselves by their crimes against 'Alī and his adherents and by their usurpation of the caliphal power[20].

Pro-Umayyad currents of greatly varying content and strength are traceable to the first half of the 8th century. It is certain that the Syrian Arabian tribes surrounded the memory of the caliphate's days of glory under Mu'āwiya and Yazīd with veneration, but these currents obtained no political significance until they lent themselves to exploitation by the early branch of the dynasty, the Sufyānids, against the later one, the Marwānids[21]. This form of tradition occupied itself primarily with Mu'āwiya's personal qualities, still a principal point with the traditionist Maslama b. Muḥārib (ca. 765–85), a member of the Sufyānids, only with the additional trait that he apparently had to discountenance the Kufic tradition's attack on Mu'āwiya. Not until the change of dynasty in 750 does this tradition appear to have taken on a legendary character when, facing the official denunciation and the *ḥadīth* scholars' doubts, it had to define its attitude towards Mu'āwiya's and Yazīd's *faḍā'il*. It is presumably owing to these attacks that in a few traditionists, 'Abdallāh b. al-Mubārak al-Marwazī (d. 797) and the Syrian Ismā'īl b. Ayyāsh, we can observe approaches to *Imām* conceptions akin to those of Shī'ism, and which must have arisen in polemics against Shiite attacks[22].

There is, however, hardly reason to think that the formation of this tradition at the end of the 8th century gained much ground or enjoyed general recognition, exept that it is expressive of a reaction against the denunciation of the two first Umayyads, who in spite of everything had been among the Prophet's *aṣḥāb* and *tābi'ūn*. Only when this denunciation under Mu'tazilism assumed the character of a principle and was associated with the attack on traditionalism did the pro-Umayyad tradition acquire a more general aim. We can, in broad outline, ascertain that minor traditionists, e.g. the Syrian Hishām b. 'Ammār ad-Dimashqī, in the mid-decades of the 9th century return to this transmission; we can follow al-Madā'inī's frequent quotations from it, only to dissociate himself promptly from it; and it is, finally, against this tradition that also al-

20 This is particularly the case in his *kitāb imāmat Mu'āwiya b. Abī Sufyān*, his *Risāla fī n-Nābita*, and his *Risāla fī amr al-ḥakamayn* (Pellat: *Mu'āwiya*, 53 *sqq.*; Jāḥiẓ: *Nābita*, 302–25; Jāḥiẓ: *Arbitrage*, 417 *sqq.*).

21 Lammens: *Omayyades*, 391 *sqq.*; cf. *AO* XXVII, 109 *sqq.*

22 *AO* XXVII, 113 *sqq.*

Jāḥiẓ turns in his hot attacks on the Mu'āwiya cult[23]. The Umayyad cult has hardly any connexion with Ḥanbalism but has arisen spontaneously, and, conversely, the Ḥanbalites with their strict disciplinary principles could hardly have acknowledged the exuberant and homely traditional formation. Common to both is, however, that they issue from the orthodoxy in the towns of the eastern provinces—the pro-Umayyad currents are known in Iraq, al-Fāris, and Khurāsān—and both turn categorically against Mu'tazilism. Thus, the scholarly as well as the the popular tradition reflects the violent and, by their principles, far reaching struggles about the middle of the 9th century concerning the justification of the Islamic tradition.

23 *AO*, 117 sq.

PART III

ATTEMPTS AT COMPROMISE 850–900

1. Introductory

Politically and culturally the history of the caliphate in the first half of the 9th century represents a transitional period. The external aspect is characterized by the splendour surrounding the court at Baghdad and by the caliphal power's most determined effort to dominate Islam's dogmatic and political development. The incipient territorial disintegration—the Umayyad Amirate in Cordoba, the polities in North Africa, the Ṭāhirids in Persia—had not yet affected the integrity of the caliphate. The internal affairs, however, presented a different picture: the bad state of the government finances, a consequence of the system of farming the collection of taxes and of granting fiefs to officers in lieu of pay, gradually deprived the caliph of his freedom of action, especially when Turkish mercenaries had definetely replaced the Arabian troops in the 830's. An additional factor in this undermining of the caliphal power consisted in the incipient Shiite infiltration into the administration, in particular into the treasury, a process that was carried to its logical consequence in 936 by the establishment of the office of Chief *Amīr;* the office of Vizir was, at any rate periodically, held by a Shiite, who for religious reasons could feel under no obligation towards the orthodox caliph, whereas his connexions with the leading bankers in Baghdad enabled him to pursue his own, fairly independent policy[1].

It is of fundamental importance to this period that the Abbasids, in the face of growing orthodox resistance, continued to insist upon their right to decide in practice what should be valid law in the Islamic society. It is in the light hereof that al-Ma'mūn—having abandoned his plan of a dynastic arrangement for the benefit of the Alids—in 827 officially established the religious preference of ʿAlī to anyone else and devised his attempts to forbid the Muʿāwiya cult[2], and that he six years later carried his policy to its logical consequence by making Muʿtazilism the official doctrine. These measures provoked violent orthodox reaction headed by Aḥmad b. Ḥanbal[3]. External circumstances as

1 Massignon, 378 *sqq.*; Sourdel: *Vizirat, passim.*

2 Mas. VII, 90 sqq.

3 On the Ḥanbali opposition and the inquisition in general, see Patton, *passim*; H. Laoust in *E.I.*², 272 *sqq.*

well as the strength of the opposition compelled al-Ma'mūn's successor, al-Mu'taṣim (833–42), to leave the turbulent capital and remove to the newly founded town of Sāmarrā'[4]. Only by help from the *miḥna* could Mu'tazilism be preserved for yet a decade until 848, when the situation became so critical that al-Mutawakkil had to abolish it as the doctrine of state and gradually accept the principles of Ḥanbalism. The immediate occasion was, to be sure, a desperate but unsuccessful attempt at liberation of the caliphate from the Turkish praetorians' stifling influence[5]; but al-Mutawakkil's capitulation was nonetheless an event of the greatest scope as a manifestation of the fact that the caliphal power had to abandon the assertion that its capacity of *Imām* entitled it to fix Islam's official religio-political line. After this time Islam's orthodox framework is established by communal precepts (*ijmā' al-umma*), even though the orthodox theologians and jurists by virtue of their authority were to be leaders.

This is not to say that vacillations were no longer apparent in the attitude of the caliphal court. The conflict between orthodoxy and Shī'ism was still in evidence, though seemingly with less stability in the second half of the 9th century than formerly and to a larger extent than ever before determined by the immediate situation. Varying factors concerning strength and contrasts at the caliphal court and correspondingly varying personal partisan standpoints made themselves felt without any firm continuity. The increasing Shī'i infiltration into the finance department and the opposition provoked by this process are also noticeable. Furthermore, the extremist Shī'ism's ominous transformation into a social-revolutionary movement (Ismā'īlism) and the beginning Ismā'īlitic risings in the provinces at the transition to the 10th century likewise compelled the caliphal court to define its attitude to the religious conflicts[6].

Compromises had no doubt proved inevitable among the many contending movements, *inter alia* in order to form a common front against the Ismā'īlitic infiltration, not only from the political, but also from the religious and cultural points of view. In the theological field the most notable contribution consisted in al-Ash'arī's (d. 935) subtle attempts to create a synthesis of the orthodox and Mu'tazilite standpoints, and the historians, too, could not remain uninfluenced by impulses from the rationalism; they are still traceable in al-Mas'ūdī's (d. 956) circumstantial and daringly constructing historical writing that once more tried to reconcile the pro-Abbasid and pro-'Alī interpretation

4 Mas. VII, 118 *sqq.*
5 Mas. VII, 190.
6 Sourdel: *Pol. rel.*, 5–21.

of the *fitna*[7]. The same tendency finds expression in the assessment of history as an ancillary science on the Aristotelian model in the literature of political science during this period. The chief result of the ninth-century struggles, however, proved to be that historical writing as well as the other *ḥadīth* disciplines preserved their independence and continued to build upon the basis of the traditional material as transmitted. The deductive systematics required by Mu'tazilism as justification of its existence did not win through decisively, and even al-Mas'ūdī has to a large extent had to follow the compilatory methods. In the introduction to his *ta'rīkh ar-rusul wa-l mulūk* Ṭabarī does indeed stress the historian's dependence upon the transmission, which ought not, however, to be used for the purpose of "rational deductions or intellectuel edification". According to himself, he loyally endeavours to reproduce what he has learned from other authors[8]. Still, the historical writing in the second half of the 9th century acquired its main character through a long series of syntheses that epitomized the work of the preceding generations. The most prominent historians of this group are al-Balādhurī, aṭ-Ṭabarī, ad-Dīnawarī, and al-Ya'qūbī. Though widely different in aptitude and in viewpoints these historians are in common in maintaining the basis of the tradition, and at the same time attest to the possibility of creating a lasting synthesis on this material. It is probable that the development of Mu'tazilism contributed to a clarification of the attitude of the orthodoxy and the moderate Shī'ism, although we cannot rule out the possibility that the impulses—or, if you like: the challenge—from Mu'tazilism may have evoked these works. To the outside world this shift of interests and methods as reflected in the historical literature manifests itself at any rate in that the hitherto current technical term *'ilm al-akhbār* is replaced by the word *ta'rīkh*, which covers the chronologically consecutive exposition[9].

7 I hope to have occasion later to account for al-Mas'ūdī's version of the 'Alī-Mu'āwiya conflict.

8 Tab. I,6–7; cf. Mahdi, 136.

9 Rosenthal: *Historiography*, 10 *sqq*.

2. Al-Balādhurī (d. 892)

It is often asserted that al-Balādhurī's works—his *kitāb ansāb al-ashrāf* as well as *kitāb futūḥ al-buldān*—surpass by far most of the classical Islamic historians' works on account of his apparent impartiality[1]. Even his contemporaries and the immediate posterity praised him as a man of great merit, and the fact that he worked under the auspices of the Abbasid court did not preclude other historians, irrespective of their personal observance, from making use of his material and his authority; even a Shiite like ash-Sharīf al-Murtaḍā justifies such procedure by declaring that "it is common knowledge that he is a recognized Sunnite authority; that he does in no way support Shī'ism; and that he is exact in everything he tells"[2]. The high estimation in which Balādhurī is held also by modern research may be due to his not suppressing the pro-Umayyad tradition. It is this circumstance that makes his rendering such a valuable historical source to us; but it cannot replace a real historiographical appraisal of his works. His honest traditional technique and loyal quotation of the evidence of both parties cannot *a priori* preclude any tendency; they do indeed give rise to the questions of why Balādhurī chose this disposition and whether it is due to a deliberate—and consequently also tendentious—scheme.

S. D. Goitein rightly draws attention[3] to *kitāb ansāb al-ashrāf's* paradoxical disposition, which does not only break the framework within which Islamic historical writing had moved hitherto, but which makes the work into a historico-genealogical-biographical monument to the strength and might of the Arab empire. He draws the conclusion that the work's "historiographic peculiarity (possibly) reflects a real historical fact". He stresses that Balādhurī's objectivity cannot be due to economic independence of the rulers, but that his relatively sympathetic exposition of the Umayyad caliphs' absolute power and strong administration may underlie the Abbasid caliphate's desire to follow

1 An exception is Rosenthal's assessment in *E.I.*[2] I, 471 sq. where his standing as a source is declared to be overrated.

2 cf. Bal.: *Ans.* V, introduction, 9, 23 sqq.

3 The following presentation rests largely on Goitein's admirable introduction to the Jerusalem edition's vol. V; cf. the same author's: *The Place of Balādhurī*, 603 *sqq.*

the same line[4]. This point of view, however, presupposes, in the first place, that the then Abbasid caliphs, whose favour Balādhurī enjoyed, recognized the legitimacy of the Umayyad caliphate, and, in the second place, that his contemporaries, too, recognized the historical reality as reflected by Balādhurī's historical technique. In other words, he is supposed to have worked according to scientifical viewpoints in the modern sense. None of these presuppositions are tenable *a priori*.

On the whole, Balādhurī's work comprises the period up to al-Manṣūr's caliphate (754–75). The Constantinople manuscript, according to which it is being published, contains 1227 folios (2454 pages)[5], of which a little more than one third (454 folios) deal with the Umayyad caliphs; in addition to this there are detailed discussions on 'Umar's and 'Alī's caliphates, respectively 70 and 57 folios. Among the Umayyads the attention is predominantly focussed on Mu'āwiya's and 'Abd al-Malik's governments, to which respectively 60 and 130 folios are allotted, whereas the first two Abbasids are given only about 30 folios each, and other prominent personalities of the Abbasid era are dealt with just as peripherically; the last detailed biography is devoted to al-Ḥajjāj b. Yūsuf, 'Abd al-Malik's awe-inspiring governor in Iraq. The main importance is thus attached to the Quraysh caliphate in Umayyad times, and within this again to the decisive periods of crisis in Islam's earliest history.

An examination of the delimitation and disposition of Balādhurī's *kitāb futūḥ al-buldān* will lead to the same result. The fact that it is limited temporally to the Umayyad age is not surprising seeing that the expansion of the empire had ceased temporarily at the middle of the 8th century, and later caliphs are consequently mentioned only sporadically[6]. Balādhurī's aim must have been to give a geographical and partly chronologically arranged depiction of the growth of the empire, of its expansion and organization. In this respect, too, his "historiographic pecularities" may be said to reflect a historical reality. But that, again, does not *a priori* preclude a tendency. It is noteworthy that each of the book's main parts ends up with an account of the arabization under 'Abd al-Malik of the State's organization and the administration[7]. It is likewise noteworthy that the occasion in the first instance is a Greek official's unreliability, and in the second instance happens at the cost of Persian officials. These few suggestions alone would indicate that even though his characterization of "the Arab Kingdom's" establishment and organization bears the impress of historical truth, the book was hardly written with scientific intentions, but for the purpose of furnishing an ideal depiction of the Arab society's gen-

4 Bal.: *Ans. V*, introduction, 15 *sq.*; this idea is taken from Margoliouth's *Lectures*, 16.
5 On the flwg., see Bal.: *Ans.* V, introduction, 11 *sqq.*; Hamidullah, 197 *sqq.*
6 e.g. Bal.: *Futūḥ*, 134, 146, 230, 299 (Hitti-Murgotten I, 206, 225, 361, 462).
7 Bal.: *Futūḥ*, 193, 300 *sq.* (Hitti-Murgotten I, 301, 465 *sq.*).

esis and structure. This work, too, bears out the impression that Balādhurī's interest in the traditional party distinctions is secondary to his treatment of the enormous constructive work underlying the organization of the empire. In this respect, too, it holds true that his handling of the sources is distinguished for its soberness, especially as compared with that of the preceding generation.

Historiographically his *kitāb ansāb al-ashrāf*, as pointed out by Goitein, breaks new ground in respect of his models and procedure. True, al-Haytham b.ʿAdī had already composed a *kitāb al-ashrāf*[8], but his Khārijite sympathies and untrustworthiness seem to have hindered his work from gaining recognition. On the other hand, Balādhurī's work has nothing in common with b. Saʿd's in its structure, no doubt because its purpose was different from that of the *ṭabaqāt* literature. And, finally, he entirely breaks that framework of chronological rendering which seems to have obtained recognition in the preceding generation. All these circumstances indicate that his aim in deviating from the customary forms cannot have been that of giving a bare exposition; he worked analytically in exactly the same way as was the case in *kitāb futūḥ al-buldān*, and chose this particular form deliberately.

From the material available it appears that Balādhurī made use of both written and oral sources, and supplemented such information as he found in the works of Abū Mikhnaf, b. al-Kalbī, al-Haytham b. ʿAdī, b. Saʿd and al-Madā'inī with oral communications from the last two; the phrase "he informed me" appears frequently, while in the normal quotation—also from b. Saʿd and al-Madā'inī—he confined himself to "he said"[9]. It is obvious that Balādhurī worked at the writings of his informants, a significant feature inasmuch as he thus gained access to the primary sources rather than to later adaptations of them. What he quoted from oral soureas, then, were mainly special supplementaries. These circumstances further enable us to date his work fairly exactly. Seeing that al-Madā'inī died in 840 and b. Saʿd in 845, and that Balādhurī quotes al-Mutawakkil (847–61) *ex vivo ore*[10], while both he and al-Muntāṣir (861–62) are referred to elsewhere as being dead, his compilation and preparation must have streched over a great many years, presumably from the 840's until some time in the 860's. His *kitāb futūḥ al-buldān* was probably commenced under al-Mustaʿīn (862–66) and hardly finished before 868–69, at the earliest [11]. Temporally the two works thus appear to come near to each other; factually they supplement each other in many ways. The important point in this connection, however, is that the planning of both works must have taken place fairly con-

8 b. Khall. no. 634 (de Slane III, 634); cf. Bal.: *Ans.* V, introduction, 11; Goitein: *Bal.*, 603.
9 Bal.: *Ans.* V, introduction, 14 *sqq.*
10 Bal.: *Futūh*, 146 (Hitti-Murgotten I, 225); *Ansāb* 345r (deGoeje, 385).
11 Bal.: *Futūh*, introduction, 2.

temporarily and while the conflict concerning Mu'tazilism was still of topical interest.

It should, finally be noted that Balādhurī's tradition technique is distinguished by great sobriety. He quotes his informants loyally, and even where he undertakes abridgements *(ikhtiṣār)* his wording often comes nearer to the sense of the original than does Ṭabarī's version[12]. Direct criticism is rarely observed in his works. One exception is his condemnation, on the authority of Hishām b. 'Ammār ad-Dimashqī, of 'Īsā b. Yazīd's indubitably corrupted information[13]. On his own part Balādhurī attests to its impossibility by comparing it with other, and according to his criterion genuine, versions of the same matter. Balādhurī's method may thus be characterized as approaching the dialectic to which we have already found tentatives in al-Madā'inī.

Balādhurī's rendering of 'Alī's conversion and relations with Muhammad[14] is highly dependent upon b. Sa'd, to whose exposition of 'Alī's *vita ante datum* and to whose veneration he, however, adds a severe criticism of the caliph[15], so that already here we meet with his dialectical method. The introductory tradition proper, which is anonymous, has the Prophet predict the caliphates af Abū Bakr, 'Umar and 'Alī, whereas 'Uthmān is passed over: that is an orthodox, though plainly tendentious transmission[16]. It is, however, immediately counterbalanced by a comment borrowed from ad-Dawraqī according to which 'Alī explains that the danger of a new Umayyad caliph was the real motive for his acceptance of the caliphate[17], a statement which in this context can hardly be absolutely positive, but rather a kind of anticlimax to the introductory transmission. The same applies to the narratives on the Shiite idolization of 'Alī which entirely lose impetus by a tradition that has 'Alī himself complain of the cult of which he was the object[18]. This is once more counterbalanced by a tradition from az-Zuhrī, who says that the traditionist Sa'īd b. Musayyab had intervened in a conflict between 'Alī and 'Uthmān to remind the latter of 'Alī's early conversion, and the former of the religious prestige surrounding

12 Bal.: *Ans.* V, introduction, 21 sqq.

13 cf. *supra*, pp. 36, 128.

14 On 'Alī's personal relations and circumstances, *Ansāb* 425r–57r (cf. Caetani X, 385–464).

15 cf. b. Sa'd. III.1. 11–19 compared with Bal. 425v–26r, 441r, 445r (Caetani X, 391 *sqq.*). In contrast to b. Sa'd, who makes 'Alī be the first believer, Balādhurī asserts, with Wāqidī as his source, that Khadīja was the first one, followed by Abū Bakr, 'Alī and Zayd b. Thābit.

16 Bal. 429r (Caetani X, 404).

17 Bal. 429r–v (Caetani X, 404 *sq.*).

18 Bal. 434r (de Goeje, 391). Balādhurī stresses repeatedly that 'Alī had nothing to do with the extremist tendency for which 'Abdallāh b. Saba' was the spokesman (though not, according to Balādhurī, the first one); Bal. 449r, 455r, 585r (Caetani X, 439; della Vida, 504).

the earliest Prophet Companions[19]. The point here is, again, an unmistakable reaction and an indubitably deliberate dissociation from the Shīʿi formation of legend, in both instances by the instrumentality of traditions that to Balādhurī must have had absolute authority in contrast to the Shiite ones; he thus repudiates that gradation of the earliest caliphs which was quite a common phenomenon in his time. On the other hand, ʿAlī does not avoid—here unlike Abū Bakr, ʿUmar and, partly, Muʿāwiya—incurring a certain comical tinge through some malicious anecdotes that are known solely from Balādhurī[20].

In contrast to the very copious description of ʿAlī's caliphate and to Ṭabarī's section on Muʿāwiya, Balādhurī's discussion on the latter's government, though just as bulky, contains but little concrete information. Muʿāwiya's reconciliation with al-Ḥasan b. ʿAlī in 661 is dealt with under ʿAlī's caliphate; even such central events as the first real Shīʿi revolt headed by Ḥujr b. ʿAdī in 671 and Muʿāwiya's action for the purpose of carrying through the election of Yazīd as his successor are treated quite peripherically. On the first of these events Balādhurī confines himself to quotation of one or two sources that disapprove of the slaying of b. ʿAdī, and on the second he bestows in this context but one single tradition, which by a *praedictum post eventum* warns Yazīd in particular against such persons—al-Ḥasan b. ʿAlī, ʿAbdallah b. ʿUmar, and ʿAbdallah b. az-Zubayr—as might conceivably contend with him for precedence[21]. The exposition of Muʿāwiya's caliphate on the whole takes the shape of an analytical, though somewhat confused, anecdotically illustrated characterization of his personality and position. A very large part of this subject-matter, which Balādhurī borrowed from many quarters—al-Madāʾinī, al-Haytham b. ʿAdī, Hishām b. ʿAmmār ad-Dimashqī, and so on—is known from other sources[22], but we see them here for the first time collected into a presumably fairly complete character sketch.

Like most of the Arabic historians Balādhurī does not deny that Muawiya was notorious for his worldliness; with ʿAmr b. al-ʿĀs as his mouthpiece he records in a tradition from al-Haytham b. ʿAdī that in their campaign against ʿAlī they both fought for the good things of this world[23]. Balādhurī goes on to declare that Muʿāwiya overcame ʿAlī by virtue of his personal qualities, his ingenuity as opposed to ʿAlī's artless probity[24], and this line finds its culmi-

19 Bal. 473v, 455v–56r (Caetani X, 405).

20 cf. deGoeje, 391; Buhl: *ʿAlī*, 6 *sq.*—In the previous biography, too, of ʿAlī's brother ʿAqīl no secret is made of the latter's disrespect for him, or of the fact that ʿAqīl sided with Muʿāwiya during the conflict.

21 Bal.: *Muʿāw.*, no.s 106, 109, 360 (cf. 361), and 390.

22 Particularly from b. Qutayba and al-Jāḥiẓ's writings.

23 Bal.: *Muʿāw.*, no. 16; cf. no. 10 (from b. al-Kalbī).

24 *Ibid.*, no. 11 (Hishām b. ʿAmmār).

nation in the rendering of an exchange of words between Mu'āwiya and 'Amr b. al-'Āṣ which indirectly established once more that religiously Mu'āwiya fails to fulfil Islam's strictest demands—the wisest man is "he that prefers religion to any other cause whatever"—but it is, on the other hand, admitted that Mu'āwiya possesses the indisputable capability of filling his place: patience, magnanimity, and self-possession[25]. The traditional regret that he did not meet all the ethical norms of Islam is thus maintained; but Baladhuri also stresses that he rose far above the *jāhiliyya* by virtue of his *ḥilm*, which is elucidated in a long series of traditions, and, furthermore, that he had the ideal *sayyid's* power to overcome antagonisms, including those of an inter-tribal nature[26]. The introduction already has it that *Anṣār* and Mu'āwiya have common ancestors in the tribal community[27]; other passages emphasize that Mu'āwiya's attempts to follow Abū Bakr's and 'Umar's line failed, but he succeeded in finding his own form, and this for the benefit of the Arabians too[28]. The Arabian character of the Umayyad Empire—the same development as can be followed in *kitāb futūḥ al-buldān*—is thus underlined, though without any idea of a denunciation of Mu'āwiya; he had personal weaknesses, but his régime is not discriminated.

Anti-Umayyad tendencies in an absolute sense will be looked for in vain in this description of Mu'āwiya. Traditions of an observance patently hostile to the Umayyads do occur, but they are in most cases balanced by comparable counter-traditions[29]. Generally speaking, Balādhurī accepts Mu'āwiya as leader of the pure Arab State—if with but little religious admiration, then no doubt with considerable veneration for his gifts as a ruler, in della Vida's formulation, "come uno dei rappresentanti più tipiche dell'ideale nazionale arabo"[30]. The emphasis on the Arab aristocracy's domination in Umayyad time, culminating under 'Abd al-Malik, has thus begun here. Reversely, it will in this connexion be of great importance to discover how Balādhurī appraises the transition from 'Alī's—also in his opinion—religiously stamped caliphate to the "Arabian Monarchy" in the chaotic years after 'Uthmān's death. Immediately, Balādhurī's description of this period will appear confused, and it is difficult to deduce from it a common denominator of his view of Mu'āwiya's showdown with 'Alī: he knows and publishes both the Kufic version of 'Alī's breach with the Syrian governor immediately after the caliph election; the earlier Kufic version

25 Bal.: Mu'āw., no. 8.

26 *Ibid.*, no.s 3–4.

27 *Ibid.*, no. 1; no. 72.

28 *Ibid.*, no. 131; cf. no. 176.

29 e.g. the indubitably apocryphal Prophet traditions *pro et contra* Mu'āwiya from Hishām b. 'Ammār and from Shī'i sources: cf. *supra*, pp. 128 *sq*.

30 Bal.: *Mu'āw.*, introduzione, xii *sq*.

of Jarīr b. ʿAbdallāh's mission; Abū Mikhnaf's rendering of the exchange of notes between the Caliph and the governor; the Syrian-Medinese accounts from Ṣāliḥ b. Kaysān and az-Ẓuhrī concerning the development of the conflict; and, finally, both the Kufic and the pro-Syrian version of the arbitration meeting, all in a manner that makes it difficult to isolate his personal opinion.

In Balādhurī the account of ʿAlī's application to Muʿāwiya is not in the nature of an ultimatum[31]; his idea must be to stress that ʿAlī merely demanded *bayʿa* from the Syrian governor without any intention of interfering in his governorship. This is further borne out by his supplementing this report with Ṣāliḥ b. Kaysān's statement that ʿAlī was disposed to let Muʿāwiya keep his post[32]. This is entirely consonant with Balādhurī's not linking Ṭalḥa's and az-Zubayr's revolt up with that of Muʿāwiya, for he states, on the contrary and with the Syrian-Medinese version as his source, that the latter did not take up arms until after the battle of the Camel, although he had contemplated launching the action of vengeance earlier[33]. Here Balādhurī repeats—i.e. at a time after the battle of the Camel—without *isnād*, but in the primary from, the report of Jarīr b. ʿAbdallah's mission to Damascus and Abū Mikhnaf's circumstantial exchange of notes[34]. It is noteworthy, however, that in Balādhurī it is now again Muʿāwiya who initiates the vengeance action. It is he who persuades Shuraḥbīl b. as-Simṭ to muster the Syrians' support in rejecting ʿAlī's demand for *bayʿa* because Muʿāwiya must above all avenge ʿUthmān's blood. The information of Muʿāwiya's agreement with ʿAmr b. al-ʿĀṣ, on the other hand, dwindles into a secondary consequence of his breach with the caliph[35].

Balādhurī's depiction of the war preparations and of the battle at Ṣiffīn does not differ essentially from Ṭabari's, they are both utterly dependent upon Abū Mikhnaf[36]. The most noticeable divergence consists in Balādhurī being considerably briefer; unlike Ṭabari[37], he has nothing at all about the Quran readers' attempts to settle the conflict before the battle at Ṣiffīn, and he also ignores Abū Mikhnaf's description of the beginning discord in ʿAlī's camp brought on by the Syrians' appealing to the Quran. Instead of these he makes

31 Bal. 467v–68r (Caetani IX, 19), from Abū Mikhnaf.

32 Bal. 468r–v (Caetani IX, 19 *sq.*). Apart from this detail, Balādhurī sets the Syrian version apart for the present.

33 Bal. 504v, 514v–15r (Caetani IX, 289, 488 *sq.*); cf. Bal.: *Muʿāw.*, no. 270 (from al-Madāinī) where b. ʿAbbās uses the same arguments as al-Walīd b. ʿUqba and such other persons as had written to Muʿāwiya concerning the murder and the vengeance (cf. Caetani IX, 36 A.H., §§ 342 and 353). It is presumably a question of a construction over the verses in the passages first quoted.

34 Bal. 494v–97r (Caetani IX, 253 *sq.*).

35 Bal. 498r–99v (della Vida, 453 and Caetani IX, 242 note 1).

36 cf. della Vida, 458 *sqq.*

37 Incidentally, also in contrast to Dīnawarī and b. al-Kathīr.

a great point of the tribal splits and the ensuing embittered struggles[38]. He inserts pro-Syrian accounts into this context in order to point out that Mu'āwiya did not lay claim to the caliphate, but merely sought vengeance for 'Uthmān; that he contents himself with receiving homage in the capacity of *Amīr* and with demanding a new caliph election, i.e. he considers 'Alī as having compromised himself by his attitude[39].

Balādhurī has borrowed the introductory part of his version of the Adhruḥ meeting from Ṣāliḥ b. Kaysān[40], and supplemented it with some variants of Abū Mikhnaf's[41]. It is impossible to determine which of the two renderings Balādhurī preferred, and it is in fact unlikely that the question was a decisive one for himself or for his assessment of the events, nor is there any reason for supposing that he has distinguished beetwen successive meetings. The crux of the matter is rather that 'Alī, irrespective of what course the arbitration hearings might have taken, was the loosing part owing to both 'Amr b. al-'Āṣ's ingenious manoeuvres and difficulties with the Khārijites.

In the first place, Balādhurī supplements Ṣāliḥ b. Kaysān's account of the arbitration negotiations with two apocryphal stories from Nāfi', 'Umar's *mawlā*, according to which 'Amr, after the negotiations with Abū Mūsā, outmanoeuvres 'Abdallāh b. 'Umar by offering him bribes for withdrawing his candidature for the caliphate[42]. Balādhurī, in an otherwise unknown tradition, goes on to say that 'Abdallah b. 'Abbās had warned 'Alī against dispatching Abū Mūsā; he had volunteered to undertake the negotiations himself for fear of the Syrians' ruses. 'Alī had turned down the offer, but regretted having done so on learning the outcome of the negotiations[43]. These traditions are no doubt both due to a late pro-Abbasid rationalization *post eventum*, and both serve to bring out the contrast between 'Alī's good will and his impotence.

In the second place, the account of the arbitration meeting is linked up very closely with the Khārijite revolt. Still, Balādhurī passes over Abū Mikhnaf's concatenation of this and the formation of a *shī'at 'Alī*[44]; instead, he takes his stand on ash-Sha'bī's rather non-committal view that "the majority (of 'Alī's men) did indeed approve of the appointment of arbitrators"; they consider arbitration a reasonable solution, despite the facts that 'Alī would have preferred to meet the Khārijites' desire for a resumption of the battle[45], and that Sahl

38 Bal. 513v–14r (Caetani IX, 487). He devotes especially much space to 'Ammār b. Yāsir's —the future Khārijite hero's—and 'Ubaydallāh b. 'Umar's death (cf. Caetani IX, 485 *sqq.*).

39 Bal. 514v–16v (Caetani IX, 488 *sqq.*).

40 Bal. 521v–23r (Caetani X, 28 *sqq.*); no reference to az-Zuhrī here.

41 Bal. 525v–27r (Caetani X, 19 *sqq.*, 22 *sqq.*).

42 Bal. 523r (Caetani X, 31 *sq.*).

43 Bal. 524r (Caetani X, 34); cf. *'Iqd* II, 291 and Bayhaqī: *Mah.*, 399 (Caetani 38 A.H., § 29).

44 cf. *supra*, p. 59.

45 Bal. 519v–20r (Caetani IX, 545).

b. Ḥunayf, the Medinese governor, also, in an otherwise unknown tradition, notes the extraordinary circumstance of not deciding a matter by force of arms[46]. This view, with Sāliḥ b. Kaysān as the source, is elaborated to the effect that the Iraqis did not want to anticipate the procedure until they had seen whether the Caliph would accept an unreasonable solution by the arbitration[47]. From here Balādhurī immediately proceeds to the arbitration meeting into which he interpolates an account of b. ʿUmar's attitude; he then continues with the report that after the Ṣiffīn battle ʿAlī returned to Kufa on 20th Rabīʿ I (37 A.H.=5th Sept. 657) and remained there for seven months (i.e. until about the 20th Shawwāl 37 A.H.=about 31st March 658) engrossed in administrative duties and the trouble with the Khārijites, until Muʿāwiya in Ramaḍān 37 A.H. (10th February–11th March 658) reminded him of his obligation to attend the arbitration hearing[48]. The reaction to the dispatch of Abū Mūsā consisted in the Khārijites' final breach with ʿAlī, and their election of ʿAbdallah b. Wahb to *Imām* on the 10th Shawwāl (21st March 658). After the futile arbitration meeting ʿAlī again urged the Khārijites to come back, and in Muḥarram 38 A.H. (9th June–8th July) he took the field against them until the battle at an-Nahrawān was joined on the 9th Ṣafar 38 A.H. (17th July 658)[49].

The immediate impression from Balādhurī's depiction of the events after an-Nahrawān is of a strongly marked process of dissolution that reaches its culmination with the murder of ʿAlī. The Caliph is encumbered with the worship of his adherents—among whom ʿAbdallāh b. Saba'[50]—and his preparations for a renewed fight against the Syrians are being interrupted by the constant Khārijite turbulence, and Khirrīt b. Rashīd's revolt[51]. The progressive disintegration is further—and more elaborately than done by Ṭabarī—illustrated by a series of Syrian-inspired attacks on ʿAlī's bases in the Arabian peninsula and Mesopotamia, and, finally the fall of Egypt[52]. In consequence hereof Muʿāwiya now finds that things have developed in his favour so much that there is no need at all for him to intervene[53].

Particularly significant is Balādhurī's consistent assertion that Muʿāwiya's

46 Bal. 524r (Caetani IX, 490).

47 Bal. 521v (Caetani IX, 545 *sq.*).

48 Bal. 523v–24r (Caetani X, 32 *sq.*).

49 Bal. 531r–32r (Caetani X, 101 *sqq.*).

50 Bal. 542r (Caetani X, 107; cf. della Vida, 495); cf. again Bal. 585 (= Jāḥiẓ: *Bayān* II, 73; Friedlaender: *b. Saba'* I, 321 *sqq.*) where Balādhurī once more repudiates the extremist Shīʿism and asserts that "the Alid faith" is founded by some anonymous persons before b. Saba'.

51 On this, Bal. 533v–58r (cf. della Vida, 497), 576v–78r (Caetani X, 192 *sqq.*).

52 Bal. 563v–76r, 579v–86r (Caetani X, 277 *sqq.*, 291 *sqq.*, 318 *sqq.*, 327 *sqq.*; della Vida, 503 *sqq.*).

53 Bal. 542r–v (Caetani X, 107 *sq.*).

acts were not to be ascribed exclusively to ambition, for his primary object in instigating the resistance was vengeance for the blood of ʿUthmān. Right from the start Balādhurī's account of the tumultuous caliph election points out very clearly that it is the leading rebels against ʿUthmān who practically force through ʿAlī's election against his will, and impose upon him an alliance with and sheltering of the murderers[54]. It is his constellation that induces Muʿāwiya to join issue with ʿAlī: "If he hands over to me the murderers of my kinsman and confirms my governorship, I will acknowledge him. This is the only condition on which I can give up the vengeance without becoming a *sūqī*, a humiliated citizen", as Balādhurī has Muʿāwiya declare in a quotation from Muhammad b. Saʿd[55].

Another salient point in Balādhurī's version is his assertion that the majority of the Iraqis approved of the arbitration agreement and that it was the Khārijites who broke the unity in ʿAlī's camp and forced him "to act against his nature"[56]. In other words, ʿAlī is the victim of movements which he himself has, in part, called forth, and which he cannot control. Balādhurī fully acknowledges the legitimacy of his caliphate; however, when the defection set in he had no choice but to draw his sword, an action that God had revealed to Muhammad[57]. There is, reversely, an obvious difference between the revolt of Muʿāwiya and the defection of the Khārijites, for while the latter give rise to the definitive process of dissolution, Muʿāwiya's proceeding is justified qua vengeance action, and his final victory favoured by the inner disintegration of ʿAlī's power. Balādhurī thus views the legitimacy of the Umayyad caliphate in a conciliatory spirit; he does not dispute their title to the caliphate, but stresses quite unsentimentally the Khārijites' responsibility.

Balādhurī's version appears at the same time to conduct a defence of the Abbasids—here most frequently identified with Banū Hāshim. Balādhurī still points to b. ʿAbbās's loyality, but makes no secret of his leaving ʿAlī in 38 A.H.; the "flight" is not, however, linked up with any decisive events, but with Abu-l-Aswad al-Duʾalī's accusation of malversation, an occurence with no relevance to the political course of events[58]. Balādhurī establishes that the Umayyads cannot justifiably accuse b. ʿAbbās of complicity in ʿUthmān's fate or blame him for supporting the one that had provided asylum for the murderers—in-

54 Bal. 465v (della Vida, 435).

55 Bal. 502r; cf. 494r–v (Caetani IX, 284 *sq.*, 253) and the opening words in Muʿāwiya's *vita*, Bal.; *Muʿāw.*, p. 1.

56 Bal. 542v (Caetani X, 108).

57 Bal. 453v–54r; cf. b. al-Athīr IV, 30 *sq.* (Caetani X, 404).

58 It is stated direct that b. ʿAbbās still followed ʿAlī after the battle at an-Nahrawān, "although other sources assert that he left him before then" (Bal. 552r without *isnād*; Caetani X, 225).

dubitably reflections of the charges preferred against ʿAlī—because Muʿāwiya's own conduct was equivocal and because he hesitated about the vengeance[59]. The primary concern of these traditions is, however, the justification of b. ʿAbbās, a late and secondary phenomenon in the tradition that does not constitute an absolute touchstone by which to appraise Balādhurī's view of b. ʿAbbās's relations with Muʿāwiya. He often—and then generally with ʿAwāna as his source—makes b. ʿAbbās recognize Muʿāwiya's services, information which is not found in other historians, and which here naturally becomes invested with a special authority, even though the author makes no secret of the Caliph's partiality for the good things of this world, and even though his recognition of the Caliph's capability as a ruler obtains a touch of gall and wormwood: "no one is worthier than he (Muʿāwiya) to be king, *malik*"[60].

A provinsional recapitulation of our analysis of Balādhurī's asssessment of the conflict will show beyond doubt that underlying his apparent impartiality lurks a conscious tendency. He accepts, of course, the legitimacy of ʿAlī's caliphate, and likewise that not only ʿAlī but also Abū Bakr and ʿUmar were better qualified religiously for the office of caliph than ʿUthmān and Muʿāwiya[61]. The distinction between the religiously infused caliphate and the *mulk* of the Umayyads is thus maintained[62]. On the other hand, he does not challenge the legitimacy of the Umayyad caliphate, and he gives its strength unqualified recognition. It was ʿAlī's heritage from ʿUthmān and the inner disintegration of the foundation for his power that paved the way for Muʿāwiya. When the defection of the Khārijites deprived ʿAlī of general recognition it was not unlawful for Muʿāwiya to receive homage inasmuch as both al-Ḥasan b. ʿAlī and ʿAbdallāh b. ʿAbbās accepted him. Balādhurī respects the legitimacy of the Umayyad caliphate even if he is not personally sympathetic towards the Syrian rulers.

It is, on the other hand, particularly difficult to place Balādhurī's work in its temporal coherence. Among the Arabic historians he is indubitably the one that comes nearest to the historical reality, but that is of little significance in this respect, even though his balanced judgment was fully recognized by his contemporaries. Balādhurī had a very large material at his disposal, and his disposition of it in his own sovereign manner makes him absolutely outstanding among the classical Arabic historical writers. The employment of his sources is extremely ingenious; his exposition of ʿAlī's caliphate rests mainly on concatenation of his excerpts from Abū Mikhnaf's writings and the Syrian-Medinese

59 Bal.: *Muʿāw.*, no.s 255, 270, 334.

60 *Ibid.*, no.s 124, 128, 134, 227, 231, 236.

61 cf. *ibid.* no. 270.

62 cf. Bal.: *Futūḥ*, 462 (Hitti-Murgotten II, 257), in which he has the narrative of Muhammad's signet-ring.

tradition with Ṣāliḥ b. Kaysān and az-Zuhrī as the final authorities. Even if Balādhurī in rare instances carries traditions—such as 'Īsā b. Yazīd's or Hishām b. 'Ammār's—that are, and perceived by himself to be, apocryphal, his precision is, also by a temporaneous yardstick, of a very high standard, often better than Ṭabarī's, and his renderings are normally quite loyal. It is particularly noteworthy that, in contrast to Ṭabarī, he prefers the original source to the later adaptation whether he has direct or indirect knowledge of it; he made his way back to Abū Mikhnaf, whereas Ṭabarī preferred the muddled source, Sayf b. 'Umar, and merely supplemented with the purer sources.

On proceding to his depiction of Mu'āwiya's caliphate we find—as mentioned above—his exposition undergoing a change of character; Balādhurī gives no consecutive description and even passes over important events; instead, he analyses. His main source is here al-Madā'inī, presumably his *kitāb akhbār al-khulafā' al-kabīr*, which constitutes the basis for 221, or 55 per cent., of the 405 traditions of this section. 30 of these traditions are culled from 'Awāna, 24 from Hishām b. Muhammad al-Kalbī, and 27 from al-Haytham b. 'Adī. It is remarkable that Abū Mikhnaf and az-Zuhrī, Ṭabarī's chief informants, are not quoted[63]. In comparison with al-Madā'inī all other sources are of minor importance within this section[64]. In the preceding sections, too, al-Madā'inī is a major informant to Balādhurī[65], but there only in the capacity of transmitter of the Kufic tradition.

Methodically, Balādhurī's analytical or, if you like: dialectical, procedure is no doubt related to al-Madā'inī's polemic collocating of pro-Umayyad narratives and his personal refutation. Balādhurī's deviation from al-Madā'inī in depiction of the *fitna* must, then, be due to divergent interpretation. To all appearances they were in unison in having the breach between 'Alī and Mu'āwiya dated after the battle of the Camel, the only difference being that Balādhurī here prefers the evidence of the Syrian-Medinese tradition, which al-Madā'inī passes over. Balādhurī also views 'Abdallāh b. 'Abbās in much the same light as his teacher did[66]. A more marked dissimilarity appears in the reading of the events after Ṣiffīn: al-Madā'inī asserts explicitly that the Khārijite rising is provoked by the arbitration award and 'Amr's treachery, whereas Balādhurī

63 az-Zuhrī is, however, cited on one occasion.

64 ad-Dimashqī, al-'Umarī, and Muhammad b. Sa'd are quoted most frequently: 32, 20, and 12 times respectively.

65 In the section on 'Uthmān's caliphate (Jerusalem edition vol. V) al-Madā'inī is quoted 163 times, i.e. more frequently than any other source; Bal.: Ans. V, introduction, 14 *sq.*; cf. della Vida, 430.

66 Both stress b. 'Abbās's loyality to 'Alī—in which respect Balādhurī builds direct on his teacher—and they are likewise in agreement that it is 'Ubaydallah b. 'Abbās, and not his brother, that joined Mu'āwiya during al-Ḥasan's short-lived caliphate (de Goeje, 392 *sq.*; Wellhausen: *Kingdom*, 109).

hardly rejects the validity of the arbitration meeting, but lays emphasis on the Khārijites' responsibility for the disintegration of ʿAlī's caliphate. The main point is, we think, that Balādhurī no longer shares in, or is able to maintain, the Kufic transmission's discrimination of the Umayyads, and so has nothing to glean from al-Madā'inī in maintaining the justification of Muʿāwiya's campaign for blood vengeance, and he also, therefore, ignores a long series of traditions on Muʿāwiya's caliphate that Ṭabarī borrowed from al-Madā'inī[67].

A salient feature in Balādhurī's physiognomy is seen to be that he recognizes the legality of the Umayyad caliphate and its effective rule; he thus naturally avoids any hiatus in the continuity of the caliphate from the early caliphs to the Abbasids. This line is quite in keeping with the general trend during the reaction against Muʿtazilism under al-Mutawakkil (847–61), a movement that found expression in Ḥanbalism. This is not to say that Balādhurī was a Ḥanbalite, even if his traditional technique, his quotations from the Ḥanbali Basrians of the pro-Umayyad tradition, and his recognition of the Syrian dynasty might seem to indicate impulses from this movement.

More telling, it seems to me, is another aspect of the same question, namely Balādhurī's showdown with Shīʿism's biased extolling of ʿAlī, and consequently also with the Muʿtazilite period's attempts to create a compromise with the pro-ʿAlī tendencies. In the same way he is nothing but consistent in deprecating the effacement of the Arab elements in Islam's earliest history, again in keeping with the general tendency of that time. His accentuation of the Arabian caliphate's absolute power can at any rate be regarded as expressive of tendencies in the viewpoints of the Abbasid caliphate in its period of disintegration. It is noteworthy that Balādhurī's narrative is brought to a conclusion almost at the time when, under al-Manṣūr, the Arab influences are beginning to give way to the Barmakids' rule, the growth of the Persian bureaucracy, and, subsequently, the Turkish military régime. There is in his work an Arab self-assertion, not in any aggressive way, but implied in its very accentuation of the grandeur of the Arabian empire. It is, moreover, a work that carries on the earlier genealogical studies and Muhammad b. Saʿd's biographical work in systematical form. Both Balādhurī's books are imbued with strict poise and admirable consistency, without doubt the best products of early Islamic historical writing.

67 cf. e.g. Wellhausen: *Kingdom,* 119, 127, 143 *sq.*—A certain divergence may naturally arise in that Balādhurī quotes Madā'inī as the latter's pupil, while ʿUmar b. Shabba (d. 875) is the normal transmitter to Ṭabarī, who is one generation younger. In Muʿāwiya's *vita* Balādhurī quotes b. Shabba only once.

3. Aṭ-Ṭabarī (d. 923)

Ṭabarī's production is above all distinguished for its vast proportions and its comprehensiveness, the fruits of such knowledge and experience as he had acquired during his journeys to the old seats of learning: Baghdad—where he resided—, Basra, Kufa, in Syria and in Egypt[1]. His economic independence, in contrast to, for instance, Balādhurī, appears to have enabled him, after his years of study, to devote himself entirely to his authorship. As a jurist of Shāfiʿite observance, though with his own physiognomy, he hardly acquired much importance[2]. But his Quran exegesis, *Jāmiʿ al-bayān fī tafsīr al-qurʾān*, and his historical writing, *taʾrīkh ar-rusul waʾl mulūk*, enjoyed an almost canonical validity, and has, like so many classical works, been maltreated by commentators and popularizers. His exegetic work represents at one and the same time an attempt to summarize what according to the criterion of his days was the authoritative traditionalistic exegetics of the Quran and to produce a book that would create an orthodox systematics with definite dissociation from Khārijites and extremist Shiites, whose testimony he entirely rejects[3]. Methodically, Ṭabarī's *tafsīr* is more remarkable for its sober, lexical, grammatical and historical commentaries than for its dogmatical originality. Characteristically his work rests on strict and narrow knowledge as evolved in the philological and historical schools; he builds upon the *sunna* of the Prophet, the Prophet Companions and Prophet Followers, supplemented with the orthodox *ijmāʿ*. His outlook is thus seen to be basically conservative[4].

The general principles that Ṭabarī adopts in his tafsir are likewise applied to his historical authorship, which in point of time seems to be of a later date than the Quran exegesis, and a kind of supplement to it[5]. Assuming this to be so we have at the same time a plausible explanation of his having disposed his work

1 On Ṭabarī, see *GAL* I, 142 *sq.*; *(S)* I, 217 *sqq.*; R. Paret in *E. I.*[1] IV,625 *sq.*; Margoliouth: *Lectures*, 101 *sqq.*

2 Only his harsh judgment of b. Ḥanbal is of significance in this connexion.

3 Goldziher: *Islam*, 50 *sqq.* He has, however, not entirely avoided influence from Shiite and Muʿtazilite points of view.

4 *Ibid.*, 52, 57 *sq.*

5 Margoliouth: *Lectures*, 101.

annalistically; year by year and event by event he builds up his exposition by means of—often several—parallel or co-ordinate traditions, normally supplemented with comments of his own; he lays down categorically how each event is to be placed and interpreted. This is one reason why Ṭabarī gives his reader, immediately and overwhelmingly, the impression of final authority.

The problems to which Ṭabarī's sources and his handling of them give rise have often been objects of study, most exhaustively by Wellhausen and Caetani. A demonstration of his sources does not occasion such difficulties as occur in the cases of Dīnawarī and Ya'qūbī, whose coherent literary presentations are without references. Ṭabarī follows the conservative traditional technique, and he does it fairly loyally; even his occasional tendentious abridgements will hardly reveal any actual falsification. The difficulties do not appear until we are to explain his peculiar choice of sources, and especially why he in long passages prefers a corrupt source like Sayf b. 'Umar to the pure ones, Abū Mikhnaf, 'Awāna and others, which he knows and frequently employs[6]. It applies generally that Ṭabarī's depiction of the revolution against 'Uthmān and of the first year of 'Alī's caliphate follows Sayf, and that his discussion on the preparations for the showdown between the Caliph and Mu'āwiya entirely follows Abū Mikhnaf, merely now and then interrupted by other sources. His description of the later part of 'Alī's rule thus acquires the character of a paraphrase of Abū Mikhnaf with rare and comparatively subordinate comments from other versions. Normally Ṭabarī quotes Abū Mikhnaf without transmitter[7]; like Balādhurī he probably builds upon his writings, an assumption that is borne out by the fact that he often, also where the exposition is broken by varying retrospective *isnāds*, follows the logical coherence in Abū Mikhnaf's depiction.

As regards the first years of 'Alī's caliphate the factual contents of the exposition are, however, entirely shifted by his quotations from Sayf b. 'Umar. His procedure may be defined by saying that for this period he follows Sayf as the chief version, but also quotes Wāqidī or 'Umar b. Shabba (d. 875) and the latter's informant, al-Madā'inī[8], as a variant of or, if you prefer: corrective

6 Strictly speaking, this problem is a personal rather than a critical-methodical one; even though Balādhurī shows signs of taking as his foundation the earliest tradition, the distinction between primary and secondary source is of course alien to Islamic historical writing. It would in this connexion, we think, be correct to say that it is the personal motives underlying Ṭabarī's selective method that require explanation.

7 Hishām b. Muhammad al-Kalbī is met with only sporadically as intermediary link, and then normally as regards specific details. This applies especially to particulars concerning the battle at Ṣiffīn (Tab. I. 3259–60, 3315, 3318–19; 3322, Caetani IX, 267, 461 *sqq.*, 466, 468).

8 Wāqidī is quoted mainly in relation to 'Uthmān's history of woe, presumably from his work on Medina. The quotations from 'Umar b. Shabba nearly all relate to the 'Uth-

to, Sayf. Ṭabarī's selection of supplementary sources may of course depend on which work would in the individual case give him the most complete information, though a more likely explanation seems to be that Ṭabarī used Madā'inī and Wāqidī as *opinio communis* in the generation after Sayf in order to elucidate, elaborate and modify the latter's categorical assertions, for the quotations from Wāqidī and Madā'inī cease at the very time when Ṭabarī leaves Sayf as the chief source. In the case of 'Umar b. Shabba—a Basrian historian with Shiite inclinations and with a faiblesse for the historical anecdote—Ṭabarī apparently selects traditions from Madā'inī that bear the impress of a moderate defence of 'Alī. They may be traditions with indirect accusations of 'Ā'isha[9] or narratives to demonstrate that Basra "out of respect for the Prophet" and 'Alī dissociate themselves from the 'Uthmāniyya, the fact notwitstanding that az-Zubayr invokes Muhammad's prophecy of the *fitna*[10].

There is hardly any reason to question Ṭabarī's confidence in Sayf b. 'Umar's version of the events. By building upon the latter's works on the *ridda* and the Arab expansion and on the *fitna* Ṭabarī's rendering has incurred a fatal lopsidedness, as demonstrated by Wellhausen. We may here add that Ṭabarī wrote perhaps a decade or two later than Balādhurī, Dīnawarī and Ya'qūbī did, and must be supposed to have been aware of their existence. It is indeed remarkable that he entirely went his own way at a time when Balādhurī's writings were at his disposal. He knew the Syrian-Medinese version, but suppresses it almost completely; he builds—paradoxically—principally upon such passages in Abū Mikhnaf as Balādhurī passes over, and chooses a particularly one-sided source for his chief version in sections of fundamental importance. The indications, then, are that his choice of sources was deliberate and, perhaps, also in contrast to that of his predecessors.

It is, on the other hand, obvious that Ṭabarī was unable to follow Sayf b. 'Umar's line of thought through consistently; he breaks off abruptly after

māniyya revolt and are probably taken from his topographical works on Basra and Kufa, which Ṭabarī cites elsewhere (*GAL* I, 137). Other sources—e.g. az-Zuhrī or ash-Sha'bī, sometimes also Shiites like al-Jarmī and Naṣr b. Muzāḥim—are used very sporadically. —As examples of Ṭabarī's special disposition may be mentioned his description of the beginning 'Uthmāniyya rising, where Sayf (Tab. I. 3091–3101, 3102, 3104–05) by means of 'Umar b. Shabba and one or two other sources (Tab. I. 3101–02, 3102–04, 3105–06) is emended; or the depiction of Mu'āwiya's contract with 'Amr, and Jarīr b. 'Abdallāh's sojourn in Syria, in which instance Sayf (Tab. I. 3249–52, 3255) is supplemented with Wāqidī and 'Umar b. Shabba (I. 3252–55, 3255–56). There is thus hardly reason to assume, as H. A. R. Gibb does (*Studies in Islamic Civilization*, 118) that Ṭabarī preferred Sayf to Wāqidī because the latter's viewpoints were stigmatized as heretical.—On 'Umar b. Shabba, see the references *supra* p. 92, note 45.

9 e.g. Tab. I. 3101–02, 3126, 3134, 3137–38 (Caetani IX, 53, 56, 58, 61).

10 Tab. I. 3136–40, 3143–44 (Caetani IX, 60 *sq.*, 119 *sqq.*).

the description of the battle of the Camel, and the last information he culled from this source concerns the contract of Muʿāwiya and ʿAmr, whereupon the variant quotations from Wāqidī and Madāʾinī are discontinued, too. And the way in which this happens is likewise characteristic. To Sayf's information that after the battle at Basra as-Sabaʾiyya began to intrigue behind ʿAlī's back and that the first germs of the Khārijite opposition were breaking through[11] Ṭabarī adds *propria auctoritate* that at that very time ʿAlī was shaking himself free of the Shīʿi sect and the pressure it had exerted on his freedom of action, and that the sect left him[12]. Undeniably a rather clumsy method of extricating himself from Sayf's version, but it reveals Ṭabarī's realizing that Sayf's points of view were no longer compatible with his own, whereupon he turns to Abū Mikhnaf and builds upon him.

In his depiction of ʿAlī's election Ṭabarī, in contrast to his normal practice, uses Sayf for supplementation of his other sources. On this controversial point he evidently sets great store by the evidence of eyewitnesses. By means of traditions from Muhammad b. al-Ḥanafiyya and ʿAbdallāh b. ʿAbbās, traditions already proved to be apocryphal, Ṭabarī establishes that with few exeptions *Muhājirūn* and *Anṣār* elected, and the "peoples" swore allegiance to ʿAlī, so that the validity of the election had been decided in an orthodoxically satisfactory manner[13]. He next ascertains on the basis of Madāʾinī and a single quotation from az-Zuhrī that Ṭalḥa and az-Zubayr joined in the oath of allegiance, "although some say that ... (they) swore allegiance against their will"[14]. Only then does Ṭabarī return to Sayf, who is made use of for dating the election and for establishing the antagonisms between the Prophet Companions and as-Sabaʾiyya, whose discontent "already (then) was instrumental in fostering discords and tumults among them"[15]. All these instances and the one exception go to show how Sayf's information forms a deliberate part of Ṭabarī's plan; the employment both of Sayf's exposition and of the variants from Wāqidī and Madāʾinī must have been very carefully arranged beforehand.

The moderating additions notwithstanding, Ṭabarī's treatment of ʿAlī's first years as caliph is strongly influenced by Sayf b. ʿUmar's judgment. By means of Wāqidī and the purely Shiite Abū Hilāl[16] Ṭabarī stresses that ʿAlī cannot for the sake of opportunism set aside his religious prestige by continuing ʿUthmān's governors in office. At a later stage he endeavours similarly, on

11 Tab. I. 3226–27 (Caetani IX, 199).

12 Tab. I. 3230 (Caetani IX, 150 *sq.*).

13 Tab. I. 3066–67 (Caetani VIII, 321 *sqq.*). On the corrupt traditions see *AO* XXVII, 111; on the orthodox caliph doctrine, see E. Tyan s. v. *bayʿa* in E. *I.*² I, 1113 *sq.* and *infra* p. 164.

14 Tab. I. 3067–72 (Caetani VIII, 322 *sqq.*).

15 cf. Ṭabarī's conclusion I. 3078, lin. 5–8 (Caetani VIII, 335).

16 Tab. I. 3083–85 and 3085–86 respectively (Caetani VIII, 339 *sqq.*).

authority from both Abū Bakr al-Hudhalī and az-Zuhrī, to show that immediately before the battle of the Camel ʿAlī was still urging his adversaries to have the Quran settle their difference[17]. In other words, he emphasizes ʿAlī's will to ward off the civil war; on the other hand, his quotations from Sayf serve to demonstrate that it is the rabid ʿAlī adherents who continually hinder him in reaching his object. In this way Ṭabarī's purpose is perceptible. He shares Sayf's assertion that the conflicts were instigated by as-Sabaʾiyya, but makes a much greater point of justifying ʿAlī. To him it is no longer just a question of placing the responsibility for the *fitna*, but also of demonstrating that ʿAlī and the Medinese and Iraqian circles that stood behind his caliphate possessed the will to take an independent and religiously pure line despite the extremist Shiites' sabotage. He maintains—presumably in contrast to Sayf—that ʿAlī did free himself of their trammels, though a true *shīʿat ʿAlī* did not materialize until the Khārijites seceded after Ṣiffīn[18].

On the other hand, the application of Sayf b. ʿUmar as the main source has inevitably exerted an influence also as regards Ṭabarī's treatment of ʿAlī's relations with Muʿāwiya. With Sayf as his source he saw the breach with the Syrian governor as irrevocable from ʿAlī's appeal directly after his election. Characteristically, he quotes no variants on this occasion; on the contrary, he emphasizes that religious sense of propriety must demand the immediate removal of Muʿāwiya from his post, needless to try to "lead them (the Syrians) to the watering place that they themselves have left"[19]. "God has entrusted the ascendancy *(sulṭān)* over Islam to us", as Ṭabarī makes ʿAlī declare in his summons to fight against the Syrians; "may be God by their help will repair the damage which the people from provinces *(ahl al-āfāq)* have caused"[20].

It is, therefore, understandable that Ṭabarī did not find it expedient to use Abū Mikhnaf's version of the exchange of notes between the two parties after the battle of the Camel, and that the application of Sayf could still affect his treatment of ʿAlī's and Muʿāwiya's showdown. ʿAmr b. al-ʿĀṣ's agreement with Muʿāwiya is, under the influence of Wāqidī and Sayf, dated prior to the arrival of Jarīr b. ʿAbdallāh, and the initiative is again transferred to ʿAmr himself. Just as in the sources, so also here: Through the prophecy of a Jewish rabbi ʿAmr has previous knowledge of the outcome of the conflict and can consequently ignore such religious considerations as might otherwise argue against this alliance; "in this year", Ṭabarī concludes, "ʿAmr gave recognition to Muʿāwiya and agreed with him to wage war on ʿAlī"[21]. Muʿāwiya's aim is

17 Tab. I. 3175–76, 3184–87 (Caetani IX, 134 *sqq.*).
18 Tab. I. 3350–51 (Caetani IX, 542).
19 Tab. I. 3085–86 (Caetani VIII, 338 *sqq.*).
20 Tab. I. 3091–94 (Caetani IX, 24).
21 Tab. I. 3249–54 (Caetani IX, 235 *sqq.*).

thus—by an undeniably inordinate interpretation of the source—already then a foregone conclusion; he is guided by his personal lust for power, and the real object of the conflict, Mu'āwiya's title to blood vengeance, is quite lost sight of. When as-Saba'iyya no longer hinders 'Alī's freedom to move, there is by the same token no longer any hindrance for him to punish 'Uthmān's murderers. Ṭabarī does, however, nowhere in his account of Jarīr's mission to Syria mention Mu'āwiya's insistence on his title to blood vengeance, but keeps narrowly to the caliph's demand for *bay'a*[22]. The initiative in the conflict, then, is althogether attributed to Mu'āwiya and 'Amr; there is no longer need for placability on the part of 'Alī, or for a scapegoat—as-Saba'iyya—to shoulder the responsibility.

Ṭabarī is thus factually in agreement with Abū Mikhnaf as regards dating the breach immediately after the caliph election, but the accusation against Mu'āwiya is aggravated through the shifts which he, like Wāqidī and Sayf b. 'Umar, undertakes after the battle of the Camel; and the report on Jarīr b. 'Abd-allāh, which he has from al-Madā'inī, is evidently meant to serve the same purpose. The rest of Ṭabarī's narrative adheres, as already mentioned, almost slavishly to that of Abū Mikhnaf, an indication that his view of this period did not differ much from the latter's. Assuming the already given interpretation of Abū Mikhnaf to be correct, he has reverted to a defence of the interests of the Abbasids and the Alids, and, conversely, also to the harsh denunciation of the Umayyads, which is in absolute contrast to Balādhurī's attitude. This conception can be sustained by Ṭabarī's chronology as well as by his assessment of 'Abdallāh b. 'Abbās and the Caliph, and of their relationship. As to the chronology, it is again the later part of 'Alī's caliphate that claims our special interest. This applies particularly to the following dates, established by Ṭabarī himself or taken from Abū Mikhnaf:

(1) The date of the arbitration agreement at Ṣiffīn is "according to what is said" set down as Wednesday the 15th Ṣafar 37 A.H. (2nd Aug. 657) with obligation for the arbitrators to meet next Ramaḍān[23].
(2) In that same year the Khārijites secede from 'Alī and his associates[24].
(3) The arbitration meeting is set down for 37 A.H. without further particulars, i.e. before 8th June 658[25].

22 Tab. I. 3254–56 (Caetani IX, 233 *sq.*). As source for Jarīr's mission Ṭabarī quotes 'Awāna, whose version, incidentically, comes very near to ash-Sha'bī's. We cannot, therefore, preclude the possibility, however faint it may appear, that the elimination of Mu'āwiya's motivation may be due to Ṭabarī's *ikhtiṣār*.

23 Tab. I. 3340 (Caetani IX, 481).

24 Tab. I. 3350 (Caetani IX, 541).

25 Tab. I. 3354 (Caetani X, 18). As a variant, which is however not made use of, Ṭabarī mentions (I. 3360) that Wāqidī dates the meeting to Sha'bān 38 A.H.

(4) When the arbitrators part, the Syrians pay homage to Muʿāwiya, whereupon he in 38 A.H. attacks ʿAlī in Egypt, Basra, etc.[26].

(5) The battle at an-Nahrawān is set down for 37 A.H., i.e. still prior to the 8th June 658, but after the arbitration meeting[27].

(6) After the battle at an-Nahrawān many people leave ʿAlī; ʿAbdallāh b. ʿAbbās, however, is still stated to be by his side[28], and not to part from the Caliph until 40 A.H., "which is confirmed by all traditionists"[29].

Ṭabarī's chronology is on the whole according to the customary pattern. It is remarkable, though, that he abridged Abū Mikhnaf's version of b. ʿAbbās's breach with ʿAlī. He omits their exchange of defamatory letters, which in Abū Mikhnaf concluded in b. ʿAbbās's threats of going over to Muʿāwiya. Even if Ṭabarī does not deny his malversation in Basra, he adds in extenuation that b. ʿAbbās took no more than what was owing to him[30]. But then, immediately prior to this, Ṭabarī recounts that "according to what is said, a truce was agreed upon between ʿAlī and Muʿāwiya (in 40 A.H.) after an exchange of letters, which is too extensive to report...(so) that ʿAlī was to have Iraq, and Muʿāwiya Syria". The initiative in this is ascribed to Muʿāwiya[31]. This passage in Ṭabarī, for which he invokes Ziyād b. ʿAbdallāh al-Bakkāʾī (d. 799/800), from Muhammad b. Isḥāq. does not only stand entirely isolated in the Arabic transmission, but is openly contradicted by other sources telling of ʿAlī's difficulties in persuading the Kufians to renewed attacks on Syria, difficulties about which Ṭabarī is practically silent. There is hardly reason to attach any

26 Tab. I. 3396 (Caetani X, 214).

27 cf. Caetani X, 77. In Tab. I. 3387–89 (Caetani X, 99 *sq.*) he states however that the majority of traditionists date the battle to 38 A.H. and quotes the otherwise unknown Abū Maryam's conception in illustration hereof; cf. also Tab. I. 3413–14 (Caetani X, 151 *sq.*).

28 Tab. I. 3340 (ash-Shaʿbī; Caetani X, 187 *sq.*).

29 Tab. I. 3453 (Caetani X, 203). He denies that b. ʿAbbās should have remained with ʿAlī and only left his son al-Ḥasan on the latter's coming to terms with Muʿāwiya (I. 3455–56; Caetani X, 203 *sq.*).

30 Tab. I. 3453–55 (Caetani X, 203 *sq.* and his note 2 to § 222).

31 Tab. I. 3452–53 (Caetani X, 330). The passage quoted *ibid.* in Caetani from Abu-l-Faraj al-Iṣfahānī (*Agh.* X, 157) concerning a certain an-Nābigha's attempt to foster dissension between ʿAlī and Muʿāwiya in order to gain the latter's favour belongs together with Busr b. Abī Arṭāt's expedition to the Ḥijāz and Yemen in that same year. In b. al-Kalbī (*Jamharat al-ansāb*, Brit. Mus. MS., fol. 138r–v; Caetani X, corr. e agg. xxix; cf. also *al-Istīʿāb*, 65 and *Agh.* IV, 131 *sq.*; Caetani *loc. cit.*) this episode is mentioned in this connexion so that the passage cannot in this context be of interest to us. On Ṭabarī's informant, al-Bakkāʾī, who was a pupil of b. Ishāq's, but is otherwise rarely quoted here (cf., however, Tab. I. 3450–52; Caetani X, 307 *sqq.*), see b. Khall., no. 247; Wüstenfeld, no. 35; Rosenthal: *Historiography*, 322; Abbott, 89, 94. Caetani mistakes Abū Isḥāq for b. Isḥāq in the *isnād.*

historical authority to this information, which is presumably due to a misunderstanding or construction on the part of his informants; Ṭabarī's placing it in this context must be seen as an attempt to gloss over b. ʿAbbās's breach with ʿAlī[32]. In its broad outline Ṭabarī's depiction of b. ʿAbbās must in the nature of things bear the mark of his two chief sources, but the overall impression of the honest mentor by the side of ʿAlī stands out here with particular pregnancy; the hero of the Abbasids never did compromise with the Umayyads, but followed ʿAlī loyally until the latter alienated him by his unfounded suspicion, and he refused to make common cause with al-Ḥasan in the latter's compromise with Muʿāwiya[33].

Ṭabarī's judgment of ʿAlī himself follows the lines accounted for in the preceding paragraph insofar as he combines the Prophet biographer, b. Hishām's semi-hagiographical depiction of Muhammad's best and unswerving supporter and associate with the Iraqian tradition's accentuation of his activities as the Prophet's successor[34]. Ṭabarī's assessment corresponds fairly well with that of the Iraqian school and, especially, that of Abū Mikhnaf. Of more significance, though, is the sharp anti-Umayyad tendency ascertainable on several points in Ṭabarī, most clearly perhaps in his treatment of the Syrian rebellion. There can be no doubt that Muʿāwiya's way to the caliphate looked to him illegal usurpation, beginning with the Syrian governor's declaration of open enmity towards ʿAlī, and culminating with his receiving homage as caliph when ʿAmr b. al-ʿĀṣ had outmanoeuvered Abū Mūsā at the arbitration hearing. At the time of Ṭabarī's authorship this sharp accusation may perhaps look somewhat paradoxical. In many ways his standpoint—as will be demonstrated below—approaches the moderate Shiite points of view as formulated by Dīnawarī and Yaʿqūbī, a factor which in conjunction with his uncompromising dissociation from the extremist Shīʿism as he saw it framed in as-Sabaʾiyya may help us in placing Ṭabarī in his temporal relation.

At the time when Ṭabarī wrote his *Annales* the Ismāʿīlitic oppositional movements were superseding Khārijism in Iraq. The Zanj risings 870–83 may still have had a Khārijite character, but from then on the Ismāʿīlitic propaganda makes headway into the lower classes in the countryside as well as towns and comes to stamp the serious revolts of the following period. In this situation the caliphal power, at any rate periodically—and especially when the constellations at the court made it opportune—tried to obtain a compromise with the moderate wing of Shīʿism, a state of affairs that logically led to the very unstable social and political balance during the following generations until the middle of the 10th century.

32 cf. Wellhausen: *Kingdom*, 104 *sqq.*, whose conjectures do not seem tenable.

33 cf. *Ibid.*, 108 note 1.

34 Sarasin, 30 *sqq.*

Though Ṭabarī never wrote under official or semi-official auspices, his standpoint in the *Annales* as well as in the Quran exegesis corresponds very well with the status of orthodoxy in this situation. It is certain that the high repute in which he was held by his contemporaries gave great weight to his pronouncements; this is attested to by the wrath of Ḥanbalism in retaliation for his attacks on them[35] as well as by the available reports on riot at his funeral in Baghdad because he was accused of having had Shiite sympathies[36]. It would be postulatory to assert that such anti-Umayyad tendencies as we find in him were directed against Balādhurī's point of view; a direct polemic is nowhere ascertainable. It is, however, beyond doubt that his attacks on Muʿāwiya for usurpation are aimed at the views prevailing in Islam, among which those of the Ḥanbali school. Like the latter, Ṭabarī makes a point of substantiating his assertions by traditions that are traced back to contemporaries, but in contrast to the Ḥanbalites he also makes a point of demonstrating that from the outset Muʿāwiya nourished ambitions of power which had nothing to do with, for instance, Balādhurī's argumentation that he acted legally in his capacity of ʿUthmān's *walī*.

In order to make his point Ṭabarī must revert to the old Iraqian tradition from the end of the 8th century, in Abū Mikhnaf in its pure, and in Sayf b. ʿUmar in a corrupt pro-Abbasid form, and sometimes resort to rather flagrant suppressions of facts[37]. In this respect, too, his standpoint—apart from the consideration of basic principles—can most aptly be compared with the Ḥanbali school's reversion to the Syrian-Medinese tradition, with the one difference that, unlike Ṭabari or Sayf, this school does not attempt to explain away the historical distribution of responsibility. Historiographically the method employed by Ṭabarī can hardly be said to represent any improvement. His rendering bears unmistakable witness of defence of the Abbasids and ʿAlī[38]; the orthodox stand is carried through less independently than was the case in his *tafsīr*, and his work lacks Balādhurī's cogency.

Tabarī's most personal contribution—also in relation to the Ḥanbalites—consists in the large-scale plan of universal history in *Annales*. And even though he (again as in his Quran exegesis) is extremely conservative and yet creates an

35 R. Paret in *E. I.*[1] IV, 625. It is characteristical that Ṭabarī in his *Annales* avoids as far as possible mentioning the Ḥanbalites' combat against the Muʿtazilism under al-Ma'mūn and his successors.

36 Margoliouth: *Lectures*, 101 *sq.*, 108.

37 cf. Wellhausen: *Prolegomena*, 144 *cum* note 2. Ṭabarī himself does not, incidentally, make any secret of his suppressing many painful things.

38 On his pro-Abbasid sympathies as illustrated by his depiction of the Abbasid revolution and settlement, see S. Moscati in *Rend. Lincei* ser. VIII:4 (1949), 323 *sqq.*, 474 *sqq.*; VIII:5 (1950), 89 *sqq.*

exposition that provides orthodoxy with a lasting ballast, it is his conspicuous merit to have given substance to the universalist basic points of view formulated by the Prophet, consistently and on an orthodox foundation. Ṭabarī's synthesis in many ways fulfils the needs of his own and next following generations better than Balādhurī's tribute to the glory of the Arab Empire, or the Ḥanbalites'—perhaps Utopian—idealism, approaches that could hardly any longer compel the same interest as Ṭabarī's attempt to place the *fitna* in the context of his own time.

4. Ad-Dīnawarī (d. ca. 895)

It is very difficult to keep track of the Shiite tradition in the 9th century. After Naṣr b. Muzāḥim's death (828) there is a marked void in our knowledge of the transmission, one reason being that such shiitizing authors as ad-Dīnawarī and al-Ya'qūbī (d. 897) differ from other historians in that they do not quote their informants. We know for certain that Shī'i or shitizing historical writing —presumably with its centre still remaining in Kufa—did exist, and in a few instances we know the names of the transmitters, but beyond that practically nothing; its framework and contents have vanished. This period has hardly seen any traditionist that might be considered to be bearer or transmitter of the Shiite tradition in the sense that Naṣr b. Muzāḥim had been. Part of the explanation may conceivably be found in the incorporation of the Kufic transmission into the orthodox tradition, or the pro-'Alī tendencies of Mu'talizism may have rendered superflous at any rate a special, moderate Shī'i tradition; we only have no certain knowledge on these points.

Naṣr b. Muzāḥim's work—and presumably not merely his *Waq'at Ṣiffīn*— and ideas seem generally and naturally to have spread, and for many generations continued to spread, within Shiite circles. His son Ḥusayn b. Naṣr is often seen as his transmitter, who again was succeded by the otherwise quite unknown Aḥmad b. 'Īsā b. Mūsā al-'Ijlī al-'Aṭṭār[1], and, this tradition was recorded directly in the now lost *kitāb fī sīrat 'Alī* by Ibrāhīm b. Dīzil al-Hamdhānī (d. 896/97)[2]. As pointed out below, Naṣr b. Muzāḥim is Dīnawarī's chief source and was also used by al-Ya'qūbī and al-Mas'ūdī. Moreover, his *Waq'at Ṣiffīn* was used by ash-Sharīf ar-Raḍī (d. 1015/16) in the latter's *nahj al-balāgha*,

1 e.g. *Agh.* IX, 5 (Caetani X, 59; cf. Tab. I. 3363–69); cf. *Maqātil aṭ-Ṭālibiyyīn* for the description of 'Alī's death (Caetani X, 410, 412, 414); Tab. I. 3111–12 (Caetani IX, 120 *sqq.*).—Aḥmad b. 'Īsā's surname, al-'Aṭṭār (perfumery merchant; cf. *E. I*². I, 751 *sq.*) is the same as Naṣr b. Muzāḥim's. Banū 'Ijl, to which Aḥmad b. 'Īsā belonged, was traditionally Shiite.

2 Caetani IX, 292 *sqq.*, 537 *sqq.*, 608, 617, 631 (according to b. Ḥajar I, no.s 2493, 2008 and III, 1602 in which he quotes a "*kitāb Ṣiffīn*" by b. Dīzīl); X, 228 (where he is quoted by adh-Dhahabī and b. al-Kathīr); cf. IX, corr. e agg., xxxi to p. 293.

and also as basis for b. Abi-l-Ḥadīd's (d. 1257) commentaries to this work[3]. As late as in post-classical times Naṣr b. Muzāḥim's version reappears in adh-Dhahabī's (d. 1348) *ta'rīkh al-Islām* and in b. al-Kathīr's (d. 1373) *al-bidāya wa-n nihāya*[4]. It is, then, an authorship of far-reaching importance.

With these details our knowledge on the subject is practically exhausted. A certain literature may have appeared in this period concerning the 'Alī figure. Balādhurī, al-Ya'qūbī, al-Jāḥiẓ, and b. al-Ḥadīd quote a long series of letters and apophthegms of rather doubtful authenticity, but such collections of *littera et dicta* need not necessarily be products of Shiite viewpoints[5]. Our lack of knowledge may be best illustrated by an example: Yāqūt mentions one Ibrāhīm b. Sa'īd b. Hilāl, a Kufian by birth who died in Iṣfahān in 283 A.H. (896/97), whose sphere of interest, as reflected in his production, seems to recall that of al-Madā'inī, though of Shiite observance. To judge by the titles, the subjects he discussed in monographs were the murder of 'Uthmān, the battle at Ṣiffīn, and the arbitration[6]; but nothing is transmitted in his name in the sources we know of. The same applies to other Shī'i authors, who to us are merely names. It is quite conceivable that the coherent presentations, as we know them from the transition from the third to the fourth century A.H. in Dīnawarī and al-Ya'qūbī, did not encourage the transmission of special monographs, and that the views of the moderate Shī'ism were so much akin to those of the orthodoxy that it did not thrive in any other form than Naṣr b. Muzāḥim's. On the other hand, the formation of the politico-revolutionary Ismā'ilism does not seem to have fostered any independent tradition. Ismā'īlism had no real, independent historical writing[7], and we do not know of any elements in the transmission to have been influenced by its ideology.

Nor does Abū Ḥanīfa ad-Dīnawarī's principal work, *al-akhbār aṭ-ṭiwāl*, seem to have been particularly well-known or esteemed by his contemporaries; it is not quoted by other authors, and his name is but rarely mentioned[8]. He does not himself normally quote his informants, and he never furnishes parallel tra-

3 Caetani IX, corr. e agg., xxxiv to p. 433, and the discussion on *Nahj al-balāgha's* authenticity and value in J. Sultan: *Études sur Nahj al-balāgha* (1940), *passim.*

4 On adh-Dhahabī, see *GAL* II, 46 *sqq.*; *(S)* II, 45 *sq.*; on b. al-Kathīr, H. Laoust in *Arabica* II (1955), 42 *sqq.* It is indeed remarkable for b. al-Kathīr to use this source, for he was no Shiite and by principle and demonstratively rejected Shiite evidence.

5 cf. Caetani X, 417 *sqq.* Both Balādhurī and Ya'qūbī cite a certain Ibrāhīm b. Ghiyāth as source, which at any rate in the former is used with b. al-Kalbī as intermediate link.

6 Margoliouth: *Lectures*, 97.—So far as the later versions allow us to identify such material as the Shiite tradition operated with, no unknown elements occur, and there is apparently no indication of any marked corruption of traditions within this circle.

7 Rosenthal: *Historiography*, 56 *sq.*; cf. *supra* p. 100.

8 Kratchkowski, 20 *sq.*, 50 *sq.*—On ad-Dīnawarī's biography, see B. Lewis in *E. I*[2]. II, 300 with the literature quoted there.

ditions on the same subject; but on the basis of information at his disposal he creates a fluent and elegant, although unevenly arranged exposition. The distortion will manifest itself even on a purely mechanical view. Whereas Dīnawarī bestows about 10 lines upon the Prophet, the first three caliphs get about 70 pages in all, and ʿAlī's caliphate over 80 pages; the Umayyads, on the other hand, are treated quite superficially in about 130 pages[9]. It is thus ʿAli's caliphate, particularly his clash with Muʿāwiya and the Khārijite revolt, to which Dīnawarī devotes his attention.

It has long been established that in his exposition of this period Dīnawarī built largely upon Naṣr b. Muzāḥim's *Waqʿat Ṣiffīn*, so far as this work went, i.e. from Jarīr b. ʿAbdallah's mission and on to the arbitration agreement at Ṣiffīn[10], Apart from some details from other sources he seems to have confined himself to this one informant. Even though Dīnawarī does not follow *Waqʿat Ṣiffīn* slavishly, but, as will be further demonstrated below, modifies its information on essential points, his dependence upon this work is quite evident and can be followed as far as Naṣr goes. The verbal similarities are striking, and also in his motivations does Dīnawarī adhere very closely to Naṣr b. Muzāḥim. As one illustration of this dependence we shall quote their accounts of ʿAlī's dispatch of Jarīr b. ʿAbdallāh to Muʿāwiya, a point concerning which Naṣr's material is not to be found in other sources[11]. The factual presentation and their phraseology are in close agreement, and ʿAlī's motivation in demanding Muʿāwiya's *bayʿa* are identical: that the legal basis for his election is the same as that of his three predecessors. The most decisive factor, however, seems to me to be that Dīnawarī's rendering of the passage of ʿAlī's letter in which he deals with the attitude of the two parties to ʿUthmān's murder may sound paradoxical, provided that one does not know Naṣr's depiction. Dīnawarī makes ʿAlī tell Muʿāwiya that he will have those guilty of the murder summoned before himself and promise to deal with them according to the Quran's commandment and the Prophet's *sunna*. This passage is only explicable by a combination of the arbitration idea, as it was subsequently developed, and a conscious reconstruction on the threats and the defamatory reference to Muʿāwiya's ancestry in Naṣr b. Muzāḥim's version. That Dinawari's source can have been none but Waqʿat Ṣiffīn is borne out by a study of his disposition. In these sections Dīnawarī never cites his informant, but the crucial point is that with reservation of a few alterations and replacements he also follows Naṣr's arrangement of the subject-matter throughout. The parallels can be ob-

9 cf. Kratchkowski, 53 *sq.*; *GAL* I, 123.

10 Brockelmann, 4 *sq.*; Caetani IX, corr. e agg., xxxiv to p. 433 and on several occasions (where the parallels, however, apply to the *Nahj al-balāgha* derived from Naṣr's work), and Vaglieri I, *passim.*

11 *Waq. Siff.*, 33 *sq.*; Din., 165.

served side by side, irrespective of the varying informants in Naṣr; his distinctions are nowhere to be seen in Dīnawarī's exposition, and, likewise, Naṣr's variants are either passed over in silence or brought into harmony with the main current of his account.

What Dīnawarī otherwise used for supplementation of his framework about the events covered by *Waqʿat Ṣiffīn* can be established only indirectly, and on this point it will hardly be feasible to set up more than a presumption. It is nevertheless noteworthy that in these sections the similarity with Abū Mikhnaf enters very largely in the picture, most strikingly in his description of the arbitration meeting and the Khārijite rising. The possibility that he—like Balādhurī and Ṭabarī—may have used Abū Mikhnaf's works cannot be ruled out. However, a number of circumstances might indicate rather that he employed one or more later adaptations of Abū Mikhnaf's transmission seeing that on some points he diverts from the latter's version of the Kufic transmission, points on which he is rather at one with later authors, especially Wāqidī, Sayf b. ʿUmar and Yaʿqūbī in their departure from Abū Mikhnaf. The probability is that in these cases he made use of the common source—presumably Hishām b. Muhammad al-Kalbī—mentioned above, even if this presumption practically defies absolute substantiation[12]. What he knew otherwise is confined to a very few details without much general significance[13]. Provided that this interpretation is correct, Dīnawarī's source material must have been extremely narrow and confined to a very few works, and as compared with some contemporary authors his horizon is strikingly limited. In his capacity of scientist, history was not exactly his real field, and that may perhaps serve to explain his narrow source material, though his work is indeed distinguished by its high quality. On the other hand, he never follows his sources slavishly, but modifies and constructs on many essential points, and these alterations would hardly be comprehensible unless Dīnawarī knew the contemporary debate on ʿAlī's caliphate.

Apart from the account of Ṣiffīn, Dīnawarī's exposition contains no exact data, and his chief points of view as regards chronology must be construed from context and composition. He takes up again the Kufic tradition's statement concerning the contact between the Caliph and the Syrian governor im-

12 *AO* XXVII, 87 *sqq.*, especially pp. 94 *sqq.*—Where Dīnawarī quotes his sources they are b. al-Kalbī or al-Haytham b. ʿAdī; Margoliouth: *Lectures*, 113; Kratchkowski, 55; cf. *index* s. nn.

13 In one passage he must have used az-Zuhrī in the description of the arbitration meeting (Din., 211 *sq.*; cf. az-Zuhrī in Tab. I. 3342–43; Caetani X, 26). Elsewhere he has one or two pieces of information of unknown origin; so Din., 172 on ʿUbaydallāh b. ʿUmar's relations with al-Hurmuzān, whom he killed as a supposed party to the murder of his father; cf. Caetani IX, 648 *sq.*, and Bal., 502v (Caetani IX, 285).

mediately after the caliph election, but he does not, in contrast to Ṭabarī, attach the same importance to it as his authorities did. Dīnawarī does not date the breach to this time, but uses the account to demonstrate that *Muhājirūn* and *Anṣar* stand behind ʿAlī and do not let themselves be intimidated "by 15,000 Syrian *shaykhs*' teaɪs over ʿUthmān's *qamīṣ*"[14]. The real breach is still—upon Dīnawarī's having accounted for the rebellion of Ṭalḥa, az-Zubayr and ʿĀʾisha[15] —dated to the time of Jarīr b. ʿAbdallāh's sojourn in Syria, when Muʿāwiya, on his brother ʿUqba b. Abī Sufyān's advice, sends for ʿAmr b. al-ʿĀs. From this point the rendering is carried on to the shipwreck of the arbitration meeting without insertion of incidental circumstances[16]. In quite the same way he treats thc Khārijite rebellion as a unity without any suggestion of their having seceded before[17]; "the Kharijites assembled and decided to unite under ʿAbdallāh b. Wahb ar-Rāsibī", as "the Iraqis had received news of how the case with the two arbitrators had passed off". By thus isolating the Khārijites Dīnawarī succeeds in giving the impression that they have not been recruited among ʿAlī's adherents and consequently have no part in breaking the unity. Finally, then, follows ʿAlī's death "some months after the battle at an-Nahrawān"[18].

This exposition thus represents a schematization of the course of events. Dīnawarī never addicts himself to annalistic historical writing, and the reason for his simplification is undoubtedly that he thereby achieves a trichotomy of which each constituent deals with a main phase of ʿAlī's caliphate, or in other words: his composition presents a conscious and factually determined tightening of the subject-matter[19]. His work is, like Balādhurī's, analytical, but follows quite different lines. The systematization is carried through with a firm hand, so that his version appears much more categorial than that of his predecessors; the chief characters appear with great pregnancy, and the contrasts between ʿAlī's honesty, Muʿāwiya's passivity (which is distinctly ascribed to his *ḥilm*), and his mentor, ʿAmr's, complete lack of scruples stand out more

14 Din., 150 *sq.* (Caetani IX, 13 *sq.*). That this is so appears from the fact that Dīnawarī omits the prophecy about al-Ḥarra in his source and, also, places the narrative of al-Mughīra b. Shuba's advice to ʿAlī after having accounted for the contact between ʿAlī and Muʿāwiya. Here b. ʿAbbās, like the common source, sides with al-Mugjīra. This leaves the impression that the matter was left in abeyance; and Dīnawarī does indeed immediately follow up this statement by saying that ʿAlī was going to Iraq to organize the fight against the refractory governor.

15 Din., 151–63 (Caetani IX, 116 *sqq.*, 160 *sqq.*).

16 Din., 164–215 (Caetani IX–X, *passim*).

17 Din., 215–25 (Caetani X, 123–31).

18 Din., 227 (Caetani X, 340).

19 Dīnawarī cuts out many superfluous details; several particulars in Naṣr b. Muzāḥim disappear, e.g. the circumstantial discussion between ʿAmr and his sons on the opportuneness of joining Muʿāwiya, the anecdotes concerning ʿAmr and Muʿāwiya, etc.

sharply in Dīnawarī than anywhere else. And he does not stop at that; with him the clear contrasts serve a definite function.

While the attitude of the earlier—including the Shiite—historians seems to have been somewhat vacillating, Dīnawarī, like Ṭabarī, defines his standpoint as regards ʿAlī's election clearly. As early as in his (incidentally, freely constructed) rendering of the Caliph's *khuṭba* on occasion of his accession, he emphasizes that the election took place with the assent of both parties, electorate and candidate[20]. The election is characterized as *bayʿa ʿāmma*, election or homage possessing general validity and admitting of no exceptions, though only *Muhājirūn* and *Anṣār* participated; and on the assumption of the elected caliph's righteousness it is inviolable. The competent electorate has, in other words, delegated the caliphal authority to ʿAlī on behalf of the Islamic society in its entirety, and the faithful must all *ipso facto* submit themselves; if not "they deny Islam's religion"[21]. This presentation, the elements of which existed already in Naṣr b. Muzāḥim, is only now carried through consistently. The first part of Dīnawarī's exposition is in complete agreement with the Sunni caliph-doctrine which indeed apprehends the *bayʿa* as a kind of contract entered into on both parties' own free will, and (by analogy with the universally accepted *ijmāʿ*) recognizing the general validity of the particular election on condition of the electorate's competence[22]. The clause concerning righteousness does not, however, exist in the orthodox caliph-doctrine, but it reveals Dīnawarī's intention. The caliph election is quite legal and the proof of the validity of the reservation as regards the course of events thus becomes a corner stone in his interpretation of ʿAlī's caliphate[23].

For this if for no other reason it will be difficult to label Dīnawarī as outright Shīʿi. On the other hand, his expounding of the special character of the

20 Din., 149 (Caetani VIII, 341).

21 Dīnawarī (165) adds explicitly that all provinces—except Syria—have complied loyally. To the enumeration of the provinces by his source, Naṣr b. Muzāḥim, he adds Egypt and the Persian provinces.

22 cf. É. Tyan in *E. I.*² I, 1113 *sq*. The Shiite caliph-doctrine does not, however, recognize the *bayʿa*, but only testamentary transference (*naṣṣ*, *waṣiyya*) of the caliphal dignity within the Prophet family. It has thus nothing in common with Dīnawarī's view as explained in this passage. In the present exposition al-Ḥasan, in a corresponding way, receives the electorate's *bayʿa* in Kufa after ʿAlī's death (Din., 230; Caetani X, 372).

23 A kind of verification hereof is immediately observed in Dīnawarī's description of the three neutral persons' (Saʿd b. Abī Waqqāṣ, ʿAbdallāh b. ʿUmar, and Muhammad b. Maslama) relations with the Caliph (Din., 151–53; Caetani IX, 116 *sqq*.). Their attitude to the election is not mentioned; their resistance does not appear until ʿAlī prepares himself to fight against the Syrians. All three stress their inability to distinguish between faith and infidelity in this situation. When al-Ashtar advises ʿAlī to punish them for violation of the preceding *bayʿa ʿāmma*, he refuses to do so. The stand of the neutrals is lawful and does not violate the homage. Dīnawarī refers this account to another context than the one where it belongs according to his source (cf. *AO* XXVII, 95 *sq*.); in con-

caliph election debars him from characterizing the conflict as *fitna*, and, so far as can be seen, he does not employ this term until Ṣiffīn, when the idea of arbitration breaks the solidarity of the Caliph's ranks. Until then the rebels are dealt with from the angle of lawfulness with, naturally, 'Uthmān's murder as the common starting point.

Dīnawarī's main interest was concentrated on 'Alī's clash with the refractory governor in Syria; but despite the still observable reflections of the contempt with which the anti-Umayyad historians regarded Mu'āwiya, the confrontation with Naṣr b. Muzāḥim gives significant indications of a number of not unessential modifications of the Shiite version. Dīnawarī thus suppresses the mention of Mu'āwiya's connection with *jāhiliyya*. With one exception the Umayyads are not referred to as *ṭulaqā'*, freedmen[24], and even the occasional comparison of the two chief characters is toned down in Dīnawarī; Naṣr b. Muzāḥim's detailed account on 'Alī's personal, religious prestige is by Dīnawarī given a twist to the effect that Mu'āwiya does not possess the Caliph's advantage of kinship with the Prophet[25]. To Dīnawarī this is—as he expressly states himself—of secondary importance inasmuch as he maintains consistently that the formal object of the conflict concerned the justification of 'Uthmān's murder and Mu'āwiya's right to act as his *walī*[26]. On this point, then, Dīnawarī approaches the views of Balādhurī, but turns away from the vulgar-Shiite argumentation of the preceding generations.

This does not, however, dispose of the justification of Mu'āwiya's course of action, for Dīnawarī immediately throws doubt on the sincerity of the Syrian governor's standpoint, by implication at first, but with growing insistency. The man who brings him the news of 'Uthmān's murder greets Mu'āwiya as caliph, but this greeting is not acknowledged since "he has not yet become Caliph". So Mu'āwiya's ambitions are not denied, but in the continuation the messenger points to the tactical strength that Mu'āwiya possesses in his *ḥilm* and in the discipline of his people[27]. The real disclosure of the relation between tactics and ambitions follows with the Caliph's offer to Mu'āwiya to judge the guilty murderers according to God's Book and the Prophet's *sunna*[28]. 'Alī's

---

sequence hereof: where his informant b. al-Kalbī makes b. 'Umar warn 'Alī against usurping the power without a *shūrā*, Dīnawarī must alter his words to the effect that he makes him implore the Caliph not to bewilder him by demanding that he define his attitude to the conflict.

24 cf. e.g. Din., 165 *sq.* (*Waq. Siff.*, 34 *sq.*), 172 *sq.* (*Waq. Siff.*, 61 *sq.*), 181 (Tab. I. 3277 from Abū Mikhnaf); an exception is Din., 199 *sq.* (Caetani IX, 506 *sq.*).

25 Din., 166 (Caetani IX, 243); cf. *Waq. Siff.*, 42 *sq.*

26 Din., 172 (Caetani IX, 248).

27 Din., 164 *sq.* (Caetani IX, 242 *sq.*).

28 Din., 165 (Caetani IX, 244). A deviation from the source that serves as a good illustration of Dīnawarī's views. Naṣr b. Muzāḥim (*Waq. Siff.*, 33 *sq.*) notes in so many words that the idea of blood vengeance is a mere pretence; cf. *supra*, p. 108.

offer is an act of justice, and the responsibility for the breach is placed entirely with Muʿāwiya. The conflict appears quite clarified in the large exchange of letters after Jarīr b. ʿAbdallāh's mission in which ʿAlī is able to dismiss Muʿāwiya's accusations and demands as tactical moves to cover up his personal power-seeking. The Caliph's acts are seen to meet the righteousness clause attached to his election; by his conduct Muʿāwiya excludes himself from the Islamic society, and ʿAlī can rightly assert at Ṣiffīn that he does indeed fight for the purpose of subjecting him to the Quran's judgment, and that the arbitration is therefore superfluous[29].

This step-by-step substantiation of the habitus of the two parties is supplemented in a different way by Dīnawarī. On the one hand, he stresses with increasing intensity the solidarity among ʿAlī's adherents until the showdown at Ṣiffīn. Muʿāwiya's standpoint is not rejected by *Muhājirūn* and *Anṣār* until he forwards a blank *ṭūmār* in reply to ʿAlī's application for *bayʿa* after his election[30]. During the exchange of views after Jarīr b. ʿAbdallāh's unsuccessful mission 10,000 of ʿAlī's adherents assume joint responsibility for the caliph murder, and the number has been doubled during the negotiations at Ṣiffīn[31]. On the other hand, Dīnawarī accentuates with increasing strength the qualms of conscience that the military encounter causes the armies of both parties, and especially the Iraqian one. He further emphasizes very strongly that the two armies were for a very long while encamped opposite each other at Ṣiffīn[32], and that the two armies fraternized lively; "everybody met his fellow (opposite number) kindly, and they hoped that the *ṣulḥ* (agreement, conciliation) would set in"[33]. So ʿAmr b. al-ʿĀṣ's Quran stratagem is not occasioned for fear of any military catastrophe, but still appears merely as a utilization of the latent feeling in either camp that "God's Book is between the two parties"[34]. The religious sense of responsibility in ʿAlī's camp manifests itself in that his companions can no longer as hitherto agree on fighting Muʿāwiya, "he who denies Islam's religion". It is this situation which Dīnawarī can make the Caliph comment upon with the phrase: "The *fitna* has broken out"[35].

And it is likewise this situation that opens the floodgates of the tragedy that

29 Din., 200 *sq.* (Caetani IX, 507 *sq.*).

30 Din., 150 *sq.* (Caetani IX, 13 *sq.*).

31 Din., 172, 182 (Caetani IX, 249, 284).

32 Dīnawarī's chronology is here rather confused. He says (162) that ʿAlī returned to Kufa after the battle of the Camel on the 12th Rajab 36 A.H., i.e. the 4th Jan. 657; the *ṣulḥ* letter is dated to the 15th Ṣafar 37 A.H., i.e. the 2nd Aug. 657 (Din., 210). It is thus out of the question that the two armies were encamped opposite to each other from Rabī I–II till Rajab; this inconsistency goes back to Naṣr's data; cf. *supra* p. 56.

33 Din., 180 (Caetani IX, 283).

34 Din., 201 (Caetani IX, 507).

35 Din., 203 (Caetani IX, 509).

is to follow, for even though the arbitration agreement, also in Dīnawarī's version, opened up the prospect of resuming the war if the two arbitrators should fail to fulfil their obligations[36], and even though the arbitration meeting *per se* is one great demonstration of 'Amr's and Mu'āwiya's manoeuvres—the latter's *ḥilm* is stressed once more—'Alī does not succeed in bridging the contrasts within his own camp, and the Khārijite rebellion is indeed expressive of the process of disintegration. In this section, too, Dīnawarī reveals his own physiognomy. The Khārijite rising is not provoked by the *ṣulḥ* letter, but by the shipwreck of the arbitration negotiations[37]. The commotion's character of a movement of terrorism is stressed here more strongly than ever before; this is what hinders 'Alī from resuming his fight against the Syrians—and thus carry out God's judgment—as had been his intention and his duty as caliph. But the upright Caliph tries even then to bring the rebels to their senses before he appeals to arms. In a protracted discussion—of which Dīnawarī makes a freehand sketch—he succeeds in refuting the Khārijites' accusations against him for *kufr*[38]; he demonstrates that the arbitration is not in contravention of God's Book, and that the fault lies with Abū Mūsā, not in his capacity of arbitrator, but because he betrays the prescribed principles.

A summing up of Dīnawarī's points of view will above all show that his purpose, like that of Balādhurī, was to analyse. He takes the legality of 'Alī's election as his foundation, and his object is to prove that the Caliph had a clear right to fight down the three rebellious movements, first and foremost that of Mu'āwiya, by military means, seeing that they are without legal justification and breaking down that unity of Islam which the caliph represents. Dīnawarī, in contrast to Balādhurī, does not attach vital importance to the caliph murder; to him the decisive turning-point is due to the fact that 'Alī's adherents are divided owing to moral scruples in the critical situation. He also differs from Balādhurī in denying the Syrian governor's action its tinge of legality. In this respect, then, Dīnawarī is in agreement with Ṭabarī, though with a particular accentuation of the idea that even if Mu'āwiya manoeuvered himself into power by illegal means, he did so, too, on the strength of his special, personal qualities. 'Alī, reversely, fulfilled all the conditions demanded of him by the righteousness clause attached to the caliphal dignity. But like contemporary historians as Balādhurī and Ṭabarī, Dīnawarī attaches great importance to the responsibility of the Khārijite opposition and rebellion—a symbol of

36 Din., 206–10 (Caetani IX, 512–15). Of the two versions in Naṣr b. Muzāḥim Dīnawarī chooses here quite logically the Shiite one.

37 Din., 215 (Caetani X, 123). It is a compositional parallel to the first sections of the treatment of 'Alī that he, as in 656, is interrupted in his action against the Syrians by a new movement of rebellion.

38 Din., 220 *sqq.* (Caetani X, 127 *sqq.*).

the nascent Ismā'īlism?—for the failure of Ali's Caliphate, even if these historians' evaluation differs in details.

Dīnawarī's exposition bears all the marks of a firm hand and admirable consistency. The treatment of his source material depends upon daring modifications of the information from his authorities, executed with an ingenuity that makes his work rise far above the clumsiness of his predecessors[39]. As a historian he, like Balādhurī, represents the summit in Islamic historical writing; both are analytical in their object, Balādhurī in the capacity of student, Dīnawarī as pragmatist; Balādhurī's views akin to those of the Ḥanbalites, Dīnawarī's shiitizing. Dīnawarī's rendering is in the nature of a defence of 'Alī, his analysis is, like Balādhurī's, concentrated on a principal idea, but pursued without the latter's careful discussing and shading. His picture of 'Alī hardly holds any reservation—as was the case in Balādhurī—and Mu'āwiya's cause hardly any extenuating circumstances. His point of view, however, are not extremist, for even though 'Alī "possesses the glory of the revelation, on the strength of which...(he) has fought down the hubristic and conquered the meek"[40], he attaches no Messianic concepts to the 'Alī figure. His assessment of the foundation of 'Alī's power is Sunnite and b. 'Abbās is treated loyally and with recognition, but without being in any way singled out. Dīnawarī, like Ṭabarī, recognizes that a new era *(dawla)* begins in the year 100 A.H. with the Abbasid opposition against the Umayyads[41], and as a Persian he naturally stresses the Khurāsānians' share in the Abbasid success. On the whole, then, Dīnawarī attempts to combine the moderate Shī'ism's veneration for 'Alī with soundly orthodox views. A univocal politico-religious placing of him seems hardly possible. It may be pointed out that according to Yāqūt he was favoured by al-Muwaffaq[42], the regent from 870, and that such points of view as he voices appear to be fairly well in agreement with the latter's. Since 878—during the serious Zanj rebellion, which still seems to have been influenced by Khārijite doctrines even if the leader claimed Alid descent—the regent evidently tried to create a more conciliatory atmosphere or to pacify the moderate Shiites (the twelfth *Imām* disappeared at that very time) by some sort of compromise between this movement and Orthodoxy[43]. Dīnawarī thus approaches Ṭabarī's standpoint, only from the Shiite side.

39 Though agreeing with Margoliouth that as a source Ṭabarī (and let us add: Balādhurī) is naturally to be preferred to Dīnawarī on account of his working method, I do not concur with him in his contention that the latter had no critical faculties (Margoliouth: *Lectures*, 113 *sq.*).

40 Din., 199 *sq.* (Caetani IX, 506 *sq.*).

41 Dīn., 336; cf. *HT* 11:V, 467 *sq.*

42 Margoliouth: *Lectures*, 112.

43 Sourdel: *Vizirat* I, 307–25; *idem*: *Pol. rel.*, 13 *sqq.*

5. Al-Ya'qūbī (d. 897)

The other outstanding shiitizing historical writer of the ninth century, Aḥmad b. Abī Ya'qūb b. Wāḍiḥ al-Ya'qūbī, belongs, like his contemporary, ad-Dīnawarī, to Persia; living far from the capital he was attached to the court of the Ṭāhirids. After the fall of this dynasty he resided—from about 260 A.H. (873)—in Egypt, but his Universal History seems to have been prepared in the eastern provinces[1]. Though an exact dating of his *Historiae*, which is carried on to the fall of the Ṭāhirids, will hardly be possible, it is, irrespective of all uncertain factors, of importance to keep in mind that it was written under the same temporal circumstances as Balādhurī's and Dīnawarī's works; in contrast to the former and possibly also to the latter it was written beyond reach of the caliphal court.

Ya'qūbī does no more than Dīnawarī state his authorities, but it is rarely difficult to ascertain his sources. His rendering represents normally a digest of Abū Mikhnaf's, possibly with Hishām b. Muhammad al-Kalbī as intermediate link, but it is supplemented from other sources on a number of points, as will appear from the survey below:

Ya'q. II. 208–09 (Caetani IX, 12); 'Alī's first measures. This passage is rather confused. His source can, as suggested by Caetani *(loc. cit.)* hardly be Sayf b. 'Umar, because Ya'qūbī would not have been able to penetrate his factual and tendentious constructions. He brings a series of details (the interregnum after 'Uthmān, the governor appointments) in common with Sayf and Dīnawarī, and his source is probably b. al-Kalbī (cf. *AO* XXVII, 91 *sq.*, 95). Ya'qubī suppresses the fact that the governor whom 'Alī dispatched to Kufa was there turned away, and says that he let Abū Mūsā remain at the request of al-Ashtar, a construction that may presuppose information from some other source, but need not necessarily do so. Ya'qūbī also entirely ignores Syria, and 'Alī's conversation with Ṭalḥa and az-Zubayr is without parallel; both this and his statement that 'Alī granted them Yamāma and Bahrayn as governorships seem to be due to constructions.

Ya'q. II. 209–11 (Caetani IX, 111 *sqq.*); Ṭalḥa's, az-Zubayr's, and 'A'isha's revolt. The nearest parallel is found in Abū Mikhnaf (Bal. 470v–75r; here, too, b. al-Kalbī appears as transmitter to Balādhurī; Caetani IX, 61 *sq.*, 63 *sqq.*).

---

1 Houtsma's comments in the *praefatio* to his edition, ii *sqq.*; Brockelmann in *E.I.*[1] IV, 1247; Margoliouth: *Lectures*, 125 *sqq.*

Ya'q. II. 214–17 (Caetani IX, 240 *sqq.*); Jarīr b. 'Abdallāh's mission and 'Amr b. al-'Āṣ's covenant with Mu'āwiya; cf. Madā'inī, from 'Awāna in Tabarī (I. 3255–56 and Bal. 494v–97r, from Madā'inī, from 'Īsā b. Yazīd; Caetani IX, 234, 240 *sqq.*). Ya'qūbī's source is thus more likely to be Madā'inī.

Ya'q. II. 217 (Caetani IX, 263); Mu'āwiya's exchange of letters with Sa'd b. Abī Waqqāṣ. The only known parallel is *Waq. Siff.*, 79 *sqq.*

Ya'q. II. 217–19 (Caetani IX, 263 sq.); 'Alī's march on Ṣiffīn and the first encounters at the watering places; cf. Abū Mikhnaf's account in Bal. 502r–04r (Caetani IX, 286 *sqq.*).

Ya'q. II. 219–21 (Caetani IX, 490 *sqq.*); the battle at Ṣiffīn. Parallels ascertainable in Abū Mikhnaf (Tab. I. 3270–72, 3333–35; Caetani IX, 274, 475 *sq.*).

Ya'q. II. 221–23 (Caetani X, 35 *sq.*); the arbitration meeting; cf. Abū Mikhnaf in Tab. I. 3354–56, 3358–60; Bal. 523v–27r (Caetani X, 18 *sqq.*), where b. al-Kalbī also appears as intermediary link.

Ya'q. II. 222 (Caetani X, 35); the account of the predictions in respect of Abū Mūsā's mistake, which cites Suwayd b. Ghafala al-Ju'fī as source; cf. Mas. IV, 383 *sq.*; Caetani's comments in the note to § 31 and *supra* p. 118 note 7.

Ya'q. II. 223–35 (Caetani X, 110 *sqq.*, 188 *sqq.*, 205, 225, 276 *sq.*, 284 *sq.*, 287 *sq.*, 314 *sqq.*); the Khārijite opposition and rebellion and the disintegration of 'Alī's Caliphate. Cf. Abū Mikhnaf in Tab. I. 3360 *sqq.* and Bal. 527 *sqq.* (Caetani X, 77 *sqq.*), the latter often with Hishām b. Muhammad as intermediary link.

Ya'q. II. 235–42 (Caetani X, 417 *sqq.*); 'Alī's letters concerning which Ya'qūbī in one passage (II. 238; Caetani X, 420) invokes Ibrāhīm b. Ghiyāth's authority. Balādhurī quotes the same letters from the same authority extensively, and with b. al-Kalbī as intermediary link.

Only in a very few cases does Ya'qūbī follow his source verbally; the renderings of his informants are in most cases transformed beyond recognition. On this, if on no other, point he differs not only from the normal *ḥadīth* scholarship, but also from Dīnawarī, who, admittedly, creates a literary and cohesive text, but which despite alterations does not diverge radically from the formulations of the sources. Ya'qūbī's rewriting is, however, lacking in that logic stringency which was a distinguishing feature of Dīnawarī's working method. His work has on the whole not freed itself from the primitive argumentation and views of the slightly earlier Shiite tradition, and his work never rises to Dīnawarī's superb technique.

Ya'qūbī's working method may be characterized by his account of the resistance that 'Alī met in al-Raqqa on his way to Ṣiffīn. Like his anonymous informant, *in casu* Abū Mikhnaf, Ya'qūbi states that 'Uthmān's followers had retired from Kufa to al-Raqqa, at which place they entrenched themselves against the Caliph. Ya'qūbī now, on the basis of a verse in Abū Mikhnaf, singles out an individual man to be their leader. But he quite suppresses that the matter was really a question of the inhabitants' unwillingness to comply with 'Alī's order to build a bridge across the Euphrates, that 'Alī desisted from crossing the river at this place, and did not return to it until al-Ashtar's threats intimidated the inhabitants into building the bridge. The narrative thus entirely loses its point and becomes nothing but a dramatic effect with which to close the rendering of the Caliph's march on Ṣiffīn, a rendering, incidentally, that suppresses every trace of such internal frictions in ʿAlī's camp as are still known in Abū Mikhnaf, Naṣr b. Muzāḥim, and Dīnawarī. On the other hand, we see a reshaping of the—to Muʿāwiya not exactly flattering—report on the quarrel about entrance to the watering places at the Euphrates, and the skirmishes between al-Ashtar and Abu-l-Aʿwar as-Sulamī assume the character of a fight about the water.

The same process of reshaping is traceable throughout Yaʿqūbī's rendering; in each instance the information in this new formulation is presented as a moral triumph for ʿAlī, though the details in Yaʿqūbi's construction of the entirety serve in fact no function beyond that of substantiating the contrasts between the two parties. So, Yaʿqūbī's procedure is notable for its moralizing purpose, and his constructions are made accordingly. His account represents a much corrupted rewriting of Abū Mikhnaf or Hishām b. Muhammad al-Kalbī and is notorious by its gross inexactitude[2]. Yaʿqūbī's selection of sources and his disposition is, on the other hand, not wholly unpremeditated, even if some details frequently may be so. The fact that for the dating of ʿAlī's breach with Muʿāwiya he rejects Abū Mikhnaf's version in favour of al-Madā'inī's does no doubt disclose a deliberate intention. The breach is linked up with Jarīr b. ʿAbdallāh's mission, on which point Yaʿqūbī meets the orthodox interpretation of the conflict; all traces of earlier clashes are suppressed.

Yaʿqūbī's depiction of Muʿāwiya contains hardly one redeeming feature. His judgment is most aptly illustrated by a construction of a kind similar to the one dealt with above. On the basis of knowledge of the distressed ʿUthmān's urgent but unavailing appeal to the Syrian governor for help, Yaʿqūbī tells that though the latter held 12.000 men in readiness, he kept them back until he had familiarized himself with the state of affairs at Medina. ʿUthmān expostulated with him and asserted that he had behaved in this way simply because he desired his death[3]. In other words, Yaʿqūbī insinuates that Muʿāwiya wished for the caliph's death in order to become "heir to the vengeance" or usurp the power. The rendering, which serves above all to characterize Muʿāwiya, appears to have been very badly thought out; on this point the historian

2 This assessment is in agreement with Lammens (*Omayyades*, 197) and L. Veccia Vaglieri (Vaglieri I, 16) in contrast to Houtsma's (*Historiae*, *praefatio*, viii, x), Noeldeke's (*ZDMG* 38, 156), Rosenthal's (*Historiography*, 115) and Brockelmann's (*E.I.*[1] IV, 1247).

3 Yaʿq. II. 205; cf. Muhammad b. as-Sā'ib al-Kalbī in Tab. I. 2984–86 (Caetani VIII, 196, 167 *sq.*). A similar and just as meaningless construction has it that ʿAmr b. al-ʿĀṣ mediated between ʿUthmān and the rebels (II. 202; Caetani VIII, 195 *sq.*); cf. al-Wāqidī (Tab. I. 2969; Caetani VIII, 148 *sq.*), where it is ʿAlī who by his intervention obtains ʿUthmān's promise of good behaviour, when the rebels arrived at Medina.

has been able to attain his object only by an extraordinarily clumsly construction. Supposing that Mu'āwiya could really have arrived with 12.000 men at Medina after the murder, the course of events would in all circumstances have turned out quite differently, and a breach with 'Alī and the rebels against 'Uthmān could hardly have been staved off till after the battle of the Camel.

Ya'qūbī's account, even as compared with the anti-Umayyad tradition in general, represents a severe downgrading of Mu'āwiya who in one passage is labelled "idolater from Mecca". He has evidently not doubted that 'Uthmān's death was richly deserved[4]; the revolt of the 'Uthmāniyya, described as a manifestation of the frustrated ambitions of the two leaders[5], is, however, deliberately kept apart from that of Mu'āwiya. The invocation of the demand for blood vengeance is to Ya'qūbī's eyes a tactical affair, though 'Alī had hoped "that they (the Syrians) would lend support to the righteous guidance"; he never has the slightest doubts about Mu'āwiya's worldly designs or about the illegality of his revolt against the Caliph.

Reversely, Ya'qūbī considers it a matter of vital importance to attest to the solidarity of 'Alī's ranks. The Quran stratagem was intended to divide 'Alī from his people; but only a very few—among which al-Ash'ath b. Qays, whom Mu'āwiya according to Ya'qūbī had formerly tried to win over, and who is supported by the Yemenites—followed the call, which consequently did not provoke any disunion. The Khārijites, in Ya'qūbī's depiction, are people possessed by demons—a not uncommon conception among Shiites[6]—but, as also Dīnawarī has it, their rebellion is detached from the events at Ṣiffīn and made into a function of the two arbitrators' fraud on Islam. The arbitration is dated to Rabī' I—Ramaḍān 38 A.H., i.e. Aug. 658—Febr. 659[7], by which means the temporal margin for the Khārijite revolt and the combating of it is narrowed down as far as possible; the battle at an-Nahrawān is dated to the year 39 A.H., which commenced in March 659[8].

al-Ya'qūbī's rendering is, on the whole, characterized by the unswerving sympathy he shows to 'Alī; his principal intention must have been to prove that 'Alī's adherents had not failed him, as the orthodox tradition would assert. However, Ya'qūbī does not unreasonably extol 'Alī to the detriment of his

4 cf. Caetani's comments in *Annali dell' Islām* VIII, 195 *sqq.*

5 Ya'q. II. 208 *sq.* (Caetani IX, 12).

6 Ya'q. II. 223 *sqq.* (Caetani X, 110 *sqq.*). This conception of the Khārijites derives according to Muṣ'ab b. 'Abdallāh az-Zubayrī (d. 845) from 'Īsā b. Yazīd (cf. Caetani X, corr. e agg., xxvi and pp. 135 *sq.*). They are often referred to as demons from the rocky coast *(shayṭān ar-radhah).*

7 This is hardly because Ya'qūbī wants to follow the genuine tradition, but rather that he intentionally alters the year from 37 to 38 A.H.

8 Ya'q. II. 225 (Caetani X, 111).

predecessors, nor does he fail to appreciate the Abbasids; 'Abdallāh b. 'Abbās is dealt with in a fair way, and he even states that Muhammad b. Ḥanafiyya had relinquished his dignity of *Imām* to the Abbasids, which, then, is entirely on the same lines as the pro-Abbasid presentation. Ya'qūbī's Shiite sympathies stand out more strongly than in other Shiitizing authors, and his approach and argumentation often come near to the vulgar-Shiite ones. He does not, on the other hand, associate Messianic ideas with the 'Alī figure[9], "*abhorrens fanaticum furorem*" (Houtsma). This placing corresponds with Houtsma's information that he declared himself to be a follower of *tashayyu' ḥasan*, the attempts to bring about a compromise between the divergent views of orthodoxy and moderate Shī'ism[10]. This interpretation, if assumed to be correct, will enable us to find in the orthodox Ṭabarī as well as in the shiitizing Dīnawarī and Ya'qūbī the same disposition to try to find a compromise between the conflicting views or conciliatory trends, which on either side strive towards a common goal.

It is indeed characteristic and hardly accidental that Balādhurī's works or Ḥanbalite points of view were not to exert any decisive influence upon Islamic historical writing after the middle of the ninth century, and reversely, it is undoubtedly of the utmost significance that orthodox as well as moderately Shī'i historians from their respective views have endeavoured to approach the rival party's standpoint. The explanation must, as already referred to, be sought in the growth of Ismā'īlism and the penetration of extremist Shī'ism (particularly adherents of the Nuṣayriyya sect) into the administration, tendencies each of which involved serious danger to the existing social order. The works of Ṭabarī, Dīnawarī and Ya'qūbī all bear the stamp of the political, religious and social antagonisms of their time. They all tend to formulate an interpretation of the *fitna* bridging over the moderate differences of opinion, and suppressing extremist points of view. Their most conspicuous common feature—at this point also shared by Balādhurī—is the attempt at holding the Khārijites responsible for the failure of 'Alī's Caliphate. This may be due to the fact that the last serious revolt inspired by Khārijite doctrines—the Zanj rebellion—took place simultaneously (869–83) and that Khārijism after that time had to yield to the revolutionary Ismā'īlism. The Ismā'īlitic expansion and revolts were indeed expressive of the precarious social balance, and from the second half of the tenth century Ismā'īlism is supported by the propaganda and terror issuing from the court of the Fāṭimids in Cairo. Reversely, the Shiite infiltration into the court in Baghdad, favoured by the disintegration of Government

9 cf. Sarasin, 40 *sqq.*

10 Houtsma: *Historiae, praefatio*, ix.—Brockelmann's statement (*E.I.*[1] IV, 1247) that al-Ya'qūbī belonged to the Shiite Mūsawiyya sect cannot be substantiated from the material. (On this sect, see Friedlaender: *Heterodoxies*, 39 *sqq.*, 50 *sqq.*; R. Strothmann in *E.I.*[1] IV, 379).

finances, leads on direct to the breaking up of the sovereignty of the orthodox caliphate from within, a state of affairs that culminated in 936 with the establishment of the office of Chief Amirate *(amīr al-umarā')*, an office which, after some years in the 930's and 940's marked by high cost of living and epidemics, falls into the hands of the Shiite Būyids in 945. The historical writing here dealt with is thus on the brink of the most severe crisis in Islam's history—it is not overcome until the Seljūq Turks in 1055 remove the Būyids and subsequently commence a strong counter-offensive against the Ismā'īlitic agitation and terror—and it is no doubt by its very attempts to find a compromise that might unite all moderate forces against the radical tendencies that it acquires its principal importance.

CONCLUSION AND SUMMING UP

Conclusion and Summing up

1.

The genesis and growth of Islamic historical writing as reflected in its treatment of the *fitna* demonstrate conspicuously the intimate correlation which in all phases exists between the politico-religious development and the formation of the tradition. From its very beginning the formation of tradition and the historical writing served a social function determined by the basic teleological view as framed by Muhammad, and by all believers' vital interest in the prosperity of the *umma*. The nature of the Arab transmission will, therefore, at the same time preclude any absolute distinction between sacral and profane historical writing; the Prophet *sīra* and the work at the historical foundations of early Islam are intimately bound up with each other, and neither of them —no more than the related *ḥadīth* disciplines, jurisprudence and theology— was uninfluenced by the religious, political, and social ferments from the 7th till the 10th century.

The first tentatives to a study of Islam's earliest history belong presumably in—or are at least traceable to—the decades about the year 700, in the prevailing conflicts provoked, but not solved, by the second civil war. It is observable in poetry as well as in prose tradition, both apparently representing independent or parallel formulations of an assessment of the past, which soon assumes a definite form, and which bears all the marks of the official verity: one-sidedness, construction, and tendency for party-political purposes. Both the Umayyads and their opponents in Iraq and Persia made the cogency of poetry and the prose tradition serve their topical political propaganda; both types are indubitably based on elements of individual oral narratives, predominantly of an *ayyām* character, but moulded eclectically by the very earliest poets and *muḥaddithūn* into a shape expressive of a general idea. This applies to the Syrian—formulated by the Medinese traditionists az-Zuhrī and Ṣāliḥ b. Kaysān—as well as to the conflicting Iraqian interpretation in a number of Kufian scholars, among whom ash-Sha'bī appears to be the pioneer. These traditional elements undergo, even before the end of the Umayyad era, a gradual recasting, particularly in the Kufic transmission, where a Hāshimite and a specifically Shiite interpretation is being framed by respectively Abū Mikhnaf and such narrators as ʿĪsā b. Yazīd and Jābir b. Yazīd al-Juʿfī, though constantly polemizing against the Syrian-Medinese tradition.

The transmission is, to all appearances, set down in writing as early as in the late Umayyad age, even though the handing down still went on orally. It already then assumed the shape upon which all subsequent compilators and adapters draw; but the pro-Syrian tradition, apart from Basra where an ʿUthmāniyya school kept it up for political purposes, had but little vital force in Abbasid times. The Kufic transmission, on the contrary, is subject to a significant evolutationary process; it is transformed along individual lines by Shīʿism as well as by pro-Abbasid scholars. It is indeed striking to observe the readiness and pliancy with which the Kufic—occasionally also the Syrian-Medinese—traditional elements in the Abbasid era adapt themselves to the changing political situations up to the final years of the 9th century. Through all stages of political and religious development the historians operate with the elements existing at the end of the Umayyad caliphate, though with ever changing selection of the material available and with varying strength and adaptation. The material at disposal is moreover largely added to by new features as occasion requires by means of constructions, sometimes epic narratives, though apparently most often polemic anecdotes or variants of narratives already existing.

The historical writing during the first generations of the Abbasid period is marked by the new rulers' settling with their revolutionary past, the coalition with Shīʿism in the combat against the Syrian caliphate. The Abbasids did not from the outset possess any independent tradition, but the fight against Shīʿism is nonetheless taken up very energetically on to Hārūn ar-Rashīd, even if with varying strength and apparently crossed by attempts at reconciliation during al-Mahdī's caliphate and the Barmakid rule[1]. The struggle against Shīʿism is reflected in the historical writing by radical adaptations of the Kufic transmission by such traditionists as Hishām b. Muhammad al-Kalbī and especially Sayf b. ʿUmar. And the Abbasid propaganda is countered by Shīʿi scholars; the tradition of the extremist Shīʿism is only known fragmentarily whereas its moderate form permits us to follow the discussion in ʿUmar b. Saʿīd and Naṣr b. Muzāḥim. Both parties were at one in their scathing criticism of the fallen dynasty, while ʿAlī's ,ʿAbdallāh b. ʿAbbās's, and Shīʿism's attitude to the *fitna* occasioned fiery debates, the foci of which were the fundamental incompatibility between the views of the *umma* and the title to the caliphate

1 cf. Sourdel: *Vizirat* I, 93 *sqq.*, 127 *sqq.*, and most recently *idem*: La politique religieuse du calife ʿabbaside al-Maʾmūn (*Revue des Études Islamiques*, Année 1962 (Paris 1963)), 27 *sqq.*

taken by Orthodoxy and Shī'ism, while the Abbasids in their own interest argued for the orthodox continuity as framed by the earliest caliphs, Shī'ism defended continuation of the divine guidance in the *Imām* line.

The work of the historians in the first generations of the Abbasid era is generally distinguished by the pregnancy with which its standpoints were defined and by its conspicuous constructional activity. In the beginning of the 9th century the situation changed again when the Abbasids under al-Ma'mūn and his successors attempted to reconcile the Alids and subsequently to adopt Mu'tazilism. From its very inception this movement appears to have been the new dynasty's supporting party, but until then it had played but an insignificant role in the shaping of the historical tradition. Mu'tazilite influences are traceable only in Abū Bakr al-Hudhalī, who was personally attached to al-Manṣūr, and apart from this intermezzo—that was perhaps determined by momentary circumstances—Hārūn ar-Rashīd still maintained the anti-Alid policy until his death. But as early as in al-Wāqidī, who seems to have been favoured by Yaḥyā b. Khālid al-Barmakī and subsequently by al-Ma'mūn, we observe a much more pronounced liking for 'Alī than had hitherto been the case in the pro-Abbasid tradition, but the attempt to create a Mu'tazilite historical writing and a compromise with the moderate pro-Alid points of view reached its full development in al-Madā'inī. Instead of the bitter attacks on Shī'ism that had characterized the first generations after 750 the rulers now preferred to try to reconcile the orthodox and moderately Shiite standpoints with Mu'tazilism as the common denominator, though still without in any way relinqishing their denunciation of *ar-Rāfiḍa*. This tendency towards *tashayyu' ḥasan*, which in the historical writing is specifically found in Wāqidī and Madā'inī, may have been furthered by the radical Shī'ism's transformation into a social oppositional movement expressive of society's precarious stability, as well as by its infiltration into the administration with the consequential danger of a weakening of the orthodox caliphate's authority.

Mu'tazilism represents, however, also a rationalist attack on the Islamic tradition's fundamental principles, and towards the middle of the 9th century historical writing as well as jurisprudence and theology show signs of an orthodox reaction under Ḥanbali leadership against the prevailing dogmatic movement, though at the same time also of attempts to revise the technique of traditionalism by applying formalistic criticism of the material. Ḥanbalism's main contribution consists indubitably in its successful struggle to justify the Islamic traditionalism's existence and in its contest with the caliphal power's attempt to dominate Islam's dogmatic development. It did not, however, at this juncture obtain any lasting significance, either religiously or historiographically. It is only in al-Balādhurī, where the sober traditional criticism is matched with accentuation of the earliest caliphate's strength, that Ḥanbali-influenced points of view seem to have had an advocate of outstanding calibre.

The period from the middle of the 9th century, when al-Mutawakkil tacitly abandoned Muʿtazilism, acquired its chief stamp by new endeavours to bring about a compromise between the orthodox and the moderate Shīʿi views. It is presumably struggles of this nature that manifest themselves in the caliphal court's varying attitudes to this period's religious antagonisms, and the same trend is noticeable also in the historians' endeavours to bring about a solution by compromise, attempts at *tashayyuʿ ḥasan*. This drift towards harmonization is no doubt bound up with the dangers involved in the radicalization of Shīʿism, the emergence of the revolutionary Ismāʿīlism, and the fact that the latter movement gradually superseded Khārijism during this period; the attempts at compromise, therefore, seem to have constituted an impulse of fundamental importance all through the 9th century. The process is observable in both orthodox and moderate Shīʿi historians; among the former Ṭabarī is the central figure, and among the latter we observe similar tendencies in Dīnawarī and, somewhat more strongly shiitizing, in Ya'qūbī.

The great compilatory works and the literary adaptations at the end of the 9th century are representative of Islamic historical writing in its full development. Moreover, in Ṭabarī, Yaʿqūbī and, subsequently, in al-Masʿūdī (d. 956) the narrow Arab horizon characteristic of former authors disappears in favour of a universal historical plan that seeks to deduce the Islamic preconditions and background in the past of the Mediterranean world. These and all subsequent attempts to have Islam linked into the common historical framework rest upon the Old-Testament-Hellenistic-Christian tradition as epitomized by Eusebios and Paulus Orosius. The Arabic historians presumably received it with Christian Arabic or Syrian authors as intermediaries[2]. It is to them—contrary to mediaeval European historians—a late and secondary strain, though absorption of this material is, naturally, tantamount to drawing the full conclusions of the fundamental historical views formulated by the Quran. Only now does Islam appear as the Prophet had intended it: as fulfilment of the divine revelation.

In other respects, however, the Arabic historical writing such as it had been framed at this juncture, marks out narrow limits to its horizon, no doubt still under influence of Muhammad's teleological system. The religious and political distinctions provoked by the *fitna* required continually re-interpretation of Islam's earliest history and developed quite an overwhelming concentration on the immediate consequences of the schism. It is thus symptomatic that

2 cf. Rosenthal: *Historiography*, 66 *sqq.*; *HT* 11:V, 472.—Paulus Orosius was translated in Spain.

interest in the recording of contemporary history seems comparatively slight and still confined to the aftereffects of the classical dividing lines. His own age is entirely passed over by al-Balādhurī, and historians like Ṭabarī and Dīnawarī deal with it in a rather lapidarian and superficial way. Islamic historical writing is perhaps to a still higher degree than that of mediaeval Europe marked by a disposition to place its own age in a historical perspective or, reversely, to project topical subjects of conflicts back to the past.

In Islam the interest in contemporary history is late in coming and slow in development, and the new lines after the period here dealt with are seen chiefly within those spheres where historical or religious aims are no longer the primary ones. The first historian to historize his own age was b. al-Miskawayhi (d. 1030), the public officer with intimate knowledge of the politics of his own time and with access to archival material[3]. He as well as other authors of this mould represent, however, stages transitional to the political science as framed—e.g. by al-Māwardī (d. 1058)[4]—under Aristotelian influences. With these political theorists the historical or religious cognition is but secondary to the didactic value of the material. It is exactly this tendency that Ṭabarī rejects when he, faced with Mu'tazilism, proves unwilling to apply the historical material empirically to philosophical systematics, and maintains the traditional technique within the theocratic frames of Islam. Ṭabarī's monumental work had been built up as a defence against Mu'tazilism's attempts to introduce new rational views, and its aim was to create orthodox unity in exactly the same way in which the contemporary theological and legal *ḥadīth* science endeavoured to provide a fixed framework and lasting norms for the orthodox *ijmā'*.

2.

The reaction of the Islamic traditionists against Mu'tazilism's demand that history be used for "rational deductions and intellectual edification" (to quote Ṭabarī) was really quite natural. If the historical writing had abandoned its traditional technique in favour of Mu'tazilism's philosophic-didactic ideal, it would *ipso facto* have lost its cogency and its placing and justification as a living function within the Islamic society. The *ḥadīth* science rested axiomatically upon the evidence of "the Prophet and the pious fathers"[5], and as regards Rationalism's contention that "the whole (Islamic) society would be unable to agree upon that was false"[6], it maintained in accordance with Islam's basic

3 *GAL* I, 342 *sq.*; cf. also Rosenthal: *Historiography*, 149 *sqq.*

4 Gibb, 141 *sqq.*, 151 *sqq.*; on the development of political theory in Islam, see E. I. J. Rosenthal: *Political Thought in Medieval Islam* (Camr. 1958), *passim.*

5 Tab. I. 55–56; cf. b. Qutayba, who establishes that "no religion has so strong a historical attestation as Islam". (Sprenger: *Trad. wes.*, 1).

6 al-Khayyāṭ, no 104 (Traduction, 144 *sqq.*); cf. Wensinck, 48.

theocratic idea that historical cognition and knowledge invariably manifested God's will. The worth of the historical narrative depended therefore solely on the narrator's or transmitter's competence in furnishing a loyal rendering, and it permitted only a formal criticism of the trustworthiness of the machinery of transmission. In its full display the employment of traditions by *ḥadīth* science, as we have followed it in the historical writing, depended very largely upon judgment of the narrator's or transmitter's party-political standpoint. But either side's extremely scrupulous assessment as to whether the religious habitus of the rival party or parties endowed their statements with trustworthiness or worth as evidence, created also in practice a continuous interaction between a weighing of the tradition's substance *(matn)* and its external appearance, more particularly so in cases of insufficient data concerning the narrators. Mu'ammar b. Rashīd could disallow az-Zuhrī's authority because he had served the Umayyads[7], which circumstance, on the other hand, did not compromise him in the eyes of the Ḥanbali; but Hishām b. 'Ammār ad-Dimashqī had to condemn the Shiite transmission in 'Īsā b. Yazīd as false on the grounds of its tendentious content.

This traditional technique is, however, mainly representative of the standards of the Abbasid era, a fact that calls for reservations in respect of both chronology and quality. In the Umayyad era the attitude of the historian to his sources does not seem to have been quite the same, and especially not so rigorous, as the attitude of his successors. The earliest narrators—also described as *muḥaddithūn*—in the first half of the 8th century had at their disposal an *ayyām* material orally transmitted to them by *ruwāt* and even then tendentious. To this *ayyām* material they would, when external circumstances made it expedient, add information on political events round the *fitna*, and both elements were from the outset fashioned eclectically into a general and collective appraisal. The earliest transmission exists in two principal versions, one Iraqian, the other Syrian-Medinese; the important point, however, is that in the earliest stages they are both formulated without any attempt to invoke authority from the past; the pro-Syrian as well as the anti-Syrian tradition is shaped by scholars of the Umayyad period as regional or partisan *opinio* in the same way as the legal doctrines. In its earliest appearance, then, the tradition is rather in the nature of an authoritative interpretation of the past as framed by the traditionists of this period: az-Zuhrī, Ṣāliḥ b. Kaysān, ash-Sha'bī, and 'Awāna, but already then marked by the one-sidedness and mutual polemic that seperate the two schools.

The inclination to invest the historical—as well as the legal and theological—tradition with an earlier and religiously coloured authority by means of the

---

7 *AO* XXVII, 102 *sq.*

isnād is, on the other hand, clearly a secondary phenomenon that belongs to a slightly later period. The many contradictory testimonies notwithstanding there is no reason to think that az-Zuhrī and his contemporaries have normally made use of *isnād* to earlier informants so far as the historical transmission is concerned, and where an *isnād* does appear it is most often due to attempts by the following generation or generations—e.g. Muʿammar b. Rashīd[8]—either to project the rendering back to earlier informants or to replace the true authority with a false *isnād*. The earliest manifestation of such tendencies is found in Iraq and chiefly in traditionists of an extremist observance. To all appearances, the detailed substantiation by means of the *isnād*—and consequential shifting of the traditional concept—makes its entry in the decades round the mid-eighth century, and the pro-Umayyad ʿAbdallāh b. al-Mubārak already conceived it institutionally "as a part of the religion". These formal adaptations are not infrequently combined with interpolation into or modification of the earliest accounts; but both forms of interference bear the character of *pia fraus*, which indubitably has relation to the bitter conflicts in late Umayyad times and the need in pietistic circles to replace the standards of the Syrian régime, stigmatized as heretical, with norms that conformed to Islam's ethical ideas. So, the concept of tradition is extended; it is detached from its origin proper and becomes in itself a function of Islamic society, and this trend reaches its completion in the 9th century under influence of Muʿtazilite criticism of the traditionalism.

The methodical and conceptual changes in the Muslim historian's attitude to his sources are parallelled by shiftings in his attitude to the subject-matter with which he deals; only the requirement that he commit himself on the vital problems raised by the *fitna* remains unaltered behind all modifications. The earliest incentive to taking sides in respect of history must undoubtedly be ascribed to the Iraqian opposition's political and religious accusations against the Syrian caliphate, and, conversely, the Medinese tradition records the case for the latter's legitimacy. The Iraqian accusation had from the very beginning to do with the justification of Muʿāwiya's vengeance action against ʿAlī and unwillingness to submit to him, but in the late Umayyad period the accusations gradually assume a far wider scope. The Syrian caliphate is identified with *jāhiliyya* and described as a heathen or secular monarchy *(mulk)* incompatible with Islam. This changed yardstick is expressive of the reluctance in Iraq towards the Umayyads' attempts to adapt the administration and religious norms to the changed social structure. Reversely, the religious intensification of the accusations against the Umayyads is reflected in the formal changes within the concept and technique of the *ḥadīth* science.

Nor did the Abbasids' coming into power and the adoption of the theocratic

8 *AO* XXVII, 99 *sqq*.

principles settle the conflicts concerning the established caliphate's religious legitimacy. As against the Abbasids' claim to be representatives of the orthodox continuity in *ummat Allāh*, Shī'ism maintained invariably the divine guidance's continuation in the *Imām* tradition, represented by 'Alī and his descendants. These fundamental discords are observable in the historical writing, first in the reaction of the Abbasids against their revolutionary origin, and subsequently with growing intensity in their stand against the radicalization of the extremist Shī'ism, which in itself was expressive of society's precarious balance, and which threatened, at the same time, to enervate from within the caliphate's authority.

Traditions provoked countertraditions irrespective of all technical principles; accusation and defence, which continue to reflect Islam's religious, political, and social struggles, alternate in the historical writing. The antiquarian aspect does never obtain any prominent placing; the Muslim historian does not confine himself to a recording of facts, he interprets them over and over again in the light of topical conflicts. The most salient feature of the historical writing from the outset is indeed its admixture of polemics; this is where we must seek the fundamental incentive to its genesis, and this element remains with it until its full bloom in the Abbasid era. The Islamic historian does not work *sine ira et odio*, and it is a matter of conjecture how common it was for prominent historians like Ṭabarī to carry on their work in financial independence. From the very earliest formation of tradition we know for certain that traditionists like Ṣāliḥ b. Kaysān and az-Zuhrī acted as spokesmen for the caliphs in Damascus; Muhammad b. Isḥāq's last years were spent writing at al-Manṣūr's court; Abū Bakr al-Hudhalī is referred to as this caliph's *nadīm* (boon companion); al-Wāqidī—apparently heavily indebted—was attached to Yaḥyā b. Khālid al-Barmakī's and al-Ma'mūn's, Balādhurī to al-Mutawakkil's court; and al-Ya'qūbī wrote under the auspices of the Ṭahirids. This does not mean, of course, that all historical work in Islam's classical period must necessarily be interpreted in terms of the will of the caliphal court or of its most influential opponents; the building up of Islamic theocracy required each member to decide and act according to his standpoint as regards the *fitna*. However, the consonance between the prevailing currents and the views of the historians is generally so marked that it cannot be ascribed to mere coincidence.

None of the Islamic historians is explicit in stating his party-political standpoint or in formulating his general conception: his likes and dislikes as well as his programme and appraisal must always be deduced from the context or from his composition. Its compilatory form notwithstanding, this historical writing made heavy demands on the deductive faculty of audience or reader, and from the angle of modern research the disposition still presents valuable clues both as regards identification of these points of view in the traditionists and as regards critical evaluation of their work and their methods. It should be noted, however, that despite the transmission's fragmentary and no doubt somewhat incidental character, a knowledge of the historical material through all its phases and all its modifications affords us possibilities of a critical and historical evaluation of the mechanism and technique of the shaping of tradition behind, and independent of, the principles laid down by its authors.

The traditionist's (and the literary historian's) method is above all distinguished by being selective. There can be no doubt at all that the Syrian-Medinese or the Khārijite tradition must have been known far more extensively than historians of Abbasid times might immediately lead us to suppose. The selection among the traditions at disposal may in the nature of things be a consequence of the Islamic *ḥadīth* science's careful graduation of the opponents' religious qualities and the evidential value of their pronouncements. But even with this reservation *in mente* does the selective element assert itself in a most striking way, and cannot by any means be accidental; we have time and again been able to ascertain that from the material at his disposal—that of his own observance not excepted—the historian had selected exactly what would serve his particular points of view and his purposes. Ṭabarī prefers Sayf b. 'Umar's corrupt transmission to Abū Mikhnaf's because it meets his preconceived conditions on which to refute the extremist Shī'ism. In a corresponding manner 'Umar b. Sa'īd and Naṣr b. Muzāḥim resort to the earliest—and incidentally primary—Kufic transmission rather than associate themselves with the extremist Shiite views, while Madā'inī, reversely, makes frequent use of the secondary and extremistic tradition against the anti-Mu'tazilite opposition. The Islamic tradition, like the contemporaneous European historical writing, represents a highly developed and sophistical work on sources; its principles are critical only in so far as it selects its material on lines that are *a priori* determined by the historian's personal opinions. The applicability of the material hinges on its tendency as much as on his judgment of the informant's trustworthiness.

The second methodical main point applies to the adaptation in form and contents of the material to be utilized. The Islamic, like the European, historian lacked the ability and the possibility of differentiating earlier and later elements of the tradition, a circumstance which, incidentally, he himself veiled by his use of *isnād*; the modern notion of primary and secondary sources was, naturally, alien to the mediaeval historian. The chain of transmitters as well as the traditional subject-matter was constantly subject to very extensive adaptations varying from interpolation to consistent falsification. The earliest tradition is in fact characterized by its ingenious, polemic constructions, to which the later tradition added attempts to justify its own version by an elaborate apparatus of *rijāl*, informants, which *per fas et nefas* is concatenated into chronologically coherent chains, the *isnād*. The falsifications of tradition, however, hardly constitute a continously progressive practice. The falsifications of both matter and form seem generally to pertain either to periods during which political and religious life is marked by particularly violent ferments or to the periphery of the tradition; they find their culmination in Sayf b. ʿUmar's pragmatic historical writing, and they are met with in extremist traditionists like Jābir b. Yazīd al-Juʿfī, ʿĪsā b. Yazīd, ʿAbdallāh b. al-Mubārak, and Hishām b. ʿAmmār ad-Dimashqī.

It will hardly be practicable to weigh the significance of one against the other of these methodical possibilities. They are all manifestations of *pia fraus*, falsifications or adaptations warrantable within the framework of Muhammad's teleological system, but at the same time phenomena which in the 9th century made traditionalism an easy prey to Muʿtazilism's rational criticism. Within the confines of our material there is hardly any doubt that this challenge through the Shāfiʿite and Ḥanbalite schools' principles of traditional criticism —though highly formalistic and imperfect—led to greater soberness, above all in al-Balādhurī. The Islamic historical writing is on the whole—all individual admixtures through all stages of its development notwithstanding—characterized by two features. Its framing is determined by external, religious, political, or social conditions, and methodically it is distinguished by afterrationalizations by means of constructions, in form or matter, or harmonization of the material at its disposal.

3.

The principal object of the present study has not been an immediate determination or interpretation of the historical course of events, but rather to furnish evidence of the earliest Islamic historical writing's position and function in Muslim society, and to characterize its working methods. But the historiographical investigation can at the same time give valuable grounds also for the historical judgment of the chaotic years under ʿAlī's caliphate. The conclusions to be drawn from the investigations here undertaken for the purpose of an evaluation of the conflicts in 656–61 must above all be that none but the earliest and primary elements of the transmission have any relevance as source material. The younger tradition in Abbasid times contains apparently an overwhelming mass of new information unknown to the ealiest narratives; the most copious and, as it seems, logically most cohesive description is found in the latest historians. This specious copiousness of the late tradition is, however, only apparent. The wealth of details in the representation is in all verifiable instances due to adaptations, constructions, modifications, or combinations upon the earlier material at disposal. In no case does it seem possible to find new information in accounts from the Abbasid era that are not most naturally or logically explicable as manifestations of adaptations from the sources, and there is no reason to think that later narrators have had at their disposal any primary sources that have subsequently been lost. This applies to the work of traditionists proper as well as to that of literary historians. The historical writing in Abbasid days is of interest primarily as a monument to the age and the society in which it came into existence. The late tradition is still of value as a source in so far as it reflects Islam's religious and political development; as a source of information on the civil war after ʿUthmān's death it is of no value at all, but it ranks high as regards elucidation of the propaganda surrounding the later formation of parties.

This does not, however, mean that the earliest and primary tradition is free of contradictions or misrepresentations. We are here facing the methodically peculiar case of having access to primary sources not mutually independent, but directly and deliberately contradictory; both the Iraqian and the Syrian-Medinese version are presumably based upon historical information which, though no longer known, was embodied in the *opinio* formulated by these traditions. The earliest narrators, too, worked eclectically and tendentiously; the polemic element is a most salient feature of both poetic and prose transmission, neither of which possesses first-hand knowledge of the events in which we are here concerned. A complete and absolutely certain reconstruction of the historical development appears to be beyond the bounds of possibility; many elements within the general context and many episodes will remain unknown for ever, as they probably were to most people of their own time, too. A confrontation of the primary elements of the sources with one another will enable us to reveal their tendency and controversy, and, where practicable, we can test their concrete information by means of other, independent—Syrian and Byzantine—evidence. Only by systematic and strictly consistent criticism will it be possible to rid the sources of their afterrationalizations, and this is the only way by which to obtain a truer picture of the earliest Islam.

Bibliography[1]

I. SOURCES

Abbreviation	Source
	Baethgen, F.: Fragmente syrischer und arabischer Historiker (*Abh.K. M.* VIII: 3, Lpz. 1884).
Caetani	*Caetani, L.*: Annali dell'Islām, I–X. (Milano 1905–26).
Vaglieri II	*Vaglieri, L. Veccia*: Traduzioni di passi riguardanti il conflitto ʿAlī-Muʿāwiya e la secessione khārigita (*AIOUN*, N.S. V (1953), 1–98).
	Wensinck, A. J.: A Handbook of Early Muhammadan Tradition (Leiden 1927, rpt. 1960).
Bal.: *Futūḥ*	*al-Balādhurī*: Kitāb futūḥ al-buldān (Liber expugnationis regionum, ed. M. J. deGoeje, Leiden 1863–66).
Hitti-Murgotten	*Translation*: *Ph. K. Hitti and F. C. Murgotten*: The Origins of the Islamic State (*Studies in History, Economics and Public Law*, ed. by the Faculty of Political Science of Columbia University LXVIII: 1–2, New York 1916–24).
Bal.: *Ans.* V	*al-Balādhurī*: Kitāb ansāb al-ashrāf[2].
	The Ansāb al-Ashrāf of al-Balādhurī. Published for the first time by the School of Oriental Studies, Hebrew University, Jerusalem, vol. V, ed. by *S. D. Goitein* (Jerusalem 1936).
	Translations:
	M. J. de Goeje: Das kitāb Ansāb al-Ašrāf des al-Balādhurī (*ZDMG* vol. 38 (1884), 382–406).
della Vida	*G. Levi della Vida*: Il califfo ʿAlī secondo il "kitāb ansāb al-ašrāf" di Balāḏurī (*RSO* VI (1914), 427–507).
Bal. *Muʿāw.*	*O. Pinto e G. Levi della Vida*: Il califfo Muʿāwiya I secondo il "Kitāb Ansāb al-Ašrāf" di Aḥmad ibn Yaḥyā al-Balāḏurī (Roma 1938).
	Bar Hebraeus, Abū-l-Faraj: Historia compendiosa Dynastarum ... arabice edita et latine versa ab *E. Pocockio* (Oxf. 1663).

1 When not otherwise stated the name of the author is used as abbreviation; all special abbreviations are indicated in the column to the left. Abbreviations of titles of periodicals are the same as those employed by the *Encyclopaedia of Islam, New Edition;* see vol. I, xi sqq.

2 Generally quoted from Caetani's translation in *Annali dell'Islām* (from the Paris MS) as: *Bal.*

Din.	*ad-Dīnawarī, Abū Ḥanīfa*: Kitāb al-akhbār aṭ-ṭiwāl (Ed. *V. Guirgass*, Leiden 1888).
Kratchkowski	Préface, variantes et index, publ. par *I. Kratchkowski* (Leiden 1912).
	al-Jāḥiẓ:
Jāḥiẓ: *Nābita*	*Ch. Pellat*: Un document important pour l'histoire politico-religieuse de l'Islam. La "Nābita" de Djāhiz (*AIEO* X (Alger 1952), 302–25).
Jāḥiẓ: *Arbitrage*	*Ch. Pellat*: Une risāla inédite de Ǧāḥiẓ sur l'arbitrage entre ʿAlī et Muʿāwiya (*Mashrīq* 1958 (Cairo *s.d.*), 417–91).
b. Khall.	*ibn Khallikān*: Biographical Dictionary, transl. from the Arabic by Bn *McGuckin de Slane*, I–IV (Paris 1842–71).
al-Khayyāṭ	*Abū al-Ḥusayn b. ʿUthmān al-Khayyāt:*
	Kitāb al-Intiṣār (Le livre du triomphe et de la réfutation d'ibn al-Rawandi l'hérétique) par Abū al Ḥusayn b. ʿOthmān al-Khayyāṭ (le muʿtazil). Ed et trad. par *N. A. Nader* (*Recherches publ. sous la direction de l'Institut de Lettres orientales de Beyrouth*, tome VI (Beyrouth 1957)).
Einl. z. b. Saʿd	*ibn Saʿd, Muhammad*: Kitāb aṭ-ṭabaqāt al-kabīr (Ed. *E. Sachau* III: 1. Einleitung (Leiden 1903)).
	The Quran:
	Translation: *R. Bell*: The Qur'ān. Translated with a critical re-arrangement of the Surahs, I–II (Edinburgh 1939).
Mas.	*al-Masʿūdī*: Murūǧ aḏ-ḏahab. Les prairies d'or, ed. et trad. par *Pavet de Courteille* et *C. Barbier de Meynard*, I–VII (Paris 1861–74).
	Nasr b. Muzahim al-Minqari:
Waq. Siff.	Waqʿat Ṣiffīn li-Naṣr ibn Muzāḥim al-Minqarī ... taḥqīq wa sharḥ *ʿAbd as-Salām Muḥammad Hārūn* (Cairo 1365 A.H./ 1945–46).
an-Nawbakhtī	*an-Nawbakhtī:* Firaq al-Shīʿa, ed. *H. Ritter* (*Biblioteheca Islamica* IV, Istanbul 1931).
	Translation: M.-J. Mashkur: An-Nawbaḫti: Les sectes šīʿites (*RHR* 153 (1958), 68–78, 176–214; tome 154 (1958), 67–95, 146–72; tome 155 (1959), 62–78).
al-Qalhātī	*al-Qalhātī:*
	Kafāfī, M.: The Rise of Kharjism according to Abū Saʿīd ... al-Qalhātī (*B. Fac. Ar.* XIV: 2 (Cairo 1952), 29–48).
Tab.	*aṭ-Ṭabarī, Abū Jaʿfar Muhammad b. Jarīr:*
	Ta'rīḫ ar-rusul wa'l-mulūk. Annales quos scripsit Abu Jafar Mohammed ibn Djarir at-Tabari, cum aliis edidit *M. J. de Goeje* (Leiden 1879–1901).
	al-Wāqidī: Kitāb al-maghāzī.
Waq.-Wellh.	*Translation: J. Wellhausen:* Muhammed in Medina (Bln. 1882).
Yaʿq.	*al-Yaʿqūbī:* Historiae, ed. *M. Th. Houtsma*, I–II (Leiden 1883).

II. LITERATURE

Abbott, N.: Studies in Arabic Literary Papyri I: Historical Texts (*University of Chicago. Oriental Institute Publications* LXXV, Chicago 1957).

	Becker, C. H.: Principielles zu Lammens Sira-Studien (*Islam* IV (1913), 263–69).
	Bernheim, E.: Mittelalterliche Zeitanschauungen in ihrem Einfluss auf Politik und Geschichtsschreibung, I (Tübingen 1918).
GAL I–II, (S), I–III	*Brockelmann, C.:* Geschichte der arabischen Litteratur, I–II (Weimar 1898–1902).—Supplement, I–III (Leiden 1937–42).
Brockelmann	*Brockelmann, C.:* Der älteste Geschichtsschreiber der Schia (*ZS* IV (1923), 1–23).
Buhl: *Aliderne*	*Buhl, F.:* Alidernes Stilling til de shiʿitiske Bevægelser under Umajjaderne (*OVSF* 1910, No. 5, 355–94).
Buhl: *ʿAlī*	*Buhl, F.:* ʿAlī som Prætendent og Kalif (*Festskrift udg. af Københavns Universitet* ... November 1921).
	Butterfield, H.: The History of the Writing of History (*XIe Congrès internationale des Sciences Historiques, Rapports*, I (Sthlm. 1960), 25–39).
	Caskel, W.: Aijām al-ʿArab. Studien zur altarabischen Epik (*Islamica* III:5, Lpz. 1930).
Duri: *al-Zuhrī*	*Duri, A. A.:* Al-Zuhrī. A study on the beginnings of History Writing in Islam (*BSOAS* XIX (1957), 1–12).
Duri: *Iraq School*	*Duri, A. A.:* The Iraq School of History. To the 9th Century (*Conference on Historical Writing of the Near and Middle East*. Duplicate Manuscript, London 1958).
E.I.[1], I–IV and (S)	*Encyclopaedie des Islams*, hrsg. v. *M. Th. Houtsma* u.a., I–IV und Ergänzungsband (Leiden u. Lpz. 1913–38).
E.I.[2], I–II	*The Encyclopaedia of Islam*. New Edition, ed. by *H. A. R. Gibb* a.o., I–II (Leiden and London 1960–62).
	Faris, N. A.: Development in Arab Historiography as reflected in the struggle between ʿAlī and Muʿāwiyah (*Conference on Historical Writing on the Near and Middle East*. Duplicate Manuscript, London 1958).
Friedlaender: *Heterodoxies*	*Friedlaender, I.:* The Heterodoxies of the Shiites according to ibn Ḥazm (Rpt. from *JAOS* vols. XXVIII–XXIX. New Haven 1909).
Friedlaender: *b. Saba'*	*Friedlaender, I.:* Abdallah ibn Saba', der Begründer der Šīʿa, und seine jüdische Ursprung (*ZA* XXIII–XXIV (1909–10)).
Friedlaender: *Geschichtskonstr.*	*Friedlaender, I.:* Muhammedanische Geschichtskonstruktionen (*BKO* IX (1911), 17–34).
	Fueter, E.: Geschichte der neueren Historiographie (2. Aufl., Mnch. u. Bln. 1925).
Gabrieli: al-Ma'mūn	*Gabrieli, F.:* Al-Ma'mūn e gli ʿAlidi (*Morgenländische Texte und Forschungen*, hrsg. v. A. Fischer, Bd. II:1, Lpz. 1929).
Gabrieli: *Origini*	*Gabrieli, F.:* Sulle origini del movimento Ḫārigita (*Rend. Linc.* 1941, fasc. VI, 110–17).
	Gibb, H. A. R.: Studies in the Civilization of Islam (Boston 1962).
Goitein: *Bal.*	*Goitein, S. D.:* The Place of Balāhurī's Ansāb al-Ashrāf in Arabic Historiography (*19. Congresso internazionale degli Orientalisti, 1935* (Roma 1938), 603–06).
Goldziher: *M. St.*	*Goldziher, I.:* Muhammedanische Studien, I–II (Halle 1889–90).
Goldziher: *Litt.*	*Goldziher, I.:* Neue Materialien zur Litteratur des Ueberlieferungswesen bei den Muhammedanern (*ZDMG* Bd. 50 (1896), 465–506).

Goldziher: *Islam*	*Goldziher, I.:* Islam fordom och nu. Studier i korantolkningens historia (Sthlm. 1915).
	Hamidullah, M.: Le "Livre des Généalogies" d'al-Balāḏurīy (*BEO* XIV (1952–54), 197–211).
Horowitz: *Vak.*	*Horowitz, J.:* De Vakidii libro qui Kitāb al-Maghāzī inscribitur (Diss., Bln. 1898).
	Horowitz, J.: Alter und Ursprung des Isnads (*Der Islam* VIII (Lpz. 1918), 39–47).
Horowitz: *Biographies*	*Horowitz, J.:* The Earliest Biographies of the Prophet and their Authors (*IC* vol. II (1928), 22–50, 164–82, 495–526).
Lammens: *Moʿāw.*	*Lammens, H.:* Études sur le règne du calife omayyade Moʿāwia Ier (Beyrouth 1908).
Lammens: *Yazīd*	*Lammens, H.:* Le califat de Yazīd Ier (Beyrouth 1921).
Lammens: *Omayyades*	*Lammens, H.:* Études sur le siècle des Omayyades (Beyrouth 1930).
Laoust: *b. al-Kathīr*	*Laoust, H.:* Ibn al-Kathīr, historien (*Arabica* II (Leiden 1955), 42–88).
Laoust: *Ḥanbalisme*	*Laoust, H.:* Le ḥanbalisme sous le califat de Baghdad (*REI* 1959, 67–128).
	Loth, O.: Ursprung und Bedeutung der Ṭabaqāt (*ZDMG* Bd. 23 (1869), 593–614).
	Mahdi, M.: Ibn Khaldūn's Philosophy of History. A Study in the Philosophic Foundation of the Science of Culture (London 1957).
Margoliouth: *Mohammedanism*	*Margoliouth, D. S.:* The Early Development of Mohammedanism (London 1914).
Margoliouth: *Lectures*	*Margoliouth, D. S.:* Lectures on Arabic Historians (Calcutta 1930).
	Massignon, L.: Recherches sur les Shīʿites extrémistes à Baghdad à la fin du troisième siècle de l'Hégire (*ZDMG* Bd. 92 (1939), 378–82).
	Moscati, S.: Per una storia dell'antica šīʿa (*RSO* XXX (1955), 351–67).
	Najim, W. T.: Studies in the Writings of al-Jāḥiẓ (Thesis (Unpublished), London 1958).
	Nallino, C. A.: La littérature arabe dès origines à l'époque de la dynastie umayyade (Traduction française par Ch. Pellat, Paris 1950).
	Noeldeke, Th.: Zur tendentösen Gestaltung der Urgeschichte Islams (*ZDMG* Bd. 52 (1898), 16–33).
	Obermann, J.: Early Islam (In: R. C. Dentan: *The Idea of History in the Ancient Near East* (New Haven 1955), 237–310).
	Patton, W. H.: Aḥmad ibn Ḥanbal and the Miḥna (Leiden 1897).
	Pedersen, J.: Den arabiske Bog (Cph. 1946).
	Pellat, Ch.: Ǧāḥiẓ à Baghdad et à Samarrā (*RSO* XXVII (1952), 47–67).
Pellat: *Jāḥiẓ*	*Pellat, Ch.:* Le milieu baṣrien et la formation de Ǧāḥiẓ (Paris 1953).
Pellat: *Muʿāw.*	*Pellat, Ch.:* Le culte de Muʿāwiya au IIIe siècle de l'hégire (*SI* tome VI (1956), 53–66).
HT 11:V	*Petersen, E. Ladewig:* Stat og Historieskrivning i Islams klassiske Periode (*HT* 11th ser., vol. V (1957–59), 455–73).
AO XXIII	*Petersen, E. Ladewig:* ʿAlī and Muʿāwiyah. The Rise of the Umayyad Caliphate, 656–61 (*AO* XXIII (1959), 157–96).

AO XXVII	*Petersen, E. Ladewig:* Studies on the Historiography of the ʿAlī–Muʿāwiyah Conflict (*AO* XX4II (1963), 83–118).
	Richter, G.: Das Geschichtsbild der arabischen Historiker des Mittelalters (*Philosophie und Geschichte* 43, Tübingen 1933).
Rosenthal: *Scholarship*	*Rosenthal, F.:* The Technique and Approach of Muslim Scholarship (*Analecta Orientalia*, ed. cur. Pont. Inst. Bibl., tome 24, Roma 1949).
Rosenthal: *Historiography*	*Rosenthal, F.:* A History of Muslim Historiography (Leiden 1952).
	Sarasin, W.: Das Bild Alis bei den Historikern der Sunna (Diss., Basel 1907).
Schacht: *Origins*	*Schacht, J :* The Origins of Muhammadan Jurisprudence (Oxf. 1949, rpt. 1953).
Schacht: *Mūsā*	*Schacht, J.:* On Mūsā b. ʿUqba's Kitāb al-Maghāzī (*AO* XXI (1953), 288–300).
	Schultess, F.: Ueber den Dichter al-Nağāšī (*ZDMG* Bd. 54 (1900), 421–74).
Sourdel: *Vizirat*	*Sourdel, D.:* Le vizirat ʿAbbāside de 749 à 936, I–II (Damas 1959–60).
Sourdel: *Pol. Rel.*	*Sourdel, D.:* La politique religieuse des successeurs d'al–Mutawakkil (*SI* tome XIII(1960), 5–21).
Sprenger: *Notes*	*Sprenger, A.:* Notes on Alfred von Kremer's edition of Wáqdy's Campaigns (*JASB*, N. S. vol. XXV (1856), 199–220).
Sprenger: *Origins*	*Sprenger, A.:* On the Origins and Progress of writing down facts among the Mussulmans (*JASB*, N. S. vol. XXV (1956), 303–29, 375–81).
Sprenger: *Trad. wes.*	*Sprenger, A.:* Über das Traditionswesen bei den Arabern (*ZDM* Bd. X (1856), 1–17).
	Spuler, B.: Islamische und abendländische Geschichtsschreibung. Eine Grundsatz-Betrachtung (*Saeculum* VI (Mnch. 1955), 125–00).
	Sultan, J.: Étude sur Nagj al-Balāgha (Thèse, Paris 1940).
Vaglieri I	*Vaglieri, L. Veccia:* Il conflitto ʿAlī–Muʿāwiya e la secessione khārigita riesaminati alla luce di fonte ibāḑite (*AIOUN*, N. S. IV (1952), 1–99).
	Weil, G.: Geschichte der Chalifen, I–II (Mannheim 1842–48).
Wellhausen: *Prolegomena*	*Wellhausen, J.:* Prolegomena zur ältesten Geschichte des Islams (*Skizzen und Vorarbeiten* VI (Bln. 1899), 1–160).
Wellhausen: *Opp.-parteien*	*Wellhausen, J.:* Die religiös-politische Oppositionsparteien im alten Islam ((*Abh. G. F. Gött.*, Philol.-Hist. Kl., N. F. V no. 2, Bln. 1901).
Wellhausen: *Kingdom*	*Wellhausen, J.:* The Arab Kingdom and Its Fall (Calcutta 1927; German edition, Bln. 1902).
	Veselý, R.: Die Anṣār im ersten Bürgerkriege (36–40 d. H.) (*Archiv Orientální* 26 (Prag 1958), 36–58).
	Wüstenfeld, F.: Die Geschichtsschreiber der Araber und Ihre Werke (Rpt. from *Abh. G. W. Gött.* XXVIII–XXIX, Gött. 1882).

Abbreviations

Abh. G. F. Gött.	Abhandlungen der Gesellschaft der Wissenschaften zu Göttingen.
Abh. K. M.	Abhandlungen für die Kunde des Morgenlandes (Lpz.).
Agh.	*Abū-l-Faraj al-Iṣfahānī:* Kitāb al-Aghānī.
AIEO	Annales de l'Institut d'Études Orientales de l'Université d'Alger.
AIOUN	Annali dell'Istituto Universitario Orientale di Napoli.
AO	Acta Orientalia (Copenhagen).
BEO	Bulletin d'Études Orientales (Damascus).
B. Fac. Ar.	Bulletin of the Faculty of Arts of the Egyptian University (Cairo).
BKO	Beiträge zur Kenntnis des Orients (Halle a. S.).
BSOAS	Bulletin of the School of Oriental and African Studies (London).
HT	Historisk Tidsskrift (Copenhagen).
IC	Islamic Culture (Hyderabad).
ʿIqd.	*Ibn ʿAbd Rabbihi:* al-ʿIqd al-farīd.
JAOS	Journal of the American Oriental Society (New Hawen).
JASB	Journal of the Asiatic Society, Bengal Branch (Calcutta).
OVSF	Oversigt over Videnskabernes Selskabs Forhandlinger (Copenhagen).
REI	Revue des Études Islamiques (Paris).
Rend. Linc.	Rendiconti della Reale Accademia dei Lincei (Roma).
RHR	Revue de l'Histoire des Religions (Paris).
RSO	Rivista degli studi orientali (Roma).
SI	Stvdia Islamica (Paris).
ZA	Zeitschrift für Assyriologie (Strassbourg).
ZDMG	Zeitschrift der Deutschen Morgenländischen Gesellschaft (Lpz.).
ZS	Zeitschrift für Semitistik und verwandte Gebiete (Lpz.).

Dansk Résumé

'Alī og Mu'āwiya i tidlig arabisk tradition.
Studier over den islamiske historieskrivnings genesis og vækst til slutningen af 9. årh.

'Uthmāns drab i juni 656 og 'Alī's kalifat (656–61) spaltede det arabiske samfund op i en række partigrupperinger, der siden har delt Islam i uforsonlige modsætninger. 'Alī's kalifat lod sig kun opretholde med støtte af de kredse, der havde ståët bag 'Uthmāns mord, og spørgsmålet om drabets berettigelse mødte straks tvivl blandt de mekkanske profetfæller, hvis revolte under ledelse af Ṭalḥa og az-Zubayr blev slået ned i dec. 656 (Kamelslaget). Vigtigst var det dog, at også 'Uthmāns slægt – ummayyaderne – under ledelse af den syriske statholder, Mu'āwiya b. Abī Sufyān rejste blodhævnskravet, rettet mod 'Alī, der gav drabsmændene asyl. De to parter mødtes i sommeren 657 ved Siffīn ved Eufrat, og 'Alī måtte her gå med til at lade kalifdrabets berettigelse efterprøve ved voldgift, men denne afgørelse udløste pany en spaltning af 'Alī's tilhængere i et alidisk parti (den senere shī'isme) og i khārijismen, der konsekvent krævede en militær afgørelse af striden som gudsdom. Voldgiften synes at have fastslået ulovligheden af kalifdrabet og at 'Alī havde kompromitteret sig religiøst ved at samarbejde med drabsmændene, men den fik næppe nogen umiddelbar betydning udover at befordre opløsningen af 'Alī's magt. Kort inden voldgiften havde 'Alī slået khārijiterne ved an-Nahrawān, og selv faldt han i januar 661 som offer for et khārijitisk attentat; men allerede den foregående sommer havde Mu'āwiya ladet sig hylde til kalif og etablerede derved ummayyadekalifatet (660–750).

Denne spaltning *(fitna)* fik imidlertid følger langt udover den første borgerkrig; *fitna* er ideelt uforenelig med Muhammeds forkyndelse, men ikke destomindre en kendsgerning, der tidligt engagerede enhver troendes samvittighed. *Fitna'en* krævede bestandig tolkning i lyset af aktuelle, politiske og sociale skel, selvom disse i tidens løb gradvis ændrede karakter og indhold. Den historiske viden om *fitna'en* inddrages derved i den løbende politiske debat, og denne omstændighed understøttes af historieskrivningens nære forbindelse med profetens forkyndelse. Fortidens erfaringsmateriale indgår hos Muhammed som en organisk bestanddel af den guddommelige åbenbaring, og omvendt kædes stat og religion her sammen til en uopløselig enhed; menighedens trivsel manifesterer den guddommelige vilje, og *fitna'en* kræver derfor stadig retfærdiggørelse fra alle sider.

De ældst kendte vidnesbyrd om en historisk behandling af *fitna'en* stammer fra årtierne omkring 700, da de politiske, religiøse og sociale modsætningsforhold, som de arabiske erobreres assimilering i det nye milleu og den begyndende islamisering af den bosiddende befolkning, skabte dybe skel i det islamiske samfund; den forbitrelse, disse processer udløste især i Iraq og Persien, rettedes først og fremmest mod ummayyadekalifatet, der havde vanskeligt ved at skabe tidssvarende retningslinier for de nye samfundsvilkår. Historieskrivningen synes – ligesom retstraditionen og den dogmatiske overlevering – netop at have været et produkt af denne situation; dens genesis forklares ikke ved antikvarisk interesse, men af behovet for at tolke *fitna'en*, og den præges i overensstemmelse hermed fra første færd af polemisk eller tendentiøs efterrationalisering i aktuelt øjemed. Såvel hos tidens digtere som hos traditionskyndige kan vi følge, hvorledes den ældste tolkning af *fitna'en* udformes eklektisk: iraqensiske lærde – ash-Sha'bī – rejser tvivl om berettigelsen af Mu'āwiyas hævnaktion mod 'Alī, og medinensere som Ṣaliḥ b. Kaysān og az-Zuhrī forsvarer ummayyadernes synspunkter. I senummayyadetiden, da den shī'itiske opposition udformes under ledelse af abbasiderne (en sidegren af profetslægten), skærpes de iraqensiske anklager mod det syriske kalifat gradvis; kufiske historikere som Abū Mikhnaf rejser da spørgsmålet om ummayyadekalifatets legitimitet overhovedet, havde Mu'āwiya usurperet magten på profetslægtens bekostning ved ulovlige midler, mistede det syriske kalifat automatisk sin eksistensberettigelse.

Ummayyadekalifatets fald i 750 og etablereingen af abbasidekalifatet medførte imidlertid ingen afklaring; det nye dynasti var kommet til magten ved shī'ismens hjælp, men det undsagde straks efter magtovertagelsen sin revolutionære herkomst og måtte som støtte herfor opbygge en historisk tradition, der kunde legitimere dets adkomst til kalifatet. De første generationers historieskrivning efter 750 præges af abbasidernes opgør med shī'ismen. Abbassidevenlige historikere som Hishām b. Muhammed al-Kalbī og Sayf b. 'Umar søgte at dokumentere, at shī'ismen havde forskertset sin ret til at optræde på profetslægtens vegne ved at svigte 'Alī i kampen mod Mu'āwiya, og at abbasidernes overtagelse af oppositionen mod ummayyaderne retfærdiggjorde deres magtovertagelse. Omvendt forsvarede moderat-shī'itiske historikere som 'Umar b. Sa'īd og Naṣr b. Muzāḥim alidernes synspunkter og berettigelsen af 'Alī's tilhængeres adfærd under opgøret mod Mu'āwiya.

Striden mellem abbasiderne og shī'ismen havde i historieskrivningen (navnlig i den abbassidevenlige) været præget af voldsomme konstruktioner over det materiale, der stod til disposition. Men allerede kort efter 800 mærkes påny andre tendenser; abbassiderne synes allerede i sen-ummayyadetiden at have været intimt knyttet til mu'tazilismen, en rationalistisk, teologisk retning og samtidig tillige støtteparti for abbassideslægten. Det er denne retning, der slår igennem under al-Ma'mūn (813–33) hos historikere som medinenseren al-Wāqidī og basrenseren al-Madā'inī, der begge arbejdede under Bagdad-hoffets auspicier; hos Wāqidī fremtræder de nye tendenser snarest i form af forsøg på at tilvejebringe kompromis mellem alivenlige og abbassidevenlige anskuelser, hos Madā'inī i renere mu'tazilistisk udformning. Mu'tazilismens historieskrivning udmærker sig i modsætning til den foregående generations ved forsonlighed mod 'Alī (omend ikke mod den yderliggående shī'isme), ved sin ubarmhjertige fordømmelse af ummayyaderne (navnlig hos Madā'inī) og fremfor alt ved sin indirekte lovprisning af abbassiderne. Også denne retning mødte imidlertid modsigelse; det ortodokse, velstående borgerskab i de østlige provinser og flertallet af tidens traditionskyndige har følt den rarionalistiske teologis angreb på den islamiske traditionalisme som en fare for den bestående samfundsstruktur; historieskrivningen skal ikke tjene »rationelle deduktioner eller intellektuel opbyggelse«, skriver Tabari lidt senere.

Modstanden mod mu'tazilismen samles om en enkelt skikkelse, juristen Aḥmad b. Ḥanbal, men blandt hans tilhængere træffer vi tillige en række historikere, der til støtte for hans argumentation påny fremfører den syrisk-medinensiske tradition fra Ṣāliḥ b. Kaysān og az-Zuhrī. Den betydeligste historieskriver, som synes at have været influeret af ḥanbalismen, var al-Balādhurī, hvis hovedværker gennem deres analytiske anlæg røber anerkendelse af ummayyadekalifatets legitimitet og beundring for det klassiske araberriges storhed og omvendt en vis kritik af 'Alī, der ikke magtede sin opgave; endelig sporer vi her også stadig velvilje mod abbassiderne. Balādhurī's værker repræsenterer ved deres redelige (omend implicite) traditionskritik den islamiske historieskrivnings bedste frembringelser, men som historiografisk retning fik ḥanbalismen næppe nogen lang levetid eller dybtgående indflydelse.

Baggrunden herfor er sikkert den sociale differentieringsproces af det islamiske samfund, som havde fundet sted i den ældre abbassidetid: Skellene mellem de østlige provinsers velstående borgerskab, hvis flertal var ortodokst eller moderat-shī'itisk, og byernes og landdistrikternes proletariat uddybedes, samtidig med at økonomisk aktivitet og udvikling af kreditteknik skabte stærk kapitalkoncentration i disse områder af kalifatet. De modsætningsforhold, som disse processer udløste, gør sig også gældende i historieskrivningen. Den yderliggående shī'isme – ismā'īlismen – bliver eksponent for de ringeststillede samfundsgruppers sociale utilfredshed, og bevægelsen antager omkring 900 revolutionær karakter. Det er muligt, at det har været denne begyndende differentieringsproces og radikaliseringen af den yderliggående shī'isme, der allerede under al-Ma'mūn havde givet stødet til, at den mu'tazilitiske tradition søgte udsoning med de moderat-shī'itiske retninger ved at forsøge at etablere en historisk forbindelse mellem abbassiderne og aliderne. I hvert fald kan der ikke være nogen tvivl om, at det må have været udsoningsbestræbelser af denne art, der toner frem bag historieskrivningen i sisdste halvdel af det 9. århundrede. Både ortodokse historikere som aṭ-Ṭabari og moderat-shī'itiske som ad-Dīnawarī og al-Ya'qūbī søger i deres arbejder at formulere en fællesfront mod de yderliggående tendenser, måske mod den spirende ismā'īlisme. Ummayayderne fordømmes påny skånselsløst som ansvarlige for 'Alī's ulykke, men ansvaret for at de nåede frem til magten placeres umiddelbart enten hos den radikale shī'isme eller på khārijiterne.

Gennem alle de vekslende faser af den historieskrivning, vi her har beskæftiget os med, finder vi altså reflekserne af de brydninger, der prægede det islamiske samfunds tilblivelse. I sig selv synes den historiske tradition at have været et produkt af de modsætninger, der spaltede samfundet i sen-ummayyadetiden, og dens videre udvikling svarer fuldtud til den funktion, man kunde forvente efter den placering, den havde indtaget i Muhammeds forkyndelse. Skal vi forsøge at karakterisere dens arbejdsmetoder indenfor disse rammer, må det først og fremmest betones, hvor dominerende en plads det polemiske element indtager. Det er heri, vi må søge det grundlæggende incitament til dens genesis overhovedet, og dette særkende følger den gennem hele dens vækst frem til den fulde udfoldelse omkring år 900.

Den arabiske historiker vil naturligvis aldrig på forhånd udtrykkeligt placere sig selv religiøst eller politisk. Hans metode er i udpræget grad selektiv; hans synspunkter eller hans sympatier må altid udlæses af sammenhængen, af hans stofudvælgelse eller hans disposition. Han udvælger af den traditionsmængde, der står til hans rådighed, netop det stof, der kan tjene hans specielle synspunkter; det religiøse eller politiske formål, han sigter mod, er det primære element, og ikke historieskrivningen, der blot er hans mest hensigtsmæssige udtryksmiddel. Traditionen øver således vel kritik mod sine kilder, men ikke udfra videnskabelige eller antikvariske kriterier. Stoffet udvælges, det kombineres eller harmoniseres; historikeren konstruerer behændigt og dristigt, men aldrig hovedløst.

Som kilder til Islams ældste historie er man altså henvist til at arbejde med beretninger, der er sene og allerede i deres udspring har tjent andre formål end det historiske. Dokumentariske kilder savnes omtrent helt, og man kan kun ved konfrontation med uafhængige, syriske eller byzantinske kilder kontrollere dem, hvor det er muligt, eller med kendskab til traditionsdannelsens indre mekanisme underkaste dem prøvelse af deres sandsynlighed. Men det er vigtigt at fastholde, at kun de primære kilder fra sen-ummayyadetiden har nogensomhelst relevans for en historisk undersøgelse. Beretningernes uhyre vækst i abbassidetiden beror ikke på kendskab til nu tabte efterretninger; det er næppe i noget tilfælde muligt at påvise tabte kilder, og deres vækst beror udelukkende på traditionsbearbejdelse, konstruktioner eller tendentiøse sammenstillinger af det materiale, der stod til rådighed. Den sene tradition har ikke destomindre stadig værdi, forsåvidt som den afspejler Islams religiøse og politiske udvikling; abbassidetidens historieskrivning er ikke kilde til ʿAlī's kalifat, men til den propaganda og polemik, der omgav de sene partidannelser.

Index of Traditionists

Glossary

adab belles-lettres.
'adl, righteousness, religious habitus.
ahl al-bayt, the Prophet's family.
akhbār, noteworthy events; *'ilm al-akhbār*, knowledge of such events; *akhbārī*, transmitter of *akhbār*.
'amīl, personal agent, provincial governor.
amīr, commander, prince; *amīr al-umarā'*, chief amīr.
anṣār, Muhammad's Medinese Companions.
aṣḥāb, Muhammad's Companions.
ayyām al-'arab, "Days of the Arabs", accounts of the (particularly pre-Islamic) combats of the Arabian tribes.
bay'a, investiture through oath of allegiance; *bay'a 'āmma*, election possessing general validity, though only *muhājirūn* and *anṣār* participated.
bayt al-māl, fiscus, treasury.
bid'a, innovation.
dawla, dynasty, era, power.
dhimmīs, protected (non-Muslim) peoples.
dīn, religion, the religious burden, which God enjoins upon the caliph.
dīwān, pension register, administrative office.
faḍā'il, special quality possessed by *aṣḥāb* and *tābi'ūn*.
fiqh, science of Muslim moral law.
fisq, sin; *fāsiq*, a sinner.
fitna, scruple, particularly by defining one's attitude to the religious problems arising from 'Uthmān's murder; the schism emerging from this event.
fuqahā' (sing.: faqīh), *fiqh*-scholar.
futuwwa, chivalry.
ghulāt, extremists, especially radical Shiite sects.
ḥadīth, tradition, transmission.
ḥakam, umpire.
ḥilm, manifestation of personal tolerance, opportunism.
ḥukm, legal rule; *ḥukm Allāh*, God's judgment; *ḥukm ar-rijāl*, human judgment.
'ibra, the predecessors' warnings, history's lesson.
ijāza, the teacher's licence to his disciple to pass on his traditions.
ijmā', consensus; *ijmā' al-umma*, the universally recognized *ijmā'*.
ikhtiṣār, abridgment.
'ilm, knowledge, wisdom, science.
imām, leader in prayer; the religious dignity of the caliph.
'iṣma, infallibility.
isnād, chain of transmitters.
jāhiliyya, state of ignorance; the pre-Islamic paganism.
jihād, holy war.

khuṭba, sermon, public address in the (Friday) prayer.
kufr, infidelity; *kāfir* (pl.: *kāfirūn, kuffār*), infidel.
maghāzī, reports of the Prophet's warfare.
mahdī, person under divine guidance.
matn, the tradition's substance or factual contents.
mawlā (pl.: *mawālī*), clients, non-Arab converts.
miḥna, inquisition.
minbar, pulpit.
muḥaddithūn, bearers of ḥadīth.
muhājirūn, Muhammad's Meccan Companions.
mulk, secular power, monarchy; *malik*, king.
naṣṣ, testamentary transference (of the caliphate).
qāḍī, judge.
qamīṣ, shirt.
qurrā', Quran readers or recitators.
ar-rāfiḍa, extremist Shiites.
raj'a, second coming.
rāwī (pl.: *ruwāt*), bearers of (profane) transmission.
ra'y, opinion, legal decision based on personal opinion.
rijāl, the apparatus of informants in the isnād.
shī'a, party; *shī'at 'Alī*, Shī'ism, supporters of 'Alī and his descendants.
shūrā, election conclave.
sīra, the traditional Prophet-biography.
siyar, approved practice.
ṣulḥ, agreement, conciliation; particularly the arbitration agreement at Ṣiffīn.
sunan, laws, approved practices.
sunna, the Prophet's and his Companion's practice; *sunnī*, orthodox Muslim.
ṭabaqāt, biographical collection.
tābi'ūn, the Prophet's Followers (second generation).
tafsīr, egegesis; *tafsīr al-Qur'ān*, Quran egegesis.
ṭalīq (pl.: *ṭulaqā'*), freedman.
taqīya, caution, exemption from one's religious conviction, caused by fear.
ta'rīkh, chronologically arranged historical writing.
tashayyu' ḥasan, harmonization of divergent points of view.
umma, the Muslim community.
walī, heir.
waṣī, testamentary executor; *waṣiyya*, testament, testamentary burden.

www.ingramcontent.com/pod-product-compliance
Lightning Source LLC
LaVergne TN
LVHW050633100826
845148LV00011B/1854

9781597404716